Unseen Worlds
Adventures at the Crossroads of
Vodou Spirits and Latter-day Saints

Marilène Phipps

CALUMET
EDITIONS

Minneapolis

Minneapolis

SECOND EDITION DECEMBER 2022
Unseen Worlds: Adventures at the Crossroads of Vodou Spirits and Latter-day Saints. Copyright © 2018 by Marilène Phipps.
All rights reserved.

No part of this book may be used or reproduced in any manner whatsoever without written permission except in the case of brief quotations used in critical articles and reviews. For information, write to Calumet Editions, 6800 France Avenue South, Suite 370, Edina, MN 55435.

10 9 8 7 6 5 4 3 2

Cover and interior design: Gary Lindberg

ISBN: 978-1-960250-41-4

To the memory of Guslé Villedrouin,
my cousin and godfather.

"I am not particularly interested in giving a full account of all things… because I need the room to write about the things of God… I raised my voice to heaven, and angels came down and helped me."

(My translation from Le Livre de Mormon.
1 Nephi 6:5; 2 Nephi 4:24)

Also by Marilène Phipps

The Company of Heaven: Stories from Haiti
Crossroads and Unholy Water

Unseen Worlds

Adventures at the Crossroads of
Vodou Spirits and Latter-day Saints

Marilène Phipps

Contents

I—Innocence

1—Origins
    1. An Uncommon Dance 3
    2. Cosmic Twins 8
    3. The Sign 10
    4. In the Beginning 11
    5. An Amalgamated People 13
    6. Home 15
    7. Crossroads 17

2—Legacy
    1. Untold Stories 20
    2. Colonization of the Island 26
    3. The Founding Fathers 29
    4. Embargos and Divisions from 1806 Onward 31
    5. A Quick Survey of 200 Years 34
    6. Civil War and Continued Mayhem (1902 to 1915) 35
    7. Racism Brought Back to the Island (1915 to 1934) 37
    8. Continuing Chaos, Home Grown Racism and Colonialism 40
    9. The Year 1964 41

3—Write This in Remembrance of Us So Others Will Read and Love Us
    1. Haitian Tarzan 46
    2. Guslé's Fall 48
    3. Births 49
    4. Stepping Ahead in Time 52

4—Vodou and Me
    1. Beings I Loved 55
    2. A Cracking Noise 56
    3. Instant Motherhood 57
    4. Initiation 59

    5. A Vision 65
    6. Syncretism and Disguise 66
    7. Possession 67
    8. Victoria 71
    9. Special Guests 73
    10. Belonging 76
    11. Curtain Fall 77

5—The Pope in Port-au-Prince
    1. The Way of a Pope 83
    2. Politics and Church 84
    3. Welcoming the Pope 85
    4. The Kiss 86
    5. Fair Maiden of Papal Approval 87
    6. A Senseless Urge 89

6—Friends of My Spirit
    A Foreign Spirit
    1. Wool 92
    2. Silent Poet 93
    3. Prayer Rug 95
    4. Resting Places 98
    5. More Leaves 103
    Friars
    6. Different Yet the Same 109
    7. Friends of Circumstance 112
    8. Orphanage of the Would-Be Dead 114

7—Losing the Garden
    1. Promise Made Under Trees 118
    2. Face of a Slum 121
    3. The Jahr House 122
    4. We The People 124
    5. Middle Man 128
    6. Staging Reality 131

8—The Great Earthquake
    1. The Earthquake in the News 136

    2. The Earthquake in Mystics' Views   138
    3. The Earthquake in my Heart   141

II—Choice

9—Claiming Holy Ground
    1. All Good Sons   147
    2. Another Chance   152
    3. Plan of Salvation   155
    4. Angels Come   172
    5. Wildlife Sanctuary   177

10—Forgiveness
    1. Clayton and Me   179
    2. Blood Feud   182
    3. Aftermath   184
    4. The Issue of Satan   187
    5. A Lucid People   189

11—Fervor
    1. The Andromeda Galaxy   193
    2. A Pot of Gold   194
    3. Oliver's People   195

12—Apostasy Revisited
    1. The Great Gathering   199
    2. A Phone Conversation   200

13—Debout Les Morts! —Rise Up, Ye the Dead!
    1. Baptism for the Dead   215
    2. The Love of Children   217
    3. The Bird Who Did Not Flee   222

14—Belonging
    1. The Way We Mourn   226
    2. New Family and Heritage   228
    3. God's Beloved Children   230
    4. New Music   232
    5. The Original Egg   233

6. Going Back to the Old that Once Was New 235
  7. Renewal of Blood 236

15—Homecoming
  1. A Bird's Wish 237
  2. Leaving Home to Cry in the Desert 241
  3. Elder Rhein's Temple 243
  4. The Making of a Christian 247
  5. The First Gate 249
  6. The Lower Gate 255
  7. Home's Gates 259

References 263

Acknowledgements 264

About the Author 265

I

Innocence

1 Origins

1. An Uncommon Dance

Lightning struck the tall tree sheltering my father's tomb in the garden of my childhood. The great being went up in flames, lighting up the night like a huge star. The burning tree acted as an otherworldly torch, leading my thoughts to the beyond, where a million other stars exist as golden seeds God spreads nightly to germinate our dreams. I tell myself how it is surely such a torch that in olden days, Knight Templars held to assemble at their Asylum, before marching in the order of procession to the residence of the dead, for the secret burial service of one of their own.

But this tree-torch happened in Haiti, and not Medieval Europe. My father's grave was dug in the land where Christianity and Vodou coexist. Graham Greene wrote, "There is something peculiarly Roman in the air of Haiti: Roman in its cruelty, in its corruption and in its heroism…The auguries are still told in the entrails of beasts… Haiti is the scene of a classical tragedy."

Yet my father lived the life of an agnostic, averse to rituals. His attitude was not uncommon in a man raised during the early years of the twentieth century, even though he served as altar boy when growing up. His intensely Catholic mother, wanting this favorite child of hers to incur God's favor, insisted that he bathe early on Sunday mornings, dress in a freshly ironed white shirt and pants prepared for him by the laundress, then be guided across the street by a trusted servant to the church of Saint Louis King of France.

It was a small church built on land the family owned in the Turgeau neighborhood of Port-au-Prince, and eventually donated to the city. That neighborhood remained for a long time the area of choice for wealthy families to live, and where they established their Victorian gingerbread-style homes.

Through the years, Port-au-Prince continued to spread, along either side of the coastline, and up the many hills and mountainside above it. My father's life, and the places of residence he chose for himself as an adult, reflected this expanding movement of the city. His grave rests in the Bourdon hills of Port-au-Prince, on the way to Petionville, on land he bought when I was a child, because he wanted to escape the bells of the Dominican monastery in the nearby heights of Turgeau.

I was an adolescent growing up in Bourdon, when my father one day stopped briefly during the stroll we took in the garden, near the river. He placed one hand solemnly on my shoulder, pointed to a tropical apricot tree with the other, and said, "Someday, you must bury me under that tree."

The tree to which my father pointed, knowing it all of his life as an apricot tree, had actually nothing in common with the apricot tree of warm temperate regions, believed to originate from Armenia, and a producer of small orange-colored fruits. The Haitian apricot tree is a Mammea Americana, or South American apricot, an evergreen confined to tropical or sub tropical climates. It can grow up to sixty feet, and bears fruits up to eight inches in diameter.

What once was my father's splendid apricot tree became a charred corpse. What was the ground-area under the midday sun for the tree's large, soft mottled shade became the stage for stark projections of a multitude of sword-like extremities, roughly indented limbs, and giant black arrowheads.

Yet, how well I remember this tree's emerald elliptical leaves! Their copper-colored inner side; leaves large and strong like a man's open palm. How often I tasted its fruits—big as breadfruits, but covered with a coarse brown skin, and flesh that was a warm orange color, firm and moist—eaten fresh off the tree, or in sweet jams that had the feel of velvet on my tongue.

Everyone in the riverside slums, which keep expanding opposite our property, now fears the tree. This foreboding in slum dwellers' hearts is the same regarding people who have died—Haitians fear the dead, for they believe the dead have power. And death by lightning surely sets you apart. The tree is now a mighty guardian. It acts as a far more effective protection, albeit too late, from grave robbers looking for a fresh cadaver, than did the thick layer of concrete I paid masons to pour around my father's coffin after the funeral.

Grave robbers are driven by schemes of sorcery, undertakings usually planned and supervised by a oungan—Vodou priest, or by a sorcerer. One possible motive in digging up a grave, and this would not have been the case for my father who died in a car crash, is to retrieve the body in time to complete the process of zombification, originally started by poisoning. The poison is alleged to be a powder mixture that relies heavily on extracts from the puffer fish; symptoms of this poison mimic death; its effect last long enough for a wake, funeral, burial, and eventual recovery of the purported corpse, deep in the night, under stars and candlelight, with incantations and counter poison. Another reason to steal a body is to access, steal, and imprison the soul, which in Haiti bears the lovely name of Good Angel. The soul is considered energy that can be stored indefinitely, adding to the temple's existing spiritual corpus, and manipulated for various magical enterprises. Every slum area in Haiti, depending on its size, counts one or more active Vodou priest and temple. It was fair of me at the time to assume that any such priest living in the slums opposite our Bourdon hills property, then twice the total surface of the slums, would view my father as a powerful man of the world endowed with a soul that would be an enviable asset to his temple or sorcerer's status. It should be said that in countries where education for the masses is lacking, upward mobility practically nonexistent, and where people live with an all-pervasive sense of powerlessness, sorcery and its promise of spiritual leverage might hold an irresistible appeal. Understanding this kind of reality, the layer of concrete I had masons pour over and around my father's coffin before closing the grave may be seen as a form of life insurance I bought for his soul.

My father suffered a stroke while driving. He crashed into an electric post a few feet from the gate of his house, and died of the shock to his forehead hitting the windshield. There were no long leave-takings between us. Like that of the tree, his life was claimed brutally, released in a flash.

Death is the scandal in our lives. It is God's way to force us to turn to Him, angrily calling Him into account. But first we must suffer this naked intruder whose timing is always wrong, his manner insolent; he creates havoc in our house, then leaves the mess behind. In our despondency, we get busy in spite of the internal crash. We are motivated by a need for meaning and order—we begin assembling in the mind the sacred words of ancient texts, following the delicate path in the heart we sense is indicated by breadcrumbs received during holy services at church; in this way, we behave like modern-day Tom Thumbs, hoping to ensure divine protection for a successful, eventual journey back to the Creator of all.

We live in death's debt, appreciating all because there is an end to all. Mankind celebrates death out of love and fear. Ancient and new civilizations alike prayed, composed, feasted, and danced to make sense of it; medieval philosophers kept skulls on their desks as Memento Mori, while the Aztec Plumed Serpent god, Quetzalcoatl, descended into the land of the dead to rescue the bones of humanity, and bring them back to life; modern-day Mexican Mariachis trumpet and chirrup on their Dios de los Muertos, while children in awe of them suck on white candy skulls, and the brittle fuchsia-pink limbs of sugar-coated corpses; Tibetan skeleton dances reflect on the transient nature of things, celebrate the eternal dance of death, and the attainment of perfect consciousness, all the while performed in a monastery guarded by wild-eyed demons ringed by fire, and their sharp claws, long fangs, skull garlands, and multiple arms brandishing weapons.

In the same order of human affairs, starting on November first, All Saints' Day, the Haitian Vodou god, Bawon Samdi, indulges himself every year in numerous spirit-possessions, happening all over Haiti during ceremonies for the dead. The same can be said for Vodou ceremonies in New York, Boston, Miami, Montreal, and wherever in the Americas and Europe are found expatriate communities of Haitians. But it is not just Haitians either—Brazilians with Candomblé, Jamaicans with Obeah, and Cubans with Santeria, have the same worship systems that are ongoing adaptive interpretations of the spirit world, evolved by African people trying to make sense of their universe within the dictates of a Christian faith, imposed on them during the slave trade.

So in Haiti, Bawon Samdi abandons himself to his delight in death's disturbances, as will his many avatars, Bawon Simityè, Bawon Lakwa, Bawon Kriminèl or Papa Gede. He will commonly manifest himself in the company of a variegated cohort of deities of the dead, his children, the Gede (pronounce "Gayday"). He will arbitrarily, and consecutively take a body-and-mind hold of either onlookers or participants in an ongoing ritualized celebration. Having done so, Bawon will then disappear for a while, long enough for you to forget him, since so much music, dancing, and praying is going on. He reappears in full parade a while later, riotous, loud-mouthed and disruptive, barefooted but donned with a purple or black silken suit, black top hat and sunglasses, one lens missing, smoking a cigar, clutching a cane, and swigging out of a bottle of the hot-peppered white rum kleren he loves. You may then suddenly remember, in a single flash of insight, how these items are commonly set aside for him by the temple's Vodou Priest. Bawon will surely have scouted for his privately reserved, sacred things through the temple's many rooms and passageways. He will likely have exhibited a knowing air, a frown, a busy manner, occasionally shoving people aside; or instead, he sveltely sneaked around like a dog on a secret errand, head and tail kept low, until he found the room reserved as his altar.

After his shocking re-entry at the epicenter of the ceremony, drums pounding, his interference in the goings-on, wanting attention, and much meddling with people in the audience, Bawon Samdi will continue to swagger from one area of the temple to another, yet careful not to spill any of his kleren. Judging by his smile, the swelling in his chest, and the sprightliness in his step, he is lit up with impish glee. Spirits of the dead gulp kleren down with gusto; the hot chili pepper decoction in the white rum is strong enough to cause actual burn damage to the mouth and stomach of any drinker who is not under spirit possession. In his wild dodging about, Bawon will occasionally stop if someone piques his curiosity; there is no refusing him when he orders you to sit down with him, and proceeds to divulge your entire future. Living from the vantage point of death where either all of life has been played out, or where life is observed until time has come for death to interfere, Bawon and the Gede know our destinies, and thus are the great fortunetellers of the Vodou pantheon.

Bawon most enjoys mischief and indignation, randomly or in revenge, while the evening and a human body are his. Later in the night, as lord of graveyards, he will crawl over cobwebbed tombs during his two-day November carousal, like a four-legged tarantula, mocking God.

2. Cosmic Twins

My brother had the charm of birds. Song was his manner. He was a man in his full maturity, and when stretched on his deathbed at the Canapé Vert Hospital in Port-au-Prince, eyes aglow, he whispered a few words to me one night:

"You and I are twins."

I spent my life judging him as being so detached that I found him coming short of being a proper brother, while in fact, I came to realize too late that I had close to me someone more necessary—a double. We were the twinned-sides of the same golden coin. I began to discover that which had been imprinted on him as a gift—to successfully achieve my maturation. We were each other's guides. I was to help him finish dying, while he was to help me finish living. He had seen it all along. I had not. His passing from life was dignified and discreet but he took much of me with him then. I did not feel the tear at first. It made no sound.

"Where does it hurt?" his doctor asked him one morning during a routine visit at the hospital.

"In my soul..." my brother said.

He was willing to die, although he never stopped reveling in this island where he thought women as joyous as fruits. He commented on how it felt for him to live in a place where movements and sounds of the sweeper begin the day, rather than end it. It was not death he feared, but being trapped inside the four walls of an unshakable room, unable to commune with the sky. He never could sleep in a bedroom, even the one decorated by his mother especially for him, with portraits of herself. All day at the hospital, he pushed away the sheet the nurse kept pulling back.

"It's heavy to bear… this ailing man's sheet…"

One would prefer that death occur like tropical rains—falling suddenly, with great burst of thunder from a yellow sky, causing two children to run for cover and curl up together in a corner of their bedroom, a frightful delight burning in their eyes.

But Death often takes its time. It took two months for my brother to die. So much needed to be said in preparation: so much to pack ahead in the heart for the voyage above, and so much in the mind to fuel the passing in the here below.

Much has happened to the garden, as it did to us. We too were outgrowths of the land. Weeds, really. After he called me a twin, my brother said again, "There was a third one… but he didn't make it…"

"He? How do you know this?"

"Spirits told me…" he murmured with a smile, then said no more.

I struggled with the desire to tell him that there had indeed been a third one—evidently a brother, yet one our mother quickly aborted because she was not sure who the father was. "I became pregnant with you very soon after that abortion," she said to me. "This is also why I had to keep you… Fortunately, you look just like your father… you both do… to the extent that one wonders if I was only a vessel in this whole motherhood affair…"

My brother and I were dazzled by our mother's beauty. All men noticed her large, dark, melancholic eyes, so easily sent a-flutter; soft, sinuous red lips, a fluff and a curl in the hair—she exuded an aura of romance. And she sang such laments! Marriage to a Haitian man whom she followed to his small foreign island, and then life as an expatriate feeling restricted by the closed-minded bourgeois mores of her new society, all but put an end to her previous budding career as a soprano in Paris. Her voice became raspy from chain-smoking; she gave in to men's flattery, and allowed her magic to remain stillborn.

3. The Sign

Thirty-two years elapsed between the time a tarantula was found in my crib, and the pope's visit to Haiti in 1983; thirty-two years, and twice divorced already. The arachnid was discovered sitting still on my pillow. This was soon after I was moved from the clinic where I was born, to the family home in the Turgeau hills.

My life is an eternal dance—rebirth and death cohabit within. The devil wanted me dead from the start. That is clear. By the chill in my heart, I recognize his feel. Through the years, the spider came back in many guises, usually dressed in black, but not always.

I waited for the pope at the airport, filled with anticipation. A ghoul may perch high over one's life like it would over the door of a cathedral. It is no wonder that I did not see it. The pope emerged from the Alitalia plane as white as a tarantula is black, an insect with panache and bravado, advancing with care. The pope descended slowly from the plane. At the bottom of the metal stairway, he folded his limbs low enough to crouch, lean forward, angle his arms, spider-like, to anchor them on either side of his shoulders, and kiss the earth.

With these incidents three decades apart, both the pope and the tarantula came within inches of my face, showing awareness of my presence, yet indifferent to it. Both times I failed to recognize danger. I never imagined that a pope could have the cold, all-encompassing, impervious stare of the conqueror—the ice of power. The tarantula had entered my crib, and the pope my country; he was on my land, in my space, yet he is the one who blessed me, signifying his magnanimous tolerance of my existence; his hand moved with authority as if a scepter, in a gesture of dominion and superiority. It makes me think of Christopher Columbus meeting Anacaona—resonances of history terrorize my reason. I was just another native, and a female one at that.

No matter. Through my window I see the sunlit colors of gladioli. I am not a disembodied Vodou spirit cast out, spiraling through the stars, relentlessly wanting, never contented. I understand that one's spiritual milieu and economic circumstances at birth are not a choice; however, adulthood is the time to grapple with them, question inherited beliefs and lifestyle, evaluate their worth and effect over one's being, family, community, and country. I have been on this earth many years, spent much time sorting out what it means to grow up in Haiti, and evaluate the all-pervading, inevitable influences of Vodou over my psyche, even whilst being raised a Catholic. My purpose with this story is to tell about my upbringing, how I bore the effects of a violent political context, pulled though risky religious experiences, overcame personal loss, and how my faith in Christ proved resilient and redemptive.

4. In the Beginning

I was born in a tropical climate at a pre-dawn hour when it was still dark but cocks crowed nonetheless. Forceps yanked out of my mother a ten-pound baby, bald, jaundiced, disoriented. Glaring light aggressed me, and I ached for the hydrous milieu from which I had just been ripped. The Bourand Maternity Clinic's antiseptic, bare walls were the first to resound with my cries.

My mother's flesh was torn at what seemed the center of her being. Her blood oozed from the new wound out of which I came, while a sweaty hospital gown stuck to her skin. I had just been set down near her by a nurse when, filled with insidious resentment, my mother decided to have a look at me. She slowly lifted her chest, and propped herself on unstable elbows. She grimaced, but also smiled faintly at her success; she then frowned, narrowed her swollen eyes, and paused a moment, blinking repeatedly.

"She looks Chinese…" my mother moaned, before crumpling and sinking her head back into the pillow.

I was a white baby in a country of black people; a Haitian baby girl produced by a French mother in a culture that prizes sons, a society where thoughts of grandmothers when first meeting a newborn, are often about the skin color rather than the features and resemblances to either parent.

My father entered the room with my two year old brother, Gaëtan, who trailed hesitantly behind him, unnoticed by nurses prepping me for the crib, and for display to visitors; they were clearing away the forceps, bloody sheets, towels, trays, buckets, and all other birthing paraphernalia. The sounds they made would have been the first I heard in this world. No one thought to add music.

With dawn rising, the city would have begun to awaken soon after the delivery, initially heard pulsating in the street below the upper level of the clinic, and slowly all around—a clashing symphony of rumbling motors, whistles, horns and honks serving as accompaniment to the high-pitched chorus of a variety of loud-mouthed street vendors, advertising their trade and merchandise for the benefit of a rushing array of passers-by, "Chan-y! Chan-y! Paate Choo! Dlo! Dlo—Shoeshine! Hot pate! Water! Water!" all echoing in the room where my body would begin to twitch timidly in its first confused attempts at grasping the clouded new space I had entered.

Except for the rooster's, animal calls would only be heard later, mostly starting at dusk, and continuing all night. They would happen suddenly, and spaced enough apart to startle a newborn each time: the alarmed barking of dogs, and the abrupt braying of donkeys in neighboring hills; goats' bleats, and cows' moos sounding infrequently; roosters however tend to brag about life in high-pitched vocalizing at any time and anywhere in the city, while raucous crows announce an afternoon rain early in the morning.

At the time of my birth, Port-au-Prince was a small, provincial city with lots of green areas provided by public and private gardens, as well as by vast surrounding hills and high mountains. In the Arawak language of the first Indian inhabitants of the island, the word "Haiti" meant "land of mountains". The natives would go to the mountains to pray in order to be close to their gods. My earliest experience of the elevation of a Haitian mountain was in the arms of my father when he first lifted me in the air, and held me, chuckling proudly at my size and charm.

There was no easy apprenticeship period for nursing, whether for the mother or the newborn—it was learnt on the fly in a kind of emergency situation where pain and incompetence were shared by both parties who surrendered themselves to the necessities of the moment. Faced with giving birth at a time when families were preoccupied with preparations for the Christmas turkey, and having to accept milky substance discharging from her breast before it could be either pumped, sucked, or bitten out of her, was just too challenging for my mother to have enjoyed having to feed me, when instead she could have been donning a green silk dress to go dancing. My father's mother however was ecstatic—there were already five grandchildren about whom she boasted to anyone who cared to listen, but I was to be special for her in that she had been asked to be my godmother.

My brother was the first gentle moon I knew. He was our grandmother's fifth grandchild, and one endowed with a smile shaped like the melancholic crescents seen glowing in the night skies of Persian miniatures. The first time he leaned over my crib, wonder was established between us.

The tarantula was also a moon creature; it visited me in my crib and stood still on my pillow, late at dusk when stars begin to speckle the sky, flashing code messages. My face was turned to one side while this disconcerting hairy member of the Theraphosidae family and I reflected calmly on each other's features.

Seven years older than me, my cousin Louise remembers both my birth and my crib. "It looked like a chicken coop!" she said, still giggling at the thought decades later. "They must have put wire mesh all around that rectangular box to keep creepy-crawling roaches, rats, and tarantulas off you! We lived in the tropics, right? I guess your parents adapted to circumstances as best they could!"

This comment bears reflecting upon, if one considers the tarantula's association with death divinities in Haitian Vodou. People from the countryside who worked in the house would have undoubtedly interpreted this visit as a sign.

5. An Amalgamated People

Babies born in the Bourand Clinic were from the bourgeois mulatto class who still ruled Haiti then. They were twentieth century descendants of aristocrats or adventurers who had fled revolutionary Europe and found a tropical island inhabited by former slaves, recently rid of their colonial masters through insurrection, massacre and fire. In

1804, Haiti had become the first free, black nation. Yet these men knew nothing of the art of living in a society other than the colonial model of master and slave previously organized on the island.

European immigrants newly arrived in Haiti slipped easily into leadership roles that quickly mirrored power relations already established in feudal Europe, before and during the slave trade. They behaved the way aristocrats had in their countries, appropriating all the wealth of the land for themselves and their children, using the black population to facilitate and maintain their luxurious lifestyles.

Photos of my father's mother as a young woman, living in Haiti's sweltering heat, show her wearing the lace-lavished, high-collared, long-sleeved, ankle-length satin dresses and ostrich-feather-plumed, wide-brim, somber-colored hats that my French grandmother also wore in Paris's temperate climate.

In contrast, and responding to the comment my mother made when I was just born, bemoaning my Chinese look, I might add that the single Chinese family I ever heard about in my childhood had not arrived in Haiti until the early years of 1900, presumably running away from collapsing dynasties. By and large, they must have been a people used to economic hardships and social inequalities of imperial China, where refinements in education and the arts were extreme but reserved for privileged, restricted groups. Chinese families thus found in Haiti a foreign yet similarly stratified social structure. These newcomers to the Caribbean habit of human exploitation birthed generations of artists able to endure the deprivations of artistic life, sacrificing material comfort to the development of vision, sensibility, and spiritual purpose. They left bold legacies of surrealist paintings now preserved in the island's museums, situated in the Presidential Palace's neighborhood, and hanging alongside paintings of heroes of the slave revolution. Other Chinese families followed, as well as many families from the Middle East; with persistence, they too eventually flourished.

6. Home

In our very first house, an angel cried, feet in water. As a toddler, I stood by him in the children's basin while the Caribbean sun tickled my skin. Mosaic steps were black, white, and hard. They led to the back garden where chickens cackled in crowded coops at easy reach of the wrinkled cook who silently grabbed one, early every Sunday morning.

Fed and guarded as the chicken had been, I too fattened up and grew until I developed into a willful biped. At three years old, I was secured with an inflated rubber belt around my waist and told to jump in the pool. My survival was conditional on my learning to stay afloat, so I quickly learnt to flap, splash, paddle, kick, toss, gurgle and resurface. It was surprising how I managed. Memories of the womb might have been stirred. It could be inferred that I somehow remembered my previous ease in water before birth, and the comfort of fluids caressing my skin. I eventually became bold enough to plunge underwater, and hold my breath with open eyes.

As soon as I had grown enough to manage running off on my own, I skipped out of my mother's distracted watch. It was not difficult to escape her attention; she enjoyed a vast array of sophisticated toiletries for long stretches of time when she was not engaged with painting self-portraits in a variety of guises; prior to marrying my father, she had been a student at the Atelier des Beaux Arts—the Paris School of Fine Arts, as well as an opera singer. So it became a habitual sight for neighbors to notice me frisk and saunter on the fissured sidewalk alongside our house. Most often, I was on my way to the Virgin of the Immaculate Conception's blue grotto, a local replica of the French original in Lourdes, which stood near our house.

The place drew me like a magnet. I had somehow overheard and understood that a white figure in a dazzling light had appeared several times to the peasant girl Bernadette Soubirous, saying, "I am the Immaculate Conception," and how this manifestation of the Virgin Mary stood high up in a grotto from which miraculous water eventually sprang. The intellectual and emotional distance between the miraculous and the magic is easily crossed, especially for a child. As a small girl just learning to maneuver in a tangible world of discernible yet uncontrollable, and possibly hurtful things, I was hardly troubled, in fact was mostly attracted, by what could suddenly appear to us, manifestations coming from a realm of invisibility into which one cannot enter but may witness if the internal conditions of the heart are right. Each time I went to the Virgin's grotto, it was deserted; this state of affairs made the holy, secluded place of prayer feel like my own private space, where I would keep company with angels and saintly beings perfected in kindness, attentiveness, and beauty. Standing in front of the reproduction of the original grotto, all I knew was the wonder I felt at the dream-dazzled eyes of the lady sheltered up high, wearing a long white robe and sky-blue sash. I sat on a bench. I stared at the Immaculate gazing at heaven. I looked where she looked and thus lost myself in the azure of the immense Caribbean sky.

I was seven when we moved to the second house, a Victorian gingerbread built on the side of a hill with a stream running below. It had a surrounding gallery-porch like a girdle holding up termite-eaten green walls. I stood on my hands and put both feet up against the hollowed walls to experience an alternate way of being. My face then was at the level of the dog's eyes while he stared, tail wagging—he licked my nose and thus taught me tenderness. At night, a melancholic moonlight shone through the Victorian lace woodwork of railings surrounding the second floor balconies. Bats came out of the attic where no child's investigation was allowed. They started at dusk, coming out of a round window-hole in a continuous flurry, scattering in space. It was rumored by house workers that bats would catch in your hair and could never be pulled out without cutting it all off. It made sense then that I should cover my head with a scarf borrowed from my mother when I crouched in a dark corner of the pool terrace to watch them circle above and take turns touching the water. It seemed to me that this was a bewitching rite performed by bats each day at dusk; I watched it in a perfect state of awe until a practical, science buff cousin taught me that the goings-on were quite ordinary, seeing that bats drink in flight.

The third and last house in which my parents, my brother and I lived as a family, was built where the Victorian house had been—

concerned over the damage done by termites, my father had it demolished. The modern house remained unfinished in the ways that we still are—all four of us as interdependent as stray dogs. During meals, we each occupied one side of the eight-foot long dining table, sitting far enough from each other to feel safe. An illusion. Mosaic steps leading upstairs were black, white, and cold. I raised myself on my toes to kiss my father goodnight while he stood by the door of his chamber. My mother wore transparent blue negligées, and took a long time getting ready before going to bed.

In my bathroom, a tarantula took shelter in a hole behind the ceramic bidet. When I turned the light on in the middle of the night, I'd find it creeping about, looking like a devil's hand, with hairy fingertips pressing onto the floor. It appeared unmoving, absent even, devoid of all intent or interest, but I wasn't fooled. It knew my every move. It felt even the slightest breeze coming through the upper window that filled each night with stars speckling heaven. I saw how it shivered and swayed, daring me.

7. Crossroads

The Bourand Maternity Clinic, a plain façade, two-level building, stood at a crossroads.

One of these roads, the Laluc Road, gave its name to an all-girls school administered by French nuns who ran in long grey habits and lorded over classes filled mostly with black children, descendants of former slaves, who wore dull black shoes with thinning socks that pulled down at the back of the ankles. A minority of mulatto girls with long hair kept to playmates of their own kind in the yard during recess. A white larger-than-life statue of the Virgin Mary above the arch of the main entrance gate surveyed all the traffic below with a benevolent gaze. It was under that comforting supervision that my cousin Therese entered the school every morning, with her long blond braids, calm and confident, as if angels had kissed her from the start of life. Although four years older than me, she accepted me as a playmate when Louise was not around. We painted watercolors of Port-au-Prince bay sitting on our grandmother's terrace, nested in the hills of Bourdon above the city. Her parents nicknamed her "Poupée—Doll;" her brother, William, was "Ti Crabe—Little Crab;" my father nicknamed my brother "Lapin—Rabbit;" I was "Crapaud—Frog." Therese's was the only endearment name not associated with a beast.

The other crossing road, the Pond-Morin road, referred to as such because it runs by the Pond-Morin bridge, went South to Turgeau where we lived with a chicken coop in the back garden. In that same Pond-Morin neighborhood, near the Church of the Sacred Heart of Jesus, a little bakery produced small, square, thick, spongy breads made with lard, called ti-beurre. They were baked out of chunky sheets of dough, into which parallel lines were indented with a knife before baking, traced vertically and then horizontally, two inches apart, so that the whole could be parceled out into thirty-six smaller segments that would break off easily, letting out a welcoming sweet scent of fresh bread. They were sold in downtown Port-au-Prince by street vendors who gathered at the bakery's front door, very early every morning, right before the appointed hour when the owners opened the shop. They would stock them in the flat, flimsy straw baskets they carried on their heads all day, travelling through the crowded sidewalks of dusty streets whose every corner sheltered piles of sour orange rinds, amidst the buzzing of flies.

My father knew the baking schedules of the bakery in the lower Pond-Morin area perfectly. On days when he felt joy, he drove my brother and me, giggling in the back seat of the green Mercedes, to buy bread, fresh out of the oven. They would still be warm when we got back home, impatient to spread New Zealand butter and Haitian guava jelly with a sterling-silver knife into the vulnerable white belly of the cooked dough.

North of the bridge area and road we called Pond-Morin, the Delmas neighborhood was developing, and the first drive-in cinema in Haiti was built there. Friday night at the movies was the one family outing when my mother did not look pained and bored. She would ignore my brother and I arguing in the back as we struggled to see the screen between the heads of our parents. The cinema played French war movies while we ate ham and lettuce sandwiches layered with thick slabs of butter. Mother had grown up in France during World War II when butter was a luxury.

The Delmas road was Haiti's first highway and represented growing wealth in the country. Yet, the North-bound Pond-Morin road we used to reach it snaked through slums that spread increasingly over the years, leading all the way to the old Maïs-Gaté Airport, now the François Duvalier Airport, where it ended.

This airport bore the name of the dictator who built it while he destroyed the country—upturning its social structure, dismantling the economy, suffocating the mulatto class—murdering entire families—and bringing the peasant class to its knees, eventually to mass exodus, abandoning the country any way they could, even if it meant drowning at sea in a flimsy boat headed for the shores of Florida. These were the same people to whom he owed his election to power.

Francois Duvalier saw to it that people who passed through his airport would feel shattered as they left, whether expatriating themselves for political, personal, or economic reasons. At the Francois Duvalier airport, my family experienced innumerable separations that caused irreparable dislocations and irretrievable loss. In some way, the Pond Morin road, from its starting point at the Bourand Clinic to its ending point at the airport, saw the births of my family, and its endings.

2 Legacy

1. Untold Stories

"At the beginning of 1964, a mysterious Haitian arrived at Jack Kennedy's grave site in Arlington cemetery," historian Alex Von Tunzelmann wrote in Red Heat: Conspiracy, Murder, and the Cold War in the Caribbean. "He took a pinch of earth from each corner of the grave. He opened a flacon, and swished it around in the air above it. Finally, he plucked one dead flower from a wreath lying upon it... Papa doc, it was said, needed the earth, the air, and the flower to summon Kennedy's soul, which he would then use to direct American foreign policy...

"Having ascended, in all but name, to the status of a king, Duvalier went about investing himself with divine right. In July, he had the Lord's Prayer rewritten. 'Our Doc, who art in the National Palace for life... Thy will be done in Port-au-Prince as it is in the provinces... forgive not the trespasses of those anti-patriots who daily spit upon our country.'"(1)

Of course, reading this stuns a reasonable mind. But much of Haiti's history remains untold. The world has not cared enough. Island stories have caught the imagination of bright children and treasure hunters only. Haitian families keep their secrets in mahogany chests. There is meaning in this small fact, deep meaning that relates to the underlying substance of the past, and the sensitive nature of Haitian existence. A country's history can be studied through the geological stratification of its layers. Human lives are in layers as well, and can be examined like geology; the stories we tell of ourselves reveal the ways in which we are stratified; we are a kind of earth, dust similar to that which we are meant to become and return to; we are ancient cities that can be uncovered by archeological digs, showing how new rooms and space in us are continually added onto the old.

The West Indian Mahogany is indigenous to the Caribbean. Haiti's earth is the result of layers upon layers of humus created by layers upon layers of its native tree's matter; its leaves, red bark, russet seeds carried by ocean breeze like translucent wings of dragonflies, and the scent of its auburn tears when its trunks are cut. Arawak Indians who once inhabited the island made canoes out of mahogany; their name for the tree is not known, but African slaves later brought to the island may have been moved by its resemblance to the 'm'oganwo' tree they knew at home, and perhaps coined its present name.

The tree's wood, like the Haitian people growing alongside it, has a red-brown color and an even grain, free of voids, resistant to rot. The U.S. has become the leading importer of this most durable of all hardwoods that exhibits excellent workability, and proves so highly versatile that it is used anywhere and for anything. Mahogany has been utilized to make boats, musical instruments, sculptures, pens, tables, chairs, cupboards, beds, billiards, floors, and doors. Its presence has therefore been felt during our travels, creative endeavors, mealtimes, relaxation, dreams and leisure. The walls of the house in which I was raised were paneled with mahogany. I was cocooned in mahogany. I am mahogany, an indigenous West Indian breed, and a U.S. import. It must be pointed out how trees are seen as endowed with mystical power by the Haitian peasantry; when a child is born, the parents dig a hole, put the umbilical cord in it, and plant a small tree on top to ensure longevity.

Mainland people everywhere are nevertheless profoundly unconcerned with life in Haiti, the nature of its flora, its fauna, and its inhabitants. This disinterest has lasted since the time of Columbus first setting foot on the island (who will thereafter be credited for its discovery, thus marking the start of Haiti's recorded history), and that of President Duvalier's messenger sent to pinch soil from President Kennedy's grave.

Such disparate and far removed events are yet not unrelated, albeit admittedly singular. Haiti and America's narratives are interconnected. Plunder, betrayal, desecration, demise and rebirth are elements of every human story, and of every land.

Yet in this instance, the question must finally be asked: How did Haitians come to suffer the dictatorship of a president such as Papa Doc? A small man, a quiet country doctor who, rumor has it, once welcomed his ministers and the press, while sitting on a toilet and wearing a soldier's helmet; he then followed this public display of himself with a live radio interview, where he declared in a markedly nasal and raspy voice, "I am an immaterial being…"

How could that be—an entire population evolved in such a way that an absurd, arrogant statement come from a man dressed like a buffoon, might actually have significance or cultural relevance enough, not only for it to have been allowed to happen, but also to have inspired fear and respect? One might also wonder if Haiti has the monopoly on such political clowns.

Oddly enough, in this case, I can explain how the rogue's dress and army headgear (a grisly satire of defense ministries), adding to the braggart's statement made in a disturbingly-pronounced nasal tone, actually all pointed to features that most Haitians would identify as Bawon Samdi's, Lord of Death, and indeed an "immaterial being." While many spirits are recognizable through various personal idiosyncrasies during their instances of spirit-possession, Bawon Samdi's entire family, the Gede, all share this characteristic nasal speech sound, whereby Haitians recognize them instantly.

It should be added here that Duvalier, in his pursuit of power, was not the first politician who made artful use of Vodou to manipulate the spirit world as well as the Haitian population's psyche. The difference here was that he flaunted it where others acted in secret. The name Papa Doc itself is astutely chosen, alluding as it does not only to ancestral power and fatherly protection, but it also draws on the loyalty and fear Haitians have for major Vodou deities, such as Papa Gede, Papa Legba, and Papa Dambala. Going from the cult of these many Papa gods, to rewriting the Lord's prayer seems an easy step; replacing "Our Father who art in heaven," with "Our Papa Doc in the National Palace" has an obvious kind of madman's logic to it.

Vodou must have been, in its African origins, a series of devotional practices developed toward forming a relationship with the sacred, and evolved into magic tools used for furthering one's material gain, success, and power. In modern times, Vodou has undoubtedly been influenced by the lasting effects of colonialism on a marginalized, belittled, and abused population. A host of unnatural feelings rose in the slave population, asking for compensation, revenge, and an equally glorious place under the sun as they saw colonialists and capitalists enjoy.

While is can be pointed out that all people of the world pray to God for the purpose of improving their lot, not all religions offer these odd rituals-turned-recipes that dispatch a surprising assortment of spirits to act in the interests of supplicants, and usually at the expense of others. While Catholic saints can be asked to intervene in our favor, they cannot be sent off for a job the way Vodou deities might. While God, or one of His saints, might answer one's prayers, and improve one's condition, He will not do so if our better luck entails doing harm to another. Vodou spirits do not bother with such sensitivities—they will argue instead, that people are responsible only for themselves, and each must work independently at pleasing the gods.

The notion of the common good is absent. Vodou offers a form of worship that appears narcissistic—it seems the stage for such behavior as "each man for himself, and God for all." While Hollywood offered to the Western world a horrific interpretation of Vodou practices, much of it sprang from factual occurrences. The movie industry might only be accused of having turned up the volume too loud.

Going back to the live, helmeted Duvalier broadcast on the radio, madness is shown to be relative. Was this pre-planned theater, intended to manipulate and control the Haitian population's unconscious, its reverence for, and dread of the lord of graveyards? Or was it a true instance of spirit-possession by Bawon Samdi of the island's president? In which case, the dictator would still have inspired reverence and dread—not only because of the evident ease with which he handled possession by such a forceful, often uncontrollable deity, but because he obviously did control that deity's spirit-possession enough, that he could safely make a public display of it, in the presence of his ministers and of the local and foreign press. In this wild manner, the dictator showed how confident he felt defying the entire nation, and the world.

While there is a tacit agreement floating between state and church over the fate of the island's population, namely that the former will retain power over citizens and the latter over souls, the Roman Catholic authorities on the island would undoubtedly have been outraged by this incident, and felt it as a slap.

The reason for this is that the dance between the Catholic Church and Vodou religion was already awkward during the French colonial rule of the island, and has remained tenuous since, when not outright hostile. Anti-superstition campaigns in Haiti, as they were called, raged from the late 1920s through the early 1940s. These were years of crisis for Vodou practitioners in Haiti. The repression of popular ritual practices had already begun at the start of the US occupation of Haiti in 1915, and lasted until the Americans left in 1934. This repression was however immediately followed in 1935 by a post-occupation Haitian state's tightening of the penal laws against what were then qualified as superstitious practices. Then, between 1940 and 1942, this new law became the legal basis for the Roman Catholic Church's most severe campaign against Vodou to date, with initial military backing from the government of then Haitian President Elie Lescot.

Yet, catechisms printed in church manuals, predominantly distributed to French priests, along with newspaper reports, personal letters, and other sources, suggest that the church's campaign must also be understood as an effort to combat the spread and influence of Protestant Churches in post-occupation Haiti. Jacques Roumain, a distinguished writer renowned for his novel, Gouverneur de la Rosée— Master of the Dew, as well as co-founder of the Haitian Communist Party, founder of the Haitian Bureau of Ethnology at the height of the anti-Vodou campaign (and also a relative of my father's mother, Maria de Lespinasse), became the church's most prominent critic of the church's war against Vodou. His articles of 1942, published in Le Nouvelliste, became the basis for his longer essay on the campaign, subsequently published in French and Spanish. Then finally, in February and March 1942, the Haitian state withdrew its support of the campaign, giving as its reasons a series of disturbances happening in Port-au-Prince churches. The Catholic hierarchy in Haiti ended all so-called "anti-superstition missions" shortly thereafter.

How did life on the island ever develop such unnatural phenomena, when there must have been loveliness and much simplicity at the start of it? One can easily imagine how, pleased by the sight of long beaches, wild coconut plantations growing at the foot of steep, verdant, red-earth mountains whose valleys harbor serpentine rivers, man might have been tempted to lay down in the shade and think that the sky is an unusually promising color; he could be content in this place; it wouldn't take much courage to live here, and he has sense enough that he could thrive.

But this is where appearances are deceiving; what is beautiful wants to be looked at; it is not only the mountain that is vain. The mountain blocks what lies behind and in the distance; one can only see what is attainable at a glance. What pleases the eyes confuses reason. Who can say, "I do not love you" to a people who look through eyes tainted with warm tones? Who can be dismissive of land laden with natural stretches of sugar cane?

My ancestors surely fell to their knees, praised the flowers and the grass, and implored hills and rivers out loud, "Give me some room that I may settle here to watch my children grow, allow us breath to live long enough, and see that my children's children increase and thrive."

Yet, what comes to stand at the front door cannot be accounted for, regardless of one's well-intended pleas. What happens is eventually exposed by increments of time. History and truth are coy. It may even appear subversive if I say, "To be from Haiti is to bear a hard legacy." It is to be heir to a culture of slavery, racism, and colonialism; heir to Haiti's bold war of independence that led to the establishment of the first black republic; heir of all the slaves who fought against the indecency of exploitation; heir of Haiti's founding fathers, as well as of all leaders thereafter.

2. Colonization of the Island

The effect of the unrest of gods and ghosts cannot be truly estimated. Foreign occupation in Haiti began in 1492 when Christopher Columbus discovered the island of Hispaniola: 29,418 square miles, its greatest length being 400 miles, its width 150. Within a decade, the Spaniards decimated the indigenous Taino Indian population.

"Have we displeased the spirit of Yúcahu, that the sea might transport devils?" the welcoming Indians questioned the heavens, finding themselves mercilessly enslaved in forced labor in the mines and fields, falling ill from smallpox and other infectious diseases that the Spaniards brought on their ships, and failing miserably at rebellion. Modern scholars evaluate the general Taino population to have been of about 400,000 when the Spanish arrived. It is generally agreed that fifteen years later, their numbers had shrunk to 57,000. By 1531, the Taino population had declined to 600. Today there are no easily discerned traces of Arawak/Taino at all.

The destruction of the Indian population did not overly concern the Spaniards. The Dominican Priest Bartolome de Las Casas had written to the pope, suggesting that African blacks would tolerate the climate better than the Taino Indians did. In this way, the slave trade began, and by a man who soon retracted his views; Las Casas then spent fifty years of his life fighting slavery and the violent colonial abuse of indigenous people.

It may seem ironic now, considering the conflicts that would later repeatedly arise between the Catholic Church and Vodou, that it was a Dominican Priest who unwittingly brought the Vodou religion to Hispaniola by inspiring the importation of slaves—Africans traveled with their gods and worship systems, thus taking along the spiritual weapons and support system that gave them inspiration and courage in their misfortune, served them during revolutionary wars, and led them to freedom.

It is undeniable that creatures covet each other's pleasures and profits. People are unbelievably inventive when it comes to assault and theft; children know it; jackals know it too. Seamen learn from observing the ways of sharks. Soon enough, pirates and privateers seized the Northwestern part of the island of Hispaniola. They continuously harassed and impeded the Spaniards who eventually, in 1664, moved their holdings to the Eastern part of the island, abandoning the mines where the Indian genocide occurred. The Spaniards became ranchers, finding that flatter land and vast grazing areas were more suitable for a fruitful life and the increase of generations.

How much life changes, and yet how unchanged it remains, inducing a certain lethargy, while allowing men to carry on with their ways. These pirates and privateers, the majority of them being French, petitioned their king to legalize their status and land ownership. The buccaneers' requests were accepted; the French sovereign could be relied upon to acquiesce to such a sudden advantage. Consequently, in 1697, the western third of the island became a French colony, and called Saint-Domingue instead of Hispaniola. France profited so much from their sugar and cocoa plantations that Haiti became known as the Pearl of the Antilles.

In time, slave rebellions broke out. What else could they do? A pattern had already been set. The Indian rebellions had failed, but ghosts murmur in those places where they once bled, and touch the hearts of those who suffer still.

African slave rebellions started in 1790, after 298 years of slavery. How can we expect to understand such things? What can be deduced from human nature that people can be corralled into unrewarded servitude for 298 years? Why did the structure finally burst? Can we just say, "At about midnight a few people rose...?"

So here began the extraordinary, much-forgotten tale of Jacques Vincent Ogé, an affranchi—a freed slave—who represented the colony in France in 1790, but eventually eluded colonial police who tried to prevent him from leaving the country. Ogé managed to escape from France to England, then to the United States, and finally to Hispaniola, where he organized a "common front of people of color against the forces of white supremacy." However, the colonists outnumbered the rebels, and resistance collapsed. After yet another escape for his life, Ogé went into hiding in the eastern part of the island, in Spanish Santo Domingo.

But the spirits of the time were in high turmoil, and the slaves had not said their last word. The Haitian revolution started again after the ceremony at the Bois Caïman, or Alligator Woods. Boukman officiated, a Vodou priest said to be a mountain of a man with a face as etched and chiseled as an African stone carving. It is then, on August 21, 1791, that slaves solemnized their pact in blood. Upon a given signal, plantations would be set aflame, and a generalized slave insurrection started. The ceremony was the result of months of planning and strategizing, during which slaves met in a thick wooded area of Morne-Rouge. Legends about that final night and ceremony speak of tempestuous storm, a great fire, and the presence of Vodou deities assuaged by the blood from animal sacrifice, and sworn to help.

As both a sacred dance and religion, Vodou was expressly forbidden in the French colonies. Despite rigid prohibitions, it remained one of the few areas of totally autonomous activity for the African slaves. It most likely gave them a sense of psychological liberation and human dignity that enabled them to remain alive. Vodou brought together disparate forces in the colony, eventually uniting them to fight side by side. Vodou also became the stage where enormous and vital creative measures for spiritual survival were evolved, giving rise to an imaginative, syncretic form of worship that interweaved Christian saints the colonists imposed, and African deities the slaves loved.

In the 19th and 20th century, Vodou was widely misunderstood in the rest of the world. Hollywood has ignored its rich history and complexity, all the while portraying the religion as primitive, savage, gruesome, and perpetuated by sex-obsessed priests and participants.

Going back to the 1790s however, we see how slave rebellions grew into a full-blooded colonial war between the French, the Spaniards, and also the British, who came from Jamaica, lured by potential profit. Differing struggles for power culminated in a Haitian revolution for independence that lasted between May 18 and November 18, 1803—the final six months of violence after twelve years of bloodshed.

3. The Founding Fathers

Seen through my eyes, Haitian history took no respectable pause. In the beginning, Toussaint Louverture was a free black man and an army doctor who took the wool out of his ears, and helped the clamoring slave colony. He is the best-known leader of the Haitian revolution. Yet the man was homely, small framed, and dressed simply; abstemious, and a vegetarian, he was also a fervent Catholic opposed to Vodou; but as a leader, he inspired awe and adulation.

When a sudden slave revolt began in August 1791 after the Bois Caiman ceremony, Tousaint was at first uncommitted. In a few weeks' time he had however resolved his indecisiveness; he joined the black forces, then burning plantations and killing Europeans as well as mulattos. Once he realized the ineptitude of the rebel leaders, he took action with military and political acumen that saved the gains of that first insurrection. Collecting an army of his own, Toussaint trained his followers in the tactics of guerilla warfare.

When France and Spain went to war in 1793, Toussaint and his black commanders joined the Spaniards of Santo Domingo, the eastern two-thirds of Hispaniola. But one year later, in 1794, the opportunity Toussaint was waiting for came when France declared the end of slavery. His switch was decisive. He has been called duplicitous for his dealings with his onetime allies, Spain and Britain, when he took arms for France against these two countries on account of their refusal, unlike France, to free all slaves. In time, he emancipated the slaves, and also struggled against Napoleonic France to obtain the island's colonial sovereignty.

The man had uncommon purpose and vision. He helped transform the 1791 insurgency into a revolutionary movement. By 1800, the colony had turned into the first freed-slave society to have explicitly rejected race as the basis of social ranking.

"Well, that worked!" Toussaint must have thought with satisfaction, finding himself at last in command of the entire island. He who had been scornful of pompous titles once offered him by the British, dictated a constitution that made him Governor-General for Life, with no provision for a French official. And so may have unwittingly started a ludicrous "For Life" trend among future leaders of the country.

Feeling enough annoyance from history taking a critical look at their lives, men will undoubtedly turn in their graves. The stability of the ascetic black general's plan depended on the reliable emotions of an already rebellious group of incensed men who lost patience with domination whilst they were also easily intimidated by it. Was it a wonder then that he later found himself betrayed, led to a trap, arrested, deported to France, and locked in the dungeons of the Fort-de-Joux, where he died? After his arrest he said, "The tree of freedom has been cut down. But it will grow back, because its roots are deep and numerous!"

Jean-Jacques Dessalines served as a lieutenant under Toussaint after the 1791 slave revolt. Both of them fought in the Spanish army, both switched to the other side once France abolished slavery. Their efforts significantly helped curtail Spanish and British incursions.

By 1799, Dessalines had risen to the rank of brigadier general. Toussaint's betrayal and capture in 1802 then brought Dessalines to the top of the chain of command.

"Won't you take a seat?" His spirit-guide tempted him. There and then Dessalines took the lead in the revolution. Two years later, tired of winning battles that did not put an end to the conflict, he imagined a solution: he ordered the massacre of thousands of people of the white minority, and all royalists. "Cut their heads! Burn their houses! And take no prisoners!" Three to five thousand people died in 1804. That did it.

Feeling bliss had descended upon him, Dessalines then declared the island an independent nation, and adopted the Taino name Haïti.

He may have found this exceedingly refreshing, for he then named himself Emperor Jacques I of Haïti, and also ruler for life. He declared Haiti an all-black nation and forbade whites from owning property or land there. A harsh regimen of plantation labor was severely enforced. Some blacks felt they were enslaved all over again. Dessalines's mad delight was short-lived. The consequences of what is ill obtained are akin to making a devil's bargain; the emperor was killed only two years into his reign.

But Jean-Jacques Dessalines had not acted alone. Alexande Pétion and Henri Christophe both took part in the revolution under Dessalines as his generals, and, in accord with the treacherous spirit of the time, they conspired to kill him as well.

Such were the results: General Alexandre Pétion, perhaps as a precaution, championed ideals of democracy but kept powers for himself, whilst the unhappy Christophe went to the North with his followers, and established an autocracy. No surprise there! In 1807, Pétion was elected president of the southern part of the republic, so, in 1811, short of being able to make himself king of the whole island, as the British once offered Toussaint, Christophe retreated to the North, and, feeling safe, proclaimed himself Henri I, King of Haiti.

It is important to understand the dictates and consequences of a racist colonial system that causes such internalized self-hatred as to inspire the abused person to imitate the abuser. We must consider the vicious circle around which the two dance. Human nature, essentially as unstable as the dust, is prone to imitate. Undermining the revolutionary spirit that brought freedom and dignity, Henri Christophe instituted a nobility that copied European models: he named his legitimate son Jacques-Victor Henry as prince and heir, built himself a palace called Sans-Souci, and then a citadel known as Laferière. This stone fortress was designated as a World Heritage Site in 1982. It was built atop the highest mountain, above the coastal town of Cap-Haitian, and was meant to help defend Haiti against the French if they came back. Yet this was an absurd military tactic, the death trap of hundreds of newly freed slaves used in forced labor by Christophe, who turned out to be a similarly self-proclaimed master, no better than those previously endured under French domination.

4. Embargos and Divisions, from 1806 Onward

To be from Haiti is to be heir to embargo and the continued division of people, from the world and among themselves: the Franco-American embargo in 1806 was the first Haiti endured, happening at the time when Dessalines was assassinated, and the nation weakened by the Pétion-Christophe duet then busy dividing the pie; it is also when separation occurred between opposing groups (It was not to be the last; the unexpected always occurs, as evidenced by the most recent U.S. embargo instituted in 1993, later said to have been apologetically called by President Clinton "a devil's bargain").

But soon after 1806 already, the wild appetite for separation, and senseless arguments in the new slave-instituted republic became further evident. It would almost appear that the population missed the marginalizing spirit of the slave masters they had expelled. The division established between kingdom and republic in 1807 with the battle of Sibert, ipso facto demonstrated what the people learnt from the isolationist spirit of the Franco-American embargo imposed on them just one year earlier—they enjoyed hostility enough to repeat and perpetuate it.

No other explanation comes to mind as to why a people newly united to win their freedom should have shown so little sense. But this did not suffice: the division already started between blacks and mulattoes, during a colonial rule they found no longer bearable, and overthrew at the great expense of violence and lives, was nevertheless reinforced by the constitution of Henri Christophe's Northern black kingdom in 1811, and in 1816 by the constitution of a Southern mulatto republic under Alexandre Pétion.

It is little wonder why Western powers that profited from slavery, whether at home, in Haiti, or in other foreign colonies, felt threatened and angered by this island population now governed by former slaves

No country in the world would concede Haiti's independence. France, to start with, had just suffered a major blow to its wealth and reputation; before the Haitian revolution, Haiti, whose French name was St. Domingue, had become more lucrative for France than the Thirteen Colonies ever were for Great Britain. Then Spain's interests were also at stake, since it still had its slave-based colonial empire in the Caribbean and Latin America. Great Britain itself was at that time the predominant world power, whose profits also depended on the brutal exploitation of African slaves, with Jamaica only a few miles from Haiti. And as far as America was concerned, acknowledging Haiti's independence would have thrown slavery, then the foundation of the South's economy and prosperity, into question.

Consequently, in the 19th century, from the start, the United States and the European powers challenged Haiti's sovereignty. Ordinary arguments are useless; the servant can be made to hear only by excessive shouting, or be grabbed by the throat. Foreign powers therefore suffocated the insurrectionist island of former slaves for many decades with devastating economic and political measures. They used Haiti's severe diplomatic isolation and the wreckage resulting from its revolution against the French to control it. Haiti's ensuing problems were then made worse by these countries' cruel and punishing neocolonial policies and actions.

Trade between the United States and Haiti was formally shut down in 1806; France joined the embargo against the small island at the time, but in 1825, also imposed an indemnity of 95 million gold Francs on Haiti (ten times France's own yearly budget in those days), for its losses in the slave trade and in the exploitation of Haiti's land-resources.

Germany then joined the game. A population with a majority of illiterate people is easily toyed with. It is most necessary to have advocates, when abuse and intimidation are being employed; but what is to be done when an octopus is found invading the refuge of common fish? The number of German citizens immigrating to Haiti had slowly grown significantly, and they quickly acquired great wealth and power. Three similarly-orchestrated conflicts happened between 1872 and 1902: German warships entered the port of Port-au-Prince, demanding from the impecunious Haitian government that huge indemnities be paid to German citizens who had actually been found guilty of committing crimes in Haiti; these citizens were already deported to Germany, and their properties nationalized by the Haitian government. In each instance, the Haitian government backed down. The Haitian flag was trampled, soiled, and left on show. The Germans prevailed, receiving the sums they demanded.

Macabre humor holds a certain allure. It is found in a tale that illustrates relentless passions playing-out in and around Haiti at the time of the Haitian civil war (division again!). Battles were raging between supporters of General Nord Alexis and those of Antenor Firmin, man of state and a pioneer of Haitian anthropology: on December 6, 1902,

Admiral Killick, then head of the Haitian navy, himself a supporter of Firmin and well aware that Germany was backing Alexis instead, received word that the German warship, the Panther, was coming to sequestrate his ship, the Crête-à-Pierrot, a 940-ton gunship. Admiral Killick immediately went on board and dismissed the whole crew; he then wrapped himself in a Haitian flag and fired in the powder room, exploding the ship, while he was on board, choosing to die rather than become prisoner of the Germans, thereby adding his name to the mounting list of patriotic madmen, courageous men, or selfless men who people the Haitian ancestral tree.

"Haitians, you speak of celebrating the centennial of your Liberty," said Dr. Rosalvo Bobo in his 1903 centennial address. "It really isn't so very clever to find reasons for new delusions. We entertain the world, which only knows of our existence through revolting caricatures."

5. A Quick Survey of 200 Years

Haiti's independence was won by former slaves, instinctual leaders, and self-made warriors. They were men who had grown up on hard labor, tyranny, heedless homicide, and barbaric conquest; in victory they displayed deviant vengefulness, and demented lust for the perversities of power.

The study of history reveals the arts of savagery. Methods employed by colonial nations to control a population and maintain power over them are committed to memory, and turned against them. The contagion of cruelty spreads insidiously. A kind of free-for-all fires in the brain, and people inflict on each other the very barbarity from which they suffered. From 1804 to 2004—200 years of independence and forty-four presidents illustrate this. The illness started by colonialism unfurled like a poisoned sail exposed to the winds of time.

Of these forty-four presidents, one retired, one stepped-down, and five died in office: a derisory total of seven peaceful, orderly transitions of power. Should someone be tempted to call this a gratifying number, or an illustrative one? Of the 37 fellows left, one was ousted, nine were forced to resign, seven were overthrown, thirteen fled abroad, Henri Christophe committed suicide, one was assassinated, one was executed, Tancrede Auguste was poisoned, Oreste Zamor was murdered in jail, Vilbrun Guillaume Sam was lynched, impaled and dismembered, and Cincinnatus Leconte was blown up by a bomb.

6. Civil War and Continued Mayhem (1902 to 1915)

While reviewing two hundred years of history, one could not but hope for the possibility of remarking finally, "And there came a gust of cool air." But such a respite from the mayhem never transpired. There are conceptualizing limits to be faced in the process of analyzing a large span of time. "Let us narrow the field and see…" is the only proposition that finally makes sense.

Even with the appraisal of Haitian history in just the twentieth century—starting not in 1804 at the glorious start of independence, but almost a hundred years later, in 1902—one inevitably comes to be dismayed and declare, "They had the most lunatic hopes, these men!"

It seems that nothing had really been gained from the freedom for which they had slaughtered the French, and then each other. An irate cynic might even argue that freedom had been a disservice to a people unprepared for it. Like jackals they fled, dispersing widely, but like Jackals are want to do they would rally, fiendishly packed, but snarling at each other, and, forgetting their hatred of the French as well as the atrocities they survived, an all-consuming greed for power bewitched them. This was at the time when Rosalvo Bobo would make his famous centennial address.

We therefore start our review with the years when troops of General Nord Alexis eventually prevailed against Antenor Firmin, and at the end of Haiti's own civil war. In heaven above, Admiral Killick, who had refused his warship to the German partisans of Nord Alexis, certainly compliments himself for his bold departure from life, every muscle of his body twitching with vexation and horrifying foresight.

Born in August 1820, Pierre Nord Alexis was eighty-two when he became president, and governed between 1902 and 1908. Wisdom and peacefulness are not necessarily by-products of old age; during those six years of the octogenarian's presidency, three known massacres were recorded. Civilians were torched in their homes. Disarmed young peasants were killed by firing squads, or executed in the infirmary while being treated. Dozens of political opponents, most of them from the intellectual and social elites, were arrested, mutilated, and executed. Massillon Coicou, a prominent Haitian poet, was one of the first victims of the killings; his body was decapitated, then thrown in a mass grave.

Nord Alexis's behavior is not surprising. Heredity and statistics go hand-in-hand and for the benefit of observers. No one could have expected a lesser degree of homicidal instinct coming from the grandson of the Citadel Laferière's builder, King Henri Christophe himself, albeit one born from his illegitimate daughter. And without stopping to consider for an instant that it might show him off in a ridiculous light at this juncture, President Nord Alexis also decided to have himself proclaimed "For Life."

In 1908 at last, President Nord Alexis fled to Jamaica. Seven presidents then followed each other during the next seven years—between 1908 and 1915.

President Guillaume Sam, the last one, was able to stay in power only four months. On July 27, 1915, one hundred and sixty seven political prisoners belonging to the social and political elite of Port-au-Prince were slaughtered in their cells by army troops laboring at the task, trampling on carcasses still warm, half-swooning in ecstasy at all the fresh blood. General Charles Oscar led the troops; for his trouble, he became a folktale figure of horror in Haitian culture during carnival where he dances among other brutes. Guillaume Sam fled his presidential palace and sought refuge with the French.

"Oh… That was close!" he might have thought as he closed the door to the guest bedroom he had been graciously offered, along with diplomatic protection. But next day, he was dragged by a mob out of the French Consulate, and they lynched and dismembered him.

This incident provided a pretext for the United States to occupy Haiti.

7. Racism Brought Back on the Island (1915 to 1934)

An insurrection of armed peasants, called the Cacos, started immediately in response to the US occupation. United States Marines were outraged. When captured, many disarmed Caco prisoners were executed. Torture of Cacos, or alleged Cacos included hanging men by their genitals, forced consumption of liquids until their stomachs ruptured, and crushing the tibia bones of prisoners between two gun butts. Historians collected oral histories and testimony that speak of the execution of civilians, rapes, lynchings, the setting of houses on fire with their inhabitants inside, and burying people alive.

Some one hundred and thirty years after the Haitian slave revolution, Franklin Delano Roosevelt, President of the United States from 1933 to 1945, made a declaration about Haiti that circulates on the Internet to this day, and that may explain the United States' views and intentions towards Haiti, not only at the start of the occupation, but dating back to 1804. "We must constantly provoke the division of the barefoot masses against the Oligarchy, and push the Oligarchs to tear each other apart. This is the only way for us to have a continuing dominance of this Negro country that gained its independence in combat, which is a bad example for the 28 million Blacks in America."

"The US did not give a cent in gifts to Haiti..." historian Roger Gaillard explained many years later in an interview with Jean-Roland Antoine, "...its occupying forces gave us an elbow shove that said, 'get up from that desk, I am going to manage your country for you because you are incapable of it...' Whose fault is it? It is our own fault—blacks and mulattoes—I am not ashamed to be Haitian, but I am sad to be Haitian... Back in 1915, we had no army, no administration, no roads, no hospitals. We had been incapable of performing on our own the tasks of a nation... And these were neither revolutionary nor were they socialist tasks... The occupying forces substituted themselves in place of our dominant class to perform the tasks incumbent on us—[the educated, dominant class], but that we just could not fulfill." (TNH – 1982- my translation)

One could nevertheless swear that President Nord Alexis's ghost came all the way from his grave at the St. Louis Cemetery and murmured to US Marines in their sleep, "My people are savages. They must not be allowed to remain intact." This is not such a far-fetched idea—Nord Alexis had actually negotiated with the US during his presidency in support of American interests in the Caribbean. This is just the man he was. I can imagine his argument: The single-minded, continued performance of atrocities work in your favor. With appropriate timing, decapitation has a calming effect on a disgruntled crowd.

It came to pass however, that Charlemagne Péralte, the organizer of the Caco rebellion, was eventually killed in 1919, four years after the start of the occupation. His naked body was publicly exhibited wearing a loin cloth; he was tied to a door leaning at a slant against a drab street wall; a rope going across his chest and under his armpits hoisted his shoulder bones up at the juncture just enough to cause his lifeless arms to resemble featherless wing bones wanting to open; a Haitian flag behind his back had been mounted on a flagpole bearing a crucifix. The evocation of the crucifixion was unintended—the dissemination of a photograph of Péralte's mutilated corpse by an airplane flying over the countryside, was meant as a warning. The people lit candles and turned the image into the icon of a martyr.

By 1920, only five years after the occupation, Roger Gaillard found that the number of Cacos and other innocent victims killed had already reached 15,000. Michel Rolph Trouillot, in his 1990 book, Haiti: State Against Nation, argues that an additional 5,500 civilians were killed in the same period during forced-labor construction of roads that facilitated the movements of US occupation troops throughout the country. Any civilian attempting to flee the labor camps was killed with machetes, as were those who slowed down their pace of work.

Franklin D. Roosevelt became the first U.S. president to visit Haiti when, on July 5, 1934, he came ashore at Cap-Haitien from the U.S.S. Houston. He met with President Stenio Vincent and an agreement was signed that would have the U.S. marines out of Haiti by mid-August. The U.S. left Haiti on August 1, 1934.

It is worth mentioning that FDR had been the only U.S. president to ever visit Haiti as president until President Bill Clinton visited on March 31, 1995, he to be held responsible in history for the U.S.-led invasion of Haiti in 1994 with 20,000 troops. It would be the second occupation Haiti suffered in the 20th Century.

Nine years after his July visit to Cap-Haitien, on October 14, 1943, President Roosevelt welcomed Haitian President Henri Lescot at a White House dinner, and spoke in words that might explain continuous covetousness and ensuing betrayals in foreign policies towards Haiti—and why France, Germany, Spain, Great Britain *and* the United States had trouble letting go of "continuing dominance of this Negro country" ever since 1804. President Roosevelt said, "Those of you who have been there know it is one of the most beautiful countries in the world... It has everything above the ground, and everything under the ground... you find there the most beautiful groves and forests... a place where you can grow everything that grows... I have had the most intense interest in the Republic of Haiti, and the development of its people in a way that will never mean exploitation by any other Nation. They ought to develop for themselves, and they have every opportunity in the world to do so... And so, in this new civilization that we are coming to, of mutual aid and in a cooperative management between all the Nations of the world, I think that not only can Haiti learn a lot from us, but we can learn a lot from Haiti... It is a wonderful thing that during all these years we have had such good friends down there in the Government of Haiti."

However, Haiti's external racist troubles did not end with the American occupation brought to a close by President Roosevelt in 1934. The Dominican Republic, two-thirds of the original island of Hispaniola, had taken their independence from Haiti in 1844. Almost one hundred years later, in 1937, Rafael Trujillo, of Haitian ancestry, but at the time president of the Dominican Republic, had nearly 20,000 Haitian migrants killed during the "Operation Persil," a racist killing in defense of what was called "territorial integrity."

8. Continuing Chaos, Home Grown Racism and Colonialism (1937-1957)

During the twenty years between 1937 and 1957, seven Haitian presidents followed each other, three of them in 1957 alone.

A loathsome game of musical chairs, adding to a demonstration of criminal pathology, possibly explains this state of affairs. In June of 1957, another massacre happened, augured by the famous statement, "Ti Kòk, ou kaka—Little Cockerel, you're fucked!" which Lieutenant. John Beauvoir told the populist President Daniel Fignolé, as first notification that he was being overthrown, albeit after only nineteen days of his presidency, and forced him into exile. The Haitian army then killed three thousand of his supporters; most of the victims lived in the Port-au-Prince slum neighborhoods of Bel Air, La Saline, and Saint Martin.

"Enough is enough!" Sustained public outcry should have been heard while, at the same time, immediate punitive action would have been fitting. More likely however, reactions to the news included shrugs, annoyance, and nervous laughter. And in a little while, if you asked again, you might have been told that history tends to repeat itself, human nature being what it is. And perhaps indeed it is well not to be obstinate, to yield to selfish delights in finding oneself safe from harm, and to recognize the right to existence that men and hyenas have, and tolerate them both.

General Antonio Kebreau was responsible for the killings. The population had nevertheless lost its taste for macabre effigies at that point; this general, unlike Charles Oscar, did not make it to being paraded or embodied as a yearly carnival cartoon. Instead, while he was backed by then-politician Francois Duvalier, he proclaimed himself head of the executive branch of government, and organized elections for September 22. Had he gone too far? He apparently did not, since Duvalier won the elections. This former country doctor lost no time afterwards in proclaiming his loyalty to poor, black, disenfranchised Haitians, those people living in the Bel Air, La Saline, and Saint Martin neighborhoods, the very population recently massacred by order of his collaborator, General Kebreau.

In spite of obstacles that appear insurmountable to our understanding, Duvalier brought power to blacks in Haiti by decimating the ruling mulatto class who had up to then refused to validate his government or comply with his fantasy of integrating their ranks. The new president put up a successful defense. Duvalier, the developing dictator of a country inhabited by a population with an already-existing complex color scheme and complicated attitudes about it, had himself grown up under the US Marines occupation that reinforced existing, internalized-self-hatred issues, handed down since colonial times.

Duvalier was eight when the Americans arrived, twenty-seven when they left, and fifty when he became president. The occupation remained imprinted on his memory, as demonstrated by his use of the techniques he learnt from Americans for maintaining power. The more theatrical examples of these techniques were seen in his street displays of decapitated bodies left to rot (like those of Massillon Coicou and Charlemagne Péralte during US occupation), until a foreign ambassador might complain that it was indecorous, and unbecoming of a respectable nation.

Haitians have been in the hands of military men from 1492 onwards, whether they were Spanish, French, liberated slave generals, American Marines, or Haitian politicians using the army. When a few polished intellectuals made it to president, these were quickly dispatched. Even when in the hands of a medical doctor they first fondly named Papa Doc, Haitians found that he too ruled with the army and an unprecedented ruthless private militia, the Tontons Macoutes, or boogeymen. In Haiti, men in power have been warriors or puppets of warriors, local or foreign. Turmoil is all they know.

9. The Year 1964

My cousin Guslé Villedrouin was my father's sister's firstborn child, and my godfather. He was seventeen when Papa Doc Duvalier came to power. His father, Roger Villedrouin, was a colonel in the Haitian army, a mulatto admired for his elegant horseback riding, and a supporter of Louis Déjoie, Duvalier's opponent in the 1957 elections.

Under Duvalier, and like everyone living in Port-au-Prince at the time, Guslé was exposed to violence first hand, violence different from that which he learnt about in school. Guslé lived in times when random people were routinely killed in the streets, or arrested at night and sent to the death-dungeons of Fort-Dimanche.

There were many massacres. On April 26, 1963, Duvalier's private militia of Tontons Macoutes carried out assassinations of several families of alleged opponents to the government, after a failed attempt had been made to kidnap his son, Jean-Claude. Tonton Macoutes raided homes, killing everyone inside, including children, the elderly, and servants; their bodies were left to rot in full view in front of their houses. Eventually, the attempted kidnapping turned out to have been orchestrated by Clement Barbot, a former head of Duvalier's secret service. The matter was dropped. The militia was sent to other chores.

Most citizens were relieved to have survived this recent culling, and went about their business. A species, however lax, rarely dies out, once it exists. But if such savage outcomes are valid and acceptable for such an inefficient people, must I not also accept them as valid? Guslé did not think so, and manifested his objections. Some of us praise the progress made by humans throughout the ages. Certainly knowledge is progressing. Wonder openly walks the streets. Indeed, a greater sense of possibilities moves us. Ah... but if only memory could not be so overburdened by the sorrows of yesterday!

And so, seven portentous years after Duvalier's election to power, "on August 5th 1964, a small boat landed at Dame Marie, on the far tip of Haiti's southern peninsula," Von Tunzelmann wrote again in Red Heat. "It contained thirteen young men: twelve mulattoes and one black. They called themselves Young Haiti. They had received modest funding from the CIA, and were trained at Special Forces camp in North Carolina. They were led by Guslé Villedrouin. He was twenty-four years old, and a former member of the United States Air Force. Another member of the group had fought with Fidel Castro in the Sierra Maestra. Young Haiti's plan was consciously modeled on the Granma invasion of Cuba. Its men meant to wage a guerrilla war, and recruit peasants to swell their forces.

"In Port-au-Prince, Duvalier noticed the parallel... [and] took command of the military response. Meanwhile, five fighter planes were illegally exported from the United States to Haiti. The State Department, still working with Duvalier even though the CIA was working against him, raised no objection. Soon, the men of Young Haiti were being bombed and strafed...

"Amid the torrential rains of the hurricane season, the men of Young Haiti would hold out as guerrillas in open country for an impressive eighty-three days, and survive at least ten skirmishes with government troops. But, one by one, they were captured..." Two of them, Louis Drouin and Marcel Numa, were caught alive when hunger pushed them to risk entering a small town on market day. They would eventually be executed in a televised, public display in front of the Port-au-Prince cemetery, after having been tortured and interrogated for several weeks. The video made of their death now circulates on the Internet.

"When seven remained," Von Tunzelmann continues, "Duvalier devised a plan to smoke them out of the mountains. He would take revenge on what was, for most of them, their hometown: Jérémie. He sent to Jérémie a notoriously brutal army lieutenant, José 'Sonny' Borges... Sanette Balmir; and one of the most feared Tontons Macoutes, Saint-Ange Bontemps. Bontemps was a psychopath...

"Houses were burned. Hundreds were arrested. Some were stripped and paraded through the streets. Most were beaten and several raped. The vilest punishments were reserved for the Drouin, Villedrouin, and Sansaricq families, whose scions were fighting in the hills."(2)

Guslé and his twelve companions had walked over 200 kilometers when, trapped in a ravine near l'Asile on October 26, the last three survivors were killed in a gunfight. When they ran out of ammunitions, they threw rocks at Duvalier's troops, Guslé having cried out to them, "Mourrons comme des braves—Let's die like brave men!"

Guslé was the last to die. He was shot and beheaded. Guslé's mother fainted at that same moment in a California parking lot. She was putting groceries in the car. When she came to her senses, she simply said to her husband, "They killed him... they killed my son."

How did she know? The essence of a secret is that it should remain a mystery. In his palace, Duvalier waited for the head of his enemy to be brought to him by helicopter—he hated and wildly admired him.

Prodigious as they seem in the moment, our intuitions are meager. We value and are affected by what we hold in the hand and can see, more than by what we know in the heart—and dread. Duvalier, in his gleeful dementia, wanted Haitian citizens to hold in their hands and heart the weight and confirmation of his victory. He therefore ordered Haiti's foremost newspaper to print a large front-page photo of Guslé's head held up by the hair. Whose hands and fingers were they that participated in that revolting act?

Freedom of the press is a victory men are proud of. The law is however what the rulers decide. Guslé's mother received notice of her son's death through this photo. An image so contrary to nature has a terrible effect on us. She spent the rest of her life trying to put the pieces of her heart back together because, "You see", she said, "all the limbs of his body may only live and be remembered in my heart now."

We, the family, Guslé's family, ended then too. Our collective history ended, although Haiti's history continued in newly written schoolbooks. We each took up our individual stories, carrying these around the world in separate luggage.

Wherever we went, Guslé's head was always haunting us, or waiting when we arrived; Guslé, son of Haiti, a fortress unto himself, as each one of us became. Like him, we were all heirs of the slave revolution of 1804, heirs of the Englishman James Phipps, one of the very first foreigners to be naturalized Haitian in 1805 by Jean-Jacques Dessalines himself, father of the revolution.

Guslé was by no means the first revolutionary in our family: James Phipps's son, William Phipps, was one of the revolutionaries who overthrew President Jean-Pierre Boyer in 1843; William Phipps's son, Delmar Phipps, was one of the revolutionaries who fought against the populist President Sylvain Salnave in 1870, the only survivor of the massacre of Vencendron, his life having been saved by a peasant woman, a coal vendor who hid him in her shack among the half-dozen sacks of coal she owned, and nursed his battle wounds. No, Guslé was not the first revolutionary of the Phipps family; but he may have been the last.

"It is really simple, and clear, how all that happened to our country and to our ancestors, in an indirect but infallible way, also happened to us," Guslé's mother said several decades after her son's death. "It will continue to determine not only the choices with which we, the family, will be faced in life, but also those that we will make, taking into account, obviously, our differences of personalities. My becoming an American citizen was one of those choices; I am endlessly grateful for it, and will always honor it. Yet, memories of our birthplace continue to sustain us, while they add meaning and lend direction to our lives, keeping us joined to each other forever." She was ensconced in a rocking chair on her Florida house gallery overflowing with ferns and begonias. She seemed almost absent, focused on the evocation of the past, missing her own parents still in an almost palpable way, her grandparents and godparents as well. Having said this, my aunt became quiet for a while, absorbed in her thoughts. Her eyes appeared calm until suddenly, a kind of fire came to light them up and she spoke again. "Besides, in that itty bitty little nothing of an island, all we had was each other!"

3 Write This in Remembrance of Us So Others Will Read and Love Us

1. Haitian Tarzan

The Paramount movie theater opened its brilliant doors in 1934. It was erected on the upper edge of a freshly cemented sidewalk running along the northern side of the Champ de Mars Plaza gardens, resonant with the sound of water fountains. When standing in front of the theater, one could see beyond the gardens' orderly spread of lawns that were edged with flowering laurel bushes, and admire the gleaming white presidential palace over whose encircling high metal fencing Guslé's head is said to have been spiked for public viewing some thirty years later.

Sunday afternoon matinées at the Paramount in the nineteen-fifties were very popular—seats were filled all the way to the front, while the auditorium buzzed with the chatter of excited children, smelling of Palmolive soap with which they had been scrubbed during their afternoon toilette, before having their bodies powdered with lilac-scented talc. The floating aroma of grenadine syrup stirred into *frescos* was also an element in the thrill of the moment, enjoyed prior to the movie staring; this was a crushed-ice treat presented in a paper cup that children crunched and slurped. There was also the pink or green taffy stick *tito* that inevitably glued onto fingertips and smeared over delighted cheeks.

Between Tarzan and Zorro, Guslé saw no argument; he wanted to be both. In these action-packed movies, both princely men had panache, dramatic allure, and virtuous ethics. He found the dashing, black-clad Zorro exciting; this outlaw who defended commoners and indigenous people of the land against tyrannical officials. He felt compelled by this hero's zeal for justice and the aura of secrecy kept around his identity and movements; the grand gestures he made in risking his life were truly gripping.

But while Guslé could dress himself up as Zorro, in a black costume with a flowing Spanish cape, a flat-brimmed black sombrero, and a black mask that covered the top of the head from eye level, he still felt the powerlessness of being a child, unable to affect the surrounding poverty.

Tarzan's life in the jungle, away from civilization, wearing only a loincloth, would prove easier for Guslé to imagine and embody. As he saw it, Haiti's tropical vegetation was like Tarzan's jungle; he did not have to envision it, he was in it. The Haitian adolescent could not have thrown himself with his whole heart into empathic connection with the feral boy raised to manhood by apes, if he had not been able to identify unreservedly with him, Tarzan's physique and generous character, an athletic, tall, well-tanned man who in any situation of conflict invariably took the side of underdog.

In the days when Guslé imagined himself as Tarzan, the family house was in Turgeau, a forest-green, two-story gingerbread house, with bougainvillea blooming all year, providing brilliant color and shade over the verandah.

The mango tree was at the back of the garden, towering far above both the house and swimming pool. Twice a week, the family laundry was spread over the pool's wide, plain-cement borders to dry in the sun. Children rushed to the tree every afternoon after school, competing for ripe, fallen fruits. They rarely found them unblemished since birds would peck at them while still green and swelling along high branches of the tree, and rats would gnaw the flesh after it fell.

The day Guslé took the rope up the mango tree there were no clothes spread out to dry around the poolside. It did not matter to him that the rope was not as long as the tree was tall; that day, he meant to see the world from great heights, and swing far above the rest. He first stood briefly under the tree, gauging the elevation, assessing the order, size and display of branches. He then made a decision, and started to climb.

2. Guslé's Fall

Guslé's father was sipping coffee from a flowered English porcelain cup on the second floor balcony outside his bedroom. He was known for his stature, proud bearing, harmonious features and large mournful eyes. He liked standing there after lunch to enjoy the privacy and coolness afforded by the lush canopy of the mango tree. Suddenly, he heard a noise, and looked above his head: Guslé was standing half naked on a branch of the tree, looking down at him.

"Son, get down from there immediately!"

"Yes, Sir!"

Guslé had not yet tested the rope when his father ordered him down. But he was a self-confident boy, and already cocky in the way he walked. So, the adolescent child grabbed the rope with both hands and jumped. Ever since he had seen the movie, he had practiced in the garden with great gusto the resounding call Tarzan let out while swinging from one liana to the next. But this time gravity took the breath and song out of him, while the unsecured rope loosened under pressure and slipped off the branch, and Guslé's whole body thudded like a sack onto the swimming-pool cement.

From the small window of the secluded storage room under the stairs habitually used for groceries, Guslé's sister had watched the entire scene. Head spinning, she heard her father shout, "Nobody touch him! I am calling an ambulance!"

He should have died. Instead, he broke both legs.

Both heels were shattered too. It was thought that he would never walk again. His mother flew with him to New York, where an ambulance came to pick them up at the airport. Mother and son stayed out of the country for several months, until the casts on her boy's legs were removed.

From this accident, Guslé never even limped.

Seeing him again after several months and remembering the unconscious adolescent she had seen on the cement ground by the pool, the washerwoman who had known him since he was a baby calmly said, "Lè l potko vini—his time had not yet come."

Twelve years later, Guslé was back in New York where he met with his mother. He was there to plot and organize a rebel invasion to free his countrymen from the Duvalier dictatorship. Had he been left with even just a limp from the accident of his Tarzan days, he could not have joined the group, let alone been their leader.

"Don't go..." his mother cried, tears coming out of her green eyes. "You can't save the world... they will kill you!"

"Mother," he said, "I am a dead man already."

3. Births

She had given birth to him at home, like her mother had, her mother's mother had, and all the mothers in Haiti then and earlier, peasant women, servant women, and bourgeois women alike. The Bourand Maternity Clinic where I was born had not yet been built.

Months before Guslé's birth, an angel had come to his mother in a dream and told her that she would have a son. The birth turned out to be easy. Dr Bayardel presented her with a child who had a full head of rich black hair. She found him exceedingly hairy, and so cried, would not hold him, and could not be comforted.

Guslé was four years old when his sister, Louise, was born in the early hours of January first. He had been impatient for the birth of his sibling and caressed his mother's growing belly every day, asking, "Mother... when?"

Dr. Bayardel was at the Turgeau Club when word was sent to him that he must hurry and come help deliver the child. At the house, the doctor bumped into Guslé who waited at the bottom of the stairs, excited and full of questions.

"My daughter just slipped out of me, a quiet, smiling baby," my aunt recounted at ninety-one, still glowing with faint pride from reminiscing that birth.

As soon as he heard the cries of the newborn, Guslé fetched his child-size rocking chair out of his bedroom, dragged it to the door of his mother's room, knocked, and waited. When he was let in, he walked straight to the foot of the bed where fresh white linen sheets had just been switched from the soiled ones, and planted his chair. He quietly sat, looked up at his mother with smiling hope, offering his little arms as crib for the baby.

When friends and acquaintances at the Turgeau Club learnt about the successful birth, they came en masse to the house. They found Guslé with his infant sister in his lap, holding her with dignity, refusing to let go. His father stayed at the club, waiting for all visitors to be gone before he went to see his wife and newborn daughter.

"My husband showed no emotions over anything… or for anyone…" my aunt said in later years. "I wonder if he fell apart the day they killed him…"

Guslé had his father's large, mournful eyes, but not their detachment. He was watchful to a fault. He would run from room to room, up and down the stairs, looking to report to his mother on his sister's needs and progress, or the maid's neglect of her. "My sister has not eaten enough… My sister is waiting for her milk… My sister is crying… she is wet." His persistent devotion is recorded in a single remaining photograph of the boy holding his sister with both arms the way he would carry her all day at the time, and until she just got too big. The image shows how she already was by then too much for him to tote, hanging like a mass at the level of her brother's pelvis. Both children look at the camera.

It is hard not to see in the picture their common understanding and acceptance of the mysterious bond that links them, through common blood, ancestry and country, and what weight in the heart this would forever entail for the whole of their lives. Four-year old Guslé already reveals in the photograph how his own wellbeing largely depended on the physical presence, happiness, and fulfillment of another like him. Later, this concern expanded to others and his brotherhood with all Haitians.

"My third child was so sad a baby that he had to be my last," my aunt recounted one evening in Florida. I was startled by her comment. I had flown from Massachusetts to visit her, and collect her memories about olden days. "I was ill with smallpox and in quarantine when I carried him, " she explained. "When he was born, I had spots all over my face and body. My maid, Felicia, cured me. 'Pa fatige w, Madanm, m ap wete tout mak yo nan kò w,' she said to me—'don't worry, Missus, I am going to erase all marks from your body.' 'Did she succeed?' You would ask now. Well… did she now! Look at me. Ever seen a mark on me? 'How did she do it?' you'll ask again. And the answer lies in so simple a recipe: coconut water! She said 'rinse your skin every day with fresh coconut water, and let it dry.' And I did. But it was difficult to tolerate. It was hot! I was *burning*! But, you can see… here… there is not one mark on me! Not on my face, not on my body! Still, all the while, my new baby boy was so sad it was almost hard for me… his own mother… to endure; he never smiled, he never laughed. He looked at me as if he already was filled with thoughts too big for him to contain. I felt his reproach—how could you bring me into this? And Guslé who felt everything wild under the sun, how could he not have felt his brother's sadness and desperately wanted to resolve it by any means he might? And since we hear stories about all of us coming to this world with foreknowledge of what will become of us, stories about how we all have agreed to trials and tests of character by which we will be faced. I have wondered I tell you, if this little baby already suffered from what was to come to his big brother, to all of us… and to you."

One day when most of the days in December had already gone, at a time when all my cousins had already been born, I in turn came into this world. On the occasion of my baptism in the Catholic Church, ten-year old Guslé wore his suit all day in spite of the heat. He held me in his arms at the baptismal font and later at the house party, passionately protective while various cousins and siblings ran around on tricycles, played hide and seek, ate white sugar-frosted almonds and three-layered orange cake in-between vivid gulps of cola-flavored soda. I was his God-given child, his godchild, and the only child he would ever hold at the baptismal font.

4. Stepping Ahead in Time

It was some sixty years after my baptism that I traveled to ask my aunt some questions about Guslé and family members I never really knew. I hoped to discover emotional currents running in our ancestry. We sat by the pond in my cousin Louise's garden, the three of us—aunt, cousin, and me—sharing with each other what we managed to rescue of the past through the melancholic treasure hunt in deep recesses of forgotten memories. Questions I asked my aunt unfurled, unchecked. Did she remember their faces animated or still as statues? Were they people contained within their thoughts? Did they prefer to read alone by a kerosene lamp at night, or did they look for each other to sit and chat in the darkness of a gallery, slapping the unavoidable mosquitoes stinging their bare arms? Did they use flowers, candy, or simply words, to say what mattered about the days they shared? Did they believe it was their appearance, or their gestures, that reflected best who they were? Or thought they were? What were the attitudes of the old folks that she remembered best? Why? Who among them believed in God? How did they manifest their faith?

Early in life, I sensed how my own story is influenced, and somewhat foretold, by events in the lives of my family. In secret folds of my memory lie traces and sensations left by those I watched and heard, respected, feared, or pitied while growing up. My own trajectory in life cannot be understood without taking theirs into account. I felt that I owed it to them to recount their stories along with mine, bring the essence of our common tale to the fore; theirs laid foundations for mine, even while I must assume responsibility for any ensuing imperfection or ennoblement of the whole I might represent.

The dark surface of my cousin's garden pond was laid in front of us. I saw it as a kind of glass plate negative of the subconscious, and let my gaze idle over it. I slowly began to distinguish, moving underneath, forms of the odd inhabitants of an aqueous world they continuously stir.

Frightened by steps coming too close, frogs will usually jump into the water, sinking to its muddy depths, where leaves rot. But on this mating day, they were all afloat, immobile, borne in the drunken stupor of instinctual behavior; countless males blindly competing for dominion onto the backs of passive females; females hanging onto whatever was close enough to be grabbed—water lilies, clumps of slime, the slippery edge of the pond. In their desperate attempts to breathe, free themselves and survive, they pushed each other off with the abrupt, senseless motion of an insipid, web-toed back leg, mindless creatures as they were, rapt in the infinite patience of eternity waiting on itself; crustaceous, bulbous growths exhibiting the appearance of death, but death foretold, to judge by the next morning when the innumerable lifeless bodies of drowned females resurfaced; limp sacks floating aimlessly, having succumbed under the weight of stubborn males.

"How was your trip?" my aunt suddenly asked.

"The plane shook, shifted, and dipped many times, but was redressed each time by the pilot's sure hands," I said. "The aircraft was being kicked around, but it resisted all it could."

"My son was a US Air Force pilot..." she mumbled, "... and a good pilot too." She had reached a time of life when she must resign herself to being brought outside in a wheelchair. She wore an embroidered turquoise blouse and a light-blue necklace whose beads were held together by an invisible thread. The beads were spaced in a way that made it seem they had been sprinkled around her neck to remain there, safe between the many folds of now-faded skin. She had been very beautiful.

I knelt in front of her, kissed her hands and blew lightly on them as if they were the small goat-spine bones we used in a game of dice when I was a child—blow on them to infuse new life, energy and magic, as did God's breath on Adam and Eve. These bones could only fall on one of their four sides, as if the four cardinal points, the curvy S, the straight I, the hollow, or the mound, each repeated throw of the dice determining the direction our game took, how we fared in it.

My aunt took my face in her hands and blew on me gently too. "When I was a child," she said, "and my heart overflowed, I would write a little note to my father and leave it under his plate… he replied the same way. He rarely spoke. He liked hunting alligators on Lake Azueï on weekends with a German friend who was accidentally killed there. With this death, my father lost the only friend he ever had in Haiti… and he spoke even less afterwards… one of the few things I remember him saying is, 'If you sit long enough on the toilet, shit comes.'"

4 Vodou and Me

1. Beings I Loved

Painted like a life-sized plaster saint one stumbles on in odd corners of provincial Catholic churches, my mother was the first mythical creature I loved. In the tropical climate of a small island, my early childhood seemed idyllic, surrounded by family either living next door or at the other end of a private path filled with wonder, a lyrical trail edged by tall weeds in which I walked in the faithful company of my basset hound mutt, *Trotinette*, and occasionally spotted *kaka-zombi*—zombie-shit—the local name given to a small fist-sized bulbous growth, red with black polka dots, that in reality is a specimen of the lattice stinkhorn family of mushrooms. I thought at the time these were real zombie turds. I avoided them cautiously, but only after having thoroughly examined them.

The time however came when my father gave Trotinette away to a German friend's daughter who wore long braids alongside her blue eyes; he and his brother were getting ready to send their families abroad. I saw my heartbreak reflected in Trotinette's frantic eyes that day. I learnt about accepting fate quietly from this sweet pregnant mutt who turned up at our gate one day, no doubt to illuminate my childhood, wagging hesitantly her black two-inch tail. I also later came to understand, how those we leave behind eventually forget us, their lives evolving richly without us.

My father and uncle only wanted to protect us from the dangers of living under a dictatorship; provide their children with a proper education, by enrolling us in schools that would not be closed due to political violence. Their sister Nicole, Guslé's mother, divorced from the father of her children, had already left the country with them and temporarily settled in Puerto Rico. My brother was sent to a Swiss boarding school, a trauma he bore silently but never forgave. I left Haiti with my mother and spent the uneasy adolescence of a foreign child in France. She and I lived in a town near Paris while my French relatives, grandmother, great-grandmother, uncle, aunt, cousins, and a great-aunt whose big bosom I marveled over, all seemed to occupy a realm other than the inaudible one in which I moved like an underwater being. They treated me with tenderness and dutifulness, revealing how they saw me as exotic and fragile, different from them.

My mother was however thrilled to be back in her country, busier revisiting delights of her childhood than helping me evolve from mine. She went out to clubs at night with old and new friends, telling me to double-lock the door, leaving behind the long-lingering scent of her Guerlain perfume, called, "The Blue Hour." Every school day, I woke up alone before dawn while she still slept to recover from her night out, ate the simple breakfast I prepared with unease, left the house noiselessly, then walked in a chilled winter darkness to the station where I waited for a bus in silence alongside girls in gray coats and boys who pulled my hair.

2. A Cracking Noise

At a family gathering one Sunday after lunch, I was quietly crouching in an unseen corner of the living room filled with antique furniture to eavesdrop on an adult conversation, when my knees made a distinct cracking sound. "What was that?" I heard my great-aunt ask while turning around to check the source of the noise and, seeing me, exclaimed, "My child, you sound like an old person!"

I was filled with alarm for the rest of the day, worried that Death had surreptitiously crept up on me, moved freely inside this "house of my soul" (what a priest had said about my body during confession), and was progressively inducing my bones to become prematurely dry to such a degree that they might prove unreliable as carriers of my weight and measure through life.

These were years when the Cartesian French culture strained the adolescent turmoil flustering my nascent persona, one initially issued from, and still feeding on vivid Caribbean mores I missed. For solace and model, I sought the company of saints in churches where I sat to read their biographies. I admired these beings that sought truth, built their lives on the miraculous, and focused beyond death. In their single-minded devotion to the idea of pleasing God above all else, I saw invitation and refuge. Statues of saints showed people possessing an unearthly gaze. I somehow felt that they saw me, and cared.

3. Instant Motherhood

I was in my mid-twenties when I returned to Haiti. Prior to that, I had spent some years in America following my time growing up in France, years first spent with a marriage in Texas, a divorce in California, but later filled with what I felt as a greater purpose when I became involved with studies in anthropology at UC Berkeley.

Once in Haiti, I soon married a dashing architect, Laurent, an older divorcee I first met at a French Embassy reception, a yearly Bastille Day celebration to which my father had asked me to accompany him. Laurent was tall, had short dark hair, and moved with elegant ease. He hovered over my face all evening, his green eyes intensely focused on me, laughing excitedly, revealing the wide space between his front teeth, believed in Haiti to be good luck. He went home that night as if a man under a spell, rushing to tell his mother next door about the hope in his heart. She must undoubtedly have reacted to her son's enthusiasm with reservations, albeit amusement.

Laurent had three small daughters, children in whose young lives I must have felt like a sudden and unwanted appearance, but one they graciously accepted. The youngest immediately adopted me as a mother figure but later retracted that sentiment. I was too young for the role and the few years the marriage lasted. I was more like an older sister who organized lyrical escapades in the countryside of Haiti, bathing in out-of-the-way rivers and hidden waterfalls, picnicking in pine forests or on the shores of lakes where pink flamingos strolled and alligators lurked. They never would have discovered any of this, had it been left to their 'clubby' father who spent all his time playing golf and tennis, or their New Englander mother who, though estranged from their father, doted on her girls, sewing frilly pastel gingham dresses for them that made the girls appear like miniature pioneers among Caribbean natives.

These daughters have grown in my memory rather than receded, alive in a sphere where they remain frozen in an Olympian dream of perfect patience and beauty. I now understand that living with them was for me a timely opportunity to prolong my own childhood, and compensate for what I never had. They were to be my best chance at the experience of mothering. Interacting with these children afforded me an occasion for growth; learning selflessness, reliability, and forbearance; enjoying the fruits of a normal, mature, parental relationship. Through them, I experienced not only a continuation of childhood but also a gradual transformation into adulthood. Had I benefitted from such models while growing up myself, I might have known how to better cherish and perhaps keep close to me for the rest of life these darling beings who had been briefly entrusted to me.

But I had been a child who talked with clouds, imagining that they, like stationary church saints, saw me and cared. As an adult, I unwittingly continued that familiar and oddly sustaining behavior of looking for invisible beings of the mind's heaven after whom I sought to model myself, instead of fully embracing relationships with humans. In Haiti, I searched for them in Vodou ceremonies where such spiritual beings are known to converse with the living.

These pursuits proved disastrous to my marriage. My interest in Afro-Caribbean spirituality and culture, my embracing of black people outside my social rank, and my defiance of the prescribed norms of acceptable intellectual activities and social interactions became a great disappointment and strain for a husband who had hoped for a different wife—more of a Europe-centered elitist he could parade in high circles, not the young woman he slowly grew to resent. It did not help that Vodou ceremonies start late at night, and end at dawn. I disappeared too often, going to the deep recesses of Port-au-Prince slums or to inaccessible reaches of the primitive countryside where Laurent refused to join me. In time, he grew impatient, and occasionally violent; I grew to feeling suffocated and fearful. Seeing me pack my bag one morning, the little girls wept.

4. Initiation

Owing to the fact that Vodou divinities and Christian saints are both called "spirits," I mistook one for the other, seeking one through the other.

I had been trained at Berkeley to do field study. I thought that the anthropological framework in which all human activities are seen as functions of need, provided me with enough intellectual distance to approach a realm filled with disquiet; Vodou was associated with the sounds of drums from surrounding hills in the night, pungent smoke carried by the breeze, house-workers whose fear was palpable when they recounted finding animal organs deposited at their doorsteps during the night. They elaborated on tales of werewolves grown to monumental sizes that lurked at the crossroads, and she-devils able to remove their skins at midnight to crawl and skulk from roof to roof, looking for children whose flesh they craved. I believed myself to be a sober university graduate, wanting to separate reality from myth, a woman trusting that a single truth existed at the core of life.

Now that I was experiencing Haiti again, I soon realized that in regard to Vodou, one gets answers only through initiation and commitment to spirit worship. Having studied with social scientists, I decided to imitate their approach and play the open-minded modern anthropologist, doing field study. In my continued pursuit of saints as models, I petitioned the heavens in a novel way, sought the ancient wisdom of the African world, and went on a quest for initiation.

The farther one goes from Port-au-Prince, the bluer the sea. Still, I never saw the ocean during the whole seven days of the *Kanzo* initiation rites I was undergoing, lying on a white sheet spread on an earthen floor in a Vodou temple by the sea in Mariani, near Leogane.

Smells of the salt in the air mixed with that of the thatch roof. Sounds of waves crashing over the low stone ramparts of the circular temple came at regular intervals. My breast seemed to rock in and out of itself, following the deep movements of the waters. When the wind was softer, the ocean gave the impression to be rubbing itself, albeit with insistence, against the embankment over which the room was built; a humble, windowless space accessed through a single creaking door that broke the silence imposed on initiates, when the Vodou priest came in for the day's ritual, and food was brought. On my left, two others were present, black men stretched on the floor like me, and dressed in ankle-length white robes. A *ounsi*—a Vodou devotee assisting the priest—watched over us at all times, there to help us with private body functions, or serve as relay to the priest. She wore the grace and glow of youth, along with a simple dress that glimmered in the corner of the dim room in which she sat motionless. Candles burned above our heads, one each, little stars plucked from the heavens, golden drops come down to earth to flicker with emotion, flashing Morse codes. Many scents rose from the beaten-earth floor, permeating the air; smells of long ago rains, ancient oils, or mushrooms grown in the woods. Children prone to eat earth, like my brother was, taking a handful into the mouth as if in hope of absorbing the entire country, with its valleys, rivers, waterfalls, woods and wells, grass, moss, and wild flowers, such children would not have tasted this temple earth, primeval and hardened as it felt, packed with memories of dreams and urges left there by a succession of initiates.

Foods we were given each day were also ritual-specific. None of these dishes, to my knowledge or experience, contained mood or consciousness-altering elements; many of them only meant to cleanse internal organs, including the blood. I remember a fragrant mixture of okra and of the black mushroom that in Haiti we call *djon-djon*. I recall eating millet whose scent, texture, and taste were unlike any I have consumed before or since. The flavor of food naturally mixed with the air and the scent of the sea coming through the door. The spring water we drank tasted of the gourds in which it was collected and stored, containers fashioned from the fruit of the calabash tree. Alcohol poured on the ground in three small doses during daily rituals scheduled throughout the seven days, are offerings to the gods, not intended for initiates. (It may happen that during a particular ceremony, or in circumstances other than an initiation, that a god will offer someone a share in his private reserve of alcohol, kept in the temple for his sole purpose; when this happens, one must not refuse, lest one is willing to offend; Vodou gods are as touchy as Greek gods, or humans, when their gifts are shunned). It is not unusual to find the concept of body cleansing equated with soul cleansing in various initiatory rituals of the world's indigenous religions, whereby it is believed that physical cleansing causes a spiritual cleansing of the whole person.

It was a very healthy diet we had as initiates, such as it was: poultry beheaded in the morning, or fish just pulled out of the ocean; leafy vegetables freshly plucked from the temple's garden, and tubers newly uprooted from a nearby farmers' land; the food was flavored with herbs and spices ground a moment before preparation, then evidently cooked just prior to our eating it; and finally, our wooden food bowls were briefly passed over a small fire built in the room before they were handed to us. I believe that the brush with fire given to the food was meant to impart, symbolically and in actuality, some of the energy and life-sustaining elements contained in the fire. Similarly, it is not unusual to have the same gesture repeated with a person's hands, feet, or other limbs during a ritual for healing.

Much later, in the months and years following my *Kanzo* initiation, I would come to experience the direct healing power of fire. Victoria, a Vodou priestess I befriended long before my initiation, offered to help me with pain in my shoulders and back.

Though middle-aged at the time I met her, and initially my Hatha Yoga teacher, Victoria was a recent psychology graduate of Howard University. A full-bodied, fair-skinned, midsize woman, she seemed to glide when she walked. She favored orange attire. She usually pulled her black hair into two thick braids. The heavy-lidded eyes of a myopic gave her an otherworldly gaze. There were times when her lower lip trembled, and she dropped her gaze. Her hands were small and supple, the fingers easily arching back like those of a Hindu dancer, but with the grip of a Sumo wrestler. She made her daughter's wedding dress in a crochet lacework so fine that a mermaid would have envied it. She had an aversion to birds, beaks, and being kissed. She kept a lush garden of flowering bushes that she grew from seeds in enormous clay pots. Her mind was an encyclopedia of eclectic information. She was also the person responsible for introducing me to the priest at the Vodou temple where I was eventually initiated. Victoria had diagnosed me with suffering from what she laughingly called "the myth of Sisyphus." The fire-healing cessions occurred in her living room where she had me sit on the green mosaic floor with my back bared. She set aflame a mixture of white rum decoction and Florida cologne that she poured in a white-enameled metal plate (each priest and priestess have their own recipes for these rum-based decoctions—called *tranpe*—containing a secret blend of spices, roots, bark, and odd foods, often received in dreams; they are used primarily for healing or as offerings to the gods, but are sometimes shared socially in liqueur glasses). Florida cologne was present in all the Vodou ceremonies I have seen; it has a scent that Vodou gods generally adore, except for the Erzulies, female deities of love, who prefer the fragrance of Pompeïa. After lighting the mixture in the white metal plate, Victoria then placed her open palms in the flaming liquid, thus catching some of its substance and flames in her hands; in a series of repeated, swift gestures, she progressively applied all of the flaming liquid directly onto my skin, rubbing it vigorously; she did this until my back, at times my whole body, had literally been bathed with fire, benefitting from its energy and the rum decoction's healing substances.

As people undergoing initiation however, and as desirous we were to experience the tranquility of a seven-day ritual, we all looked forward to the daily visits from the Vodou priest. They connected to a specific ritual for the day. No visit was ever arbitrary. They broke the monotony of the complete silence otherwise kept, and allowed us a chance to sit up. They had an educational purpose as well, lessons of sorts, and made it possible to discuss with the priest anything on our minds. We ate during these rituals, or afterwards; the visits had this added joy to them, and were perhaps an attempt to associate rituals, gods, and food in our subconscious.

Besides being festive, food is comforting; it is uniquely connected to deep layers of our consciousness, those involved with a mother's initial breastfeeding and caring. These are our defining first experiences of love, the singular warmth we hold deep within the cells of our body (and provided that the mothering experience goes as it is meant to), and that accompanies or rescues us throughout life.

Needless to say that it is challenging to lay on a hard floor in silence for seven days, confronted day and night with a self-imposed, inner reflective mirror. This journey inside is emotionally arduous, even with company, and a kind of brotherhood, with strangers slowly develops.

The three of us wore a chastened face that week. For a few days, we were people outside the trappings, rules, and limitations of country, culture, society, or bank account. We were souls. Nakedness was the garment we sought. We prayed that this nakedness would attract spirits to us; we hoped that they would come to claim us as god-entrusted children meant for them to nurture and educate.

At the close of these seven days of *Kanzo* initiation rites, we were celebrated in a brilliant coming-out ceremony. All the *ounsis* of the temple were gathered on the parvis of the initiation house, out of which we were brought with dances and chants. Three drummers played the rhythms and songs of each of the gods said to be *dancing* in our heads. These deities are identified by the Vodou priest during the seven days of initiation, through dreams and other kinds of revelations. "Dancing" is the word used to refer to the presence and motion of spirits in a person's head, but also to their protection, inspiration, demands, and control. Each initiate wore the ceremonial dress prepared beforehand as part of the many things to be made ready before initiation. My own dress was as long and flowing as I felt a queen should wear on such a day. The sea wind loved it, playing with its skirts as if to wear it too. The day was heaven's it seemed, a feast of blue and white, the colors of the Immaculate I cherished since childhood. The initiates were the white stars and the dancing clouds of a blue universe of ocean and sky. Each initiate received a heavy ceremonial necklace made of multicolored, opaque-glass beads, called *grenn maldyòk*, interspersed with old colonial coins that could be bought at the downtown Port-au-Prince Iron Market. But each necklace was specific to each initiate. The colors of the beads stood for the flag colors of seven deities who presented themselves to the priest during initiation as protectors of a particular initiate; one of these spirits, referred to as the *Mèt Tèt*—Master of the Head—has most power in that person's archipelago of spirits.

It feels odd now for me to remember my necklace of spirits. Eagerness to discover that day the identities of my protectors, eventually developed into profound disquiet. The last image I have of this sumptuous necklace is a scattering of beads and coins after I had cut and flung it into one of the many crossroads of the old Port-au-Prince.

The colors, I came to discover, were not just lively color combinations. The necklace was not just a stunning ornament that only required reverent treatment. The necklace had a life of its own. I found that the colors themselves acted as powerful magnets to specific forces prowling in the universe, while at first they had only seemed to be innocuous echoes of flags habitually taken out during ceremonies.

Flag colors are emblems of the gods, and always shown in pairs: for example, red and blue indicate warrior gods; green and white, the snake god; pale blue and pink, the sacred twins. A Vodou temple holds particular devotion to their priest's personal and family gods. The coming out of the flags is an important and magnificent ritual in itself, even if it only opens of the ceremony. Brilliantly ornate flags embroidered with sequins are paraded with chanting and drums, and repeatedly bowed to. Some of the world's best museums keep such flags in their collections, unaware of their active power. Museum curators do not realize that the much-celebrated Vodou artists who embroidered them, created the flags for the glory of the gods they worship, the dissemination of their presence and power throughout the earth.

In time, I progressively discovered how Vodou deities resemble Greek gods, how they vary in stature, and battle for power over people and the world. On earth too, human ambition and greed corrupt the spiritual arena. Like their gods, people compete for status and material gain. Spirits come to be viewed as assets, commonly used as intercessors or tools towards wealth.

5. A Vision

The Vodou Priest informed me that my *Mèt Tèt* was a warrior god. I responded with an amused smile because of Joan of Arc—the virgin peasant girl who successfully led the armies of Charles VII against the English during the Hundred Years' War, is the guardian saint I chose during my Catholic Confirmation ceremony when I was eight.

Joan's visions started when she was twelve. Archangel Michael and Saint Catherine explained how they were sent to prepare her for a divine mission. At her trial for heresy some years later, Joan claimed to have done nothing more than obey God's orders. She could have saved her life by denying her visions and her God. She did not. She was nineteen when she was burnt at the stake.

I experienced a vision of my own at the beginning of my *Kanzo* initiation. I had long stretches of meditative hours for several days afterwards, to savor and ponder over this visit from a spirit, while I was laid on the floor. The woman in my vision was just a crone. She sat still, unsmiling and mute. I had only a side view of her body ensconced in a white rocking chair. Her face however was fully turned into a frontal view while she stared at me from five feet away. Her large eyes might have been softened by wrinkles subduing their contour, but they were not. Her pupils were black and cold, her hair white. She wore an ankle-length white dress of delicate cloth. Light around her in that obscure, barren room was a thin, unearthly glow. The Vodou Priest identified her as Aïzan, an ancient spirit whose ritual song I still remember after thirty years, *"Aizan velekete, imamou sègwèlo, rele Aizan..."* These songs are in *langaj*—a secret tongue that only the Vodou gods understand, and that the *oungan* is sometimes able to interpret. Protector of family, Aïzan presides over the harvest. Her colors are yellow and white, as were paper flags and banderoles strung along streets of Port-au-Prince to celebrate Pope John Paul II at his 1983 visit to Haiti. Surprisingly however, while remaining the single vision I had during my initiation at the temple, Aïzan was not one of the protective spirits included in my initiate's necklace. Perhaps she had only come in anger, thinking me a fraud.

A later attempt to paint an oil portrait of the crone in my vision and show my friend Victoria what I had seen only revealed an aged version of me. I quickly covered it with white canvas ground paint. Victoria asked if she could use the discarded canvas for one of her craft projects, but returned it soon after. "There is blinding light coming out of it," she complained. "I can't see what I'm doing. There was power there. You ruined it."

6. Syncretism and Disguise

The richness, diversity, and complexity of the Haitian Vodou pantheon and rites are a result and reflection of the human exodus from the African continent—Africans sold into the slave trade, started by Columbus in 1505, brought with them to Haiti the spirit worship traditions of their various regions of origin, mostly from Western and Central Africa, families of spirits now identified in Haiti under group names, Rada, Petwo, Bizango, San Pwèl, Kongo, each recognizable through distinct psychological features and behavior, as well as preferences in rhythm, food, drinks, scents, and dress— the old Creole song tells us: *Ian Ginen m te ye, se Ian Ginen m tonbe*—I came from Africa (Guinea), I landed in Africa.

Social scientists of the past coined the word "syncretism" to explain Haitian religion and worship system, whereby saints and Vodou spirits—*lwa*—are combined to form one entity—their similarities enhanced, their differences overlooked—a practice started during the time of slavery when Africans were forced to abandon the worship of their regional, African deities, for that of Christian Gods; they devised this imaginative, disguised way, unbeknownst to their colonial slave masters, to continue ancestral devotion while pretending to pray to Catholic saints, but actually were invoking divinities who shared recognizable traits with the saints; this syncretic kind of worship goes on to this day. For example, calling for Danbala, the snake-god, is the same as praying to Saint Patrick, while the Virgin Mary's many names and manifestations in Catholicism offer ideal counterparts to the numerous African female divinities.

I progressively came to perceive spirit possession however, as infiltration of a person's body by forces whose intent and needs are not always honorable or clear, even if deities are responding to human invitations. These are expressed through elaborate, finely articulated ceremonies whose ritual vocabulary must be respected if the outcome is to be successful, meaning that spirits will enter our reality level by taking hold of human bodies through which they'll partake of offerings, oftentimes also choosing to dance, sing, or spend time conversing with eager participants. Once spirits leave the body under their control and the person regains consciousness, it is often too short a time span until they must be placated again. I grew uneasy with Vodou spirits' hunger for our world and their invasive appetite for the feel of a human body.

7. Possession

Some Vodou devotees are more prone to spirit possession than others. While Gede spirits are famous for taking hold of a person's consciousness unrequested and unwelcomed, mostly because they are lewd, debauched, and thus exhibit a generally embarrassing behavior and manner of speech, there are instances of spirit possession that occur outside ceremonies, and even outside of one's home. Furthermore, some people have such a finely tuned relationship with a particular spirit, and with possession by that spirit, that the switch of consciousness is almost imperceptible to an outside observer, or even perhaps to the person experiencing it. This kind of subtle spirit-possession can often be observed during a visit to a Vodou priest or priestess for a consultation of some sort, or even at a *bòkò*'s—a witchdoctor—men sought after for black magic, making zombies, but also for healing, and counteracting the sorcery done by another *bòkò*.

These subtle types of spirit-possession are called *je klè*, meaning open-eyed, indicating that the spirit has taken hold of the person, but that the person is still conscious, albeit not in control, and only acting as a conduit.

I was neither a Vodou devotee prone to spirit possession, nor one with a finely tuned relationship with a particular spirit when I first experienced spirit-possession, as well as that very hunger Vodou spirits have for using our bodies. I was not even an initiate at the time, but merely an anthropologist wannabe, who accompanied Victoria to ceremonies at night all over the Port-au-Prince slums and countryside. I was so eager to learn and discover all there was, moving with absolute fearlessness, that Victoria nicknamed me "Zombie Activist," and later shortened it to, "Zomb." She meant that my lack of fear, my curiosity and level of energy were such, that I was like the blind, a potential danger to myself, a being powered by a will existing outside my better judgment. I was twenty-six.

Victoria was marvelous at coining two-word character definitions of person. She rid herself of her second husband that way, a very learned literary man, full of wit and intellectual passion. But passion for his wife, he had none. Night after night, Victoria mulled in bed while he snored. Finally, at 3:00 am one night, she had her eureka moment; she knew what to say to hurt him deeply, the way only our intimates do. She shook the man until he groaned from discomfort. As soon as he opened an eye, she yelled, "You're nothing but a *Macrocephalic* RUNT!" And *that* did it. She got her divorce.

I have not forgotten the night when I had my first experience of spirit-possession. I was passively watching a ceremony for a Nago spirit in an innocuous Vodou temple of a gray Port-au-Prince slum, sitting with Victoria and other special guests in the first row of onlookers, when a sudden impulse got a hold of me, and without reason, I stood up.

I had no choice. I had to get up. Once I was up, I could not make any other movement. It seemed that a mountain stood with, and within me—I was an upsurge from the earth, a heavy, homogeneous mass, feeling infinitely tall, calm, distanced, cocooned in clouds.

The fire at the center of the room, the drums, the many dancing *ounsis* in red, and the clamor of their chants receded far away. It is many years since this happened to me. My recollections of the details of the ceremony may not be fully accurate. But the memory of what I experienced is indelible.

I remember how it was that very night, when I could hear and see all that was going on all around me, but felt removed, and alone.

The stillness in me was ancient; it was observing the goings-on with my eyes, but it was not my own.

I observed impassively how the *oungan*, noticing me standing, suddenly held up his right hand, and ordered the ceremony to stop—it had to shift gear—the drumming, the songs, the intent of the moment. With one glance at me, he knew that a different spirit had come unexpected; no matter that the ceremony was for another, the visitor needed a proper welcome; homage had to be paid.

So the drums stopped; the dances stopped; all sounds stopped; confusion temporarily seized the temple.

The priest calmly wiped the sweat off his brow with a white scarf, and then wrapped it back around his neck. So much is said with a scarf in a ceremony—a wave, a welcome, a caress, a slap, a reproach. But this scarf asked for a pause.

Holding high his ceremonial *ason* in his right hand, a scepter of sorts, the *oungan* grabbed a clay jar of water and a calabash bowl containing white flour. He summoned the drummers and the *ounsis* for them to follow him, and he brought them at my feet, little me, incomprehensibly feeling a hundred feet tall at that moment, as well as immensely, and irretrievably sad. The sorrows of the universe had accumulated in my throat, but could not be expressed. Yet the priest understood; he knew these feelings; he knew the being come in this way, at that moment.

One word and name from him to the drummers and to the *ounsis*, and all were informed that here was a spirit—a *lwa*—of the Rada family, a *Danti*—an ancient one—remote, respectable, a *white* spirit, meaning kind, slow-moving, different from a fire spirit, not red, but a *lwa* come from inaccessible lands inhabited by those who will not be commanded to do evil. In his beginning address to the god in me, facing me, the priest prayed in *langaj*—addressing the *lwa* with the words of respect meant for him only, looking him in the eyes, my eyes.

When the prayer ended, the *ounsi*s began singing the god's song, and the drummers matched it with the proper rhythm. The priest kneeled down and traced (with flour streaming out of his fingers the way a Tibetan sand mandala is drawn), a specific *vèvè* on the ground—the god's sacred, symbolic representation. He then poured water out of the clay jug three times. Afterwards, he backed up a little from me so he had space to turn and face the four cardinal points one at a time, genuflecting while raising and rattling his *ason* each time, the *ason* resonant from the meshwork of *maldjòk* beads and snake bones surrounding it. I saw and heard everything. I was conscious, yet as if pushed in some frozen corner of my being, feeling the tears of the god running down my cheeks.

But the fire gods had been patient enough! They had waited while the intruder was being fussed over. This was their ceremony, their honoring, their reward for all they had done for the Vodou priest in whose head they danced, masters of the place.

I don't recall how the transition was made. Perhaps I no longer was as open-eyed in spirit possession as I had been, but I found myself swirling barefooted on top of the table where god offerings had previously been laid. I was spiraling, and spiraling, arms open wide, uncontrollably delighting and delighted. And when the table proved too restrictive, I lifted my body in just one swirling hop, and landed on the beaten ground in a continuous spinning dance. It was not me, this whirl, this long-haired eddy, this flow, this rush, this turmoil, this furiously rhythmic spiraling energy that all were watching—the drummers, the *ounsis*, the strangers, the *oungan*, Victoria—but those however were indeed my feet, my bare legs, my breast, my arms outstretched, my fingers reaching, my laughter, my spirit, it was me, absolutely all of me, wide open.

I came home at dawn finding that my husband had waited up for me. My eyes had come back to him still filled with stars, and I had lots to tell that was inexpressible, though I tried. But Laurent was not interested. He had no sympathy for my pain either—the soles of my feet were blistered, burst open, and scraped raw from my spiraling dance; the pain had been made worse from having had to walk on these two huge open sores, out of the interminable back alleyways of the slums in the dead of the night, piss and rats and all.

8. Victoria

Victoria was a *manbo*—a Vodou priestess—who approached Vodou through her intellect, familiar as she was with Carl Jung's theories—she believed Vodou spirits to be archetypes manifesting themselves out of our collective psyche, and not actual forces taking over a person's body and mind during possession. She only chuckled when a white-haired *oungan* warned her, tugging at a slim old beard: "Archetypes you say? Oh yeah… wa gen tan konnen—you'll soon find out…"

Victoria dazzled every priest of every Vodou temple of Port-au-Prince and Jacmel with the remarkable array of spirit possession she manifested—warrior gods, crusaders, seafarers, peasants, iron workers, healers, seers, witchcraft makers, trickster divinities of the dead, female divinities of motherly or romantic love, prostitutes, child-eaters, mermaids, as well as Aïzan, my crone of the harvest who came to me in a vision. She was possessed by ancient, slow, wise divinities, and by young, reckless, evildoing ones known to empower gangs of witch doctors who run through the countryside at night when cocks don't crow, calling for monstrous incarnations at the crossroads to whom they feed animals and men. Victoria's spirit possessions were not the hysterical, inarticulate, groaning, mouth-foaming variety that journalists and Hollywood have publicized, but experiences where the spirit sits with quiet composure, speaks lucidly, then departs with a faint silence. She was proud of the richness and variety of her spirit-possessions. *Oungans and manbos* flash and snob each other with their spiritual assets, the way women do with diamonds and diadems. There was one exception: Ti Pete Lakwa—Little-Fart-of-the-Cross, the worst foul-mouthed Gede spirit, a comical gossip of unusual arrogance. About this one, Victoria would not be teased.

Here indeed, the joke was at her expense. She found it a deeply humiliating one. Victoria, usually a refined intellectual, and a well-mannered lady, would not only take on the personality of a man when under spirit possession by Ti Pete Lakwa, but that of a rogue who delighted in revealing compromising secrets about the lives of people in town; he discussed any or all matter that she had been told in confidence. Victoria's Gede would babble incessantly, laughed at his own jokes, slapping his thighs; if anyone in the audience objected, or tried to silence him, he would protest loudly, insult the silencer, and make singularly grotesque mocking noises; one of these would be to swell his cheeks with air to bursting point, while puckering his lips in a most hideous manner that imitated the convulsive motions of a chicken's rectum, and let it all out as a booming fart.

Victoria's sophisticated notions about archetypes were here exposed to her detriment—she was aware how one might observe this spirit of hers, and wonder at those secret aspects of her deep inner self that found expression through such an insidious, tasteless character. The fact that he was found comical in Victoria's entourage was perhaps less a factor of his own personality, and more because he was such a contrast to the Victoria we knew. Little-Fart-of-the-Cross invited himself anywhere and at any ceremony, Gede or not. In order to make him disappear, Victoria would have had to cease all her Vodou research and activities altogether, especially the private-worship ceremonies held in her home, and attended only by her private circle of friends. It is at the end of these home ceremonies that Ti Pete Lakwa was likely to come up, having waited for the right moment when people would relax with all guards down, indeed the best time to embarrass not only Victoria, but her friends among themselves.

The Gede are the divinities of death. Lakwa—The Cross (from the original colonial French "la croix")—is their generic family surname. Bawon Samdi is their father. They are all men, except for Grann Brijit, their mother; a woman possessed by a Gede, as Victoria could be, will speak and think of herself as a man throughout the possession, referring to the person being possessed as the *chwal*—meaning the "horse"—an animal being mounted, regardless of that person's actual gender. When possessed by Ti Pete Lakwa, Victoria's psyche, perceptions of women, and sexual attractions were those of a man. Bawon Samdi on the other hand is the dead; oftentimes, during spirit possessions by him, the *chwal* is catatonic, corpse-like, and is prepped for the morgue, with face powdered white in imitation of death's pallor, and body covered with a white sheet. Victoria quite liked possession by Bawon Samdi, being Father of the Dead. There was status there. While having a spirit called Little-Fart take over her mind and control her public behavior was deeply offensive to her customary feminine elegance and scholarly achievements.

Ceremonies for the Gede generally involve the sacrifice of male goats. These fare badly. They are carried to the stage on their backs, feet tied together, genitals hanging; the testicles are grabbed with one hand by the priest, then swiftly cut with the other; the animal is left to bleed, with blood collecting in a white vessel; it is a long while before the goat's throat is finally slit open, putting an end to the deafening cries of the suffering creature. Satisfied with the sacrifice, Gede then looks for roasted plantain and tubers, all the while clutching a cigarette and his chili peppered *Kleren*, guzzling it down in large quantities between mouthfuls of food throughout the evening.

Possessions by the Gede happen most often in groups. They are mischief-makers, rabble-rousers, and lewd dancers. Their propensity for obscenity manifests itself with dizzying liberality. Like death itself, they disturb, destabilize, and shock. Looking at you through the smoke of dark glasses, one lens of which is always missing, Gede will counsel, caress, and curse all in the same breath.

9. Special Guests

Jean Leregard and his German wife Nora were owners of the temple by the sea where I was initiated, and where they also ran a nightly Vodou show for tourists. Jean's skin was as strong and black as his wife's was delicate and fair. They were both striking examples of classical beauty, each within their own racial categories; they were tall, with a noble bearing of the head, broad-shouldered, long-limbed, exhibiting poise and gracious manner at all times. Both evoked Greek gods. But Nora was as languorous as Jean was industrious. She spent her days eating canned delicacies ordered from Europe, sitting and hosting close friends in the only air-conditioned room of the temple, hers and Jean's bedroom, and where the scent of French perfume permeated the air.

Jean and Nora were both oungan and manbo—father and mother of the gods. Spirit possessions witnessed by tourists during the nightly show were not faked. However, neither Jean nor Nora officiated during the show. For that, they hired Chantale.

Nora and Chantale were disdainful of each other. Chantale saw Nora as a useless white woman whose only advantage over her in maintaining Jean's affection was her fair complexion. Nora tolerated Chantale's strutting around the temple as if she were irreplaceable, because in fact, she was. Chantale was an indefatigable, wiry woman who spent nine years of her life as a zombie, living in a barrel, subsisting on food also given to pigs. Jean is the one responsible for saving Chantale, for initiating her, making a Vodou priestess out of her, and giving her the responsibility of the nightly tourist show. Neither one would recount the circumstances of their meeting. While *manbos* are usually big, slow women, in need of a solid body meant to withstand the possible brutality of a spirit possession, Chantale was delicately built. She made up for it in willfulness. She sang loudest in ceremonies. To all but Nora, she offered a smile that lit up a room.

Victoria and I went regularly to the nighttime ceremony at the Leregard's temple, sometimes several times a week. We considered Jean and Nora as close friends and colleagues of sorts, all of us involved with doing field study in Vodou. We sat at the table reserved for Jean and Nora, in the same area where tourists watched the show. World-renowned psychologists, anthropologists, and journalists were often guests at the table with us. They mostly came to investigate Vodou, each in their own professional field, but oftentimes they were looking for health treatments, or secret initiation.

These were exciting, intellectual times for me. We shared elevated purpose within the remote island where fate had us be born. Jean was princely, always dressed in white pants and white guayabera shirt, while Nora wore kaftans with richly embroidered *vèvès* that respected the color preference of the spirit for whom the ceremony was dedicated. On Wednesday nights, she wore a red kaftan with white embroidery for the Ogou, warrior spirits; on Thursdays, she wore a pink kaftan for the Erzulies, goddesses of love, exhibiting a huge heart-shaped *vèvè* embroidered on her breast.

It was a Wednesday night that I discovered how Vodou spirits might fall in love. Anminan was god of lightning. He would possess a man, always young, muscular, handsome, often the same one among the male *ounsis* participating in the ceremony. He arrived when the fire was at the highest, the hottest, drums most furious, and the dancing wildest. Sitting at Jean and Nora's table, we recognized his arrival by the uproar among the *ounsis*. Stretching our necks, we'd see Anminan standing boldly, front stage, bare-breasted, legs apart, arms raised wide, holding a burning log on which he chewed, and with which he beat his chest repeatedly. It was not a Tarzan cry coming out of him, but a song of pure bravado, boasting, "Mwen se zèklè yan yan, mwen se loray di mwa daout!—I am the lightning yeah yeah, I am the thunder in the month of August!" It was then that I braced myself for what I knew would come; Anminan would suddenly leap off the ceremony's stage, run towards the table where we sat, and stop in front of me; he'd shake his shoulders with a kind of defiance, hit the floor three times with the black log he held in a tense grip, and slowly bow. With his chest and face all charred and shining with sweat, Anminan had come to declare his love.

    He did not speak. He frowned. His feelings were serious. I knew—his great theatrical act would not stop until I got up. He would then walk backward with arms open as if to clear the way for me, while I walked toward him, at the center of the ceremony. All he really wanted from me was to notice him, look him in the eyes, pirouette and curtsy with him three times in the ritual manner I had been taught during initiation, and bow. That done, he would calm down, and I could go, walk swiftly back to my seat, embarrassed yet delighted. How had he even come to notice my existence, surging as he did from the darkness of the beyond of which we know nothing? Anminan not only made me feel how special I was to him, but he showed it to everyone present.

    Victoria and Nora each had a shame-inducing Gede of which neither ever spoke. But Nora's was worse. Nora's Gede would come so discreetly onto her that in spite of her height and the full-length embroidered kaftan that emphasized her statuesque presence, no one would notice her get up with great composure from her chair next to Jean's, walk quietly towards her private living area, and disappear from the ceremony.

Her return could however not be missed. Nora's Gede invariably presented himself with face entirely charred black from a thick piece of coal gotten from the back kitchen. He wore dark glasses, one lens missing. The whole bottom part of Nora's sumptuous kaftan, from the ankles all the way up to her waist, was gathered and shoved into one of Jean's white undershorts that Gede had stolen from the bedroom drawers, and slipped on. Nora's white legs then seemed no shapelier than a monstrous toddler's extending from oversized diapers. Six feet tall Nora thus never failed to create both disturbance and hilarity among the tourists who easily recognized the dress and blond hair of the stately white woman who had so elegantly welcomed them earlier at the start of the ceremony. Her husband groaned, but remained composed, seated among his guests. He had to appear calm, while letting his wife's spirit possession play itself out in spite of the indignity.

Nora's Gede invariably marched past Chantale, saluted, and entered the ceremonial stage to join the other *ounsis*, some of whom were already visited by their own Gede. It was always impressive how this European woman, albeit not raised with African rhythms and dance, could gyrate her hips in front of a stupefied crowd as loosely and obscenely as any Haitian might. An entirely different being from Nora was evidently present. It would take days afterwards for her to clean her pale white skin of coal dust sunk deep into the pores.

10. Belonging

In those benevolent days of involvement with Vodou, my true devotion was to Victoria. If archetypes may be invoked, Victoria was my Great Mother, a tree of life and love, a friend who cooked and baked for two days to celebrate my twenty-seventh birthday.

Her dog Poncho, usually hirsute and ill-mannered, friendly only to those who intimidated him, more prone to running around the neighborhood than to watch the gate of his mistress's house, showed how he could sit politely for two days by the back door if he so chose, waiting for scraps. Poncho was even bathed for the event, throughout which he behaved impeccably, and was seen to chase, bite, and burst only one red balloon.

I was earnest in my search for the spiritual in Vodou. Having a string of spirits interested in me gave me a feeling of connection to the divine as well as to the larger Haitian family and culture. Mine was a novel feeling of belonging I had never known before. Seen as white and unwelcomingly privileged in an impoverished black country, or viewed in France as brown-skinned and socially declassed in a white country, adding to the fact of being raised by ill-matched parents from disparate cultural legacies, I was now able to modify my definition of family, expanding the number of people it comprised. Haitians involved in Vodou worship admitted me into their midst as family because we shared an understanding of a spiritual heritage, along with recognition and acceptance by respected African spirits. They called me *pitit kay*—house child—our child.

Learning these secret layers of the people's religious psyche in ways my own family never cared to, I acquired a lyrical understanding of the average Haitian's perception of the universe and of a person's place in it. This gave me a new ability to read the subtext of conversations overheard, incidents witnessed or recounted, as if suddenly I were part of a secret society whose rules and organizing principles were shared only by a select, poetic, and spiritual elite. I learnt a language using codes that connected, signified, and reconnected in constantly evolving, creative ways. Put in another way, I had become a member of another family at whose head was Victoria as sole parent. I did not mind being acolyte, servant, and sorcerer's apprentice. I had entered another culture, the culture within my culture, whose cyphers were dramatically different from those of my birth family, and would have been deeply threatening to them. In grasping these intricate layers of the Haitian psyche I had not previously even guessed at, I felt that I had been accepted as a sister in the profound meaning of the word. I not only became part of a family, I also became part of a people. It was exhilarating.

11. Curtain Fall

More than anything, it was the lyricism and sheer drama in Vodou ceremonies that captivated me. As sincere as my spiritual interest was, it spoiled; as reassuring as was finding a tangible presence of the divine in my life, it was befouled; as exciting as the ability to communicate with the gods, it all paled when compared to the sustaining attraction of Vodou for me—the unmatched dramatic lyricism found in the unfeigned, instinctual, theatrical elements of human religious expression.

I never tired of the joy everyone had in gathering for a ceremony, and watching the stage being set—the complex, geometric *vèvès* ritual designs drawn on the earth-beaten floor; the colorful sequined flags of the gods brought into the light and hung in display all around; textures and scents of foods ceremoniously presented in time-polished calabash bowls; candles lit in clay bowls or in dried half-orange cups, and set at the base of trees; the deep incrustation of knowledge in the faces of the old, the glowing abandonment of the young; the mute resignation of sacrificial pigeons, roosters, goats, or bulls brought from secluded areas outside the temple; the unspeakable anticipation of death, and the frightful manifestation of the invisible into form. I never wearied of the explosive life in drums, the rhythmic lament in songs that articulated the most profound human needs, the exuberance and defiance in dance. Each Vodou ceremony is a creation following ancient, strict modalities, yet each one is impossible to duplicate and always feels new. A complete exposition of human emotions and psychological situations is presented each time in constantly shifting proportions and correspondences from an unwritten script whose vocabulary and grammar are expressed through the visual and symbolic. All human drama is there, charted in rituals based on an ancient understanding of complex designations, characteristics, and spiritual functions of the various families of gods. It is no wonder that Victoria interpreted it all through Carl Jung's archetypes. It is as if indeed all is connected and meaningful in our universe. Try all theories, or intellectual interpretations of the world as we might, it is up to us to find the real sense of it all. It may take a lifetime, and a lifetime is all we have, but truth is there somewhere waiting to be found.

And yet, perhaps because it was theater of a kind, one day the curtain fell. Something suddenly shifted in Victoria's demeanor, and her face closed before me. Although never stated or explained, I knew—I was no longer welcome. The joyous smile she once always had when I came to her gate, was no longer there.

I felt shame in my sorrow, as if her rejection of me was just. I struggled to believe that she desired to protect me from an evil she sensed in Vodou, and whose nature she progressively understood in a different way than she initially had. The old Vodou priest had indeed warned her: "Archetypes you say? Oh yeah… wa gen tan konnen—you'll soon find out…"

Whilst too proud to admit that she had been mistaken, and that indeed here was a world she entered with all intellectual confidence, but had underestimated and wrongly interpreted, perhaps Victoria rejected me out of a maternal instinct to preserve my life.

It had not been long before my own demise that Victoria's lover, a Protestant minister from Bermuda whom she had met at an African religion conference, had suddenly died in mysterious circumstances. She would not discuss his death. I think that she felt responsible. He was not meant to die yet. He was a splendid totem of a man, a black colossus, with the laughter and the health of a prizefighter.

While Victoria was embarrassed by this relationship outside of marriage with a man who did not belong to the society she knew, and gossiped about her, Alfred on the other hand, would delight in parading and spoiling Victoria, buying first class seats for their frequent flights outside of Haiti. Victoria's extensive and comparative studies in Vodou, Candomblé, and Santeria, caused Alfred to be increasingly curious about Haitian Vodou, and he asked Victoria to be introduced to the Leregard couple. She did so, but reluctantly, and after prolonged hesitation. Alfred then requested initiation from her. Victoria refused. She once said to me that, "Spiritual knowledge, and therefore spiritual power, must not be given to anyone without careful consideration of what that person is likely to do with it."

I found out later that Alfred had succeeded in convincing Jean Leregard to initiate him, unbeknownst to Victoria; she felt it as deep treachery from both men since neither said a word to her about it at the time. Alfred also subsequently purchased a magic charm from Jean to acquire some form of power; this type of charm is called a *pwen* in Haiti. It was soon after that Alfred suddenly fell ill in Bermuda, and died quickly. He was already dead when Victoria learnt that he had been ill. She was disconsolate at never having had a chance to try and heal him, using her knowledge and powers of a *manbo* to counteract the evil at work. She began to suspect foul play from Jean, and even more so from Nora who, the closer one became to her, displayed in her comments and manner little true respect for the *lwas*, as well as a narrow understanding of forces at play in Vodou. Whilst Jean was a true intellectual, Nora used Vodou for attention and glory; her growing resentment at Jean getting all the attention from visitors, as well as attracting international renown as a historian and priest of African religions, had begun to show in pouts and snide remarks. I had noticed how she seemed to consider all initiates in Jean's temple as his or her property; she expressed the subtle, yet deep feeling that the initiates' spiritual strength was part of the temple's, and that all sacred, albeit personal, belongings of initiates were to remain in the temple. So when Victoria distanced herself from the Leregards, admitting to me her complete loss of trust in them, and finally cut all ties, it was a tragic demise for all of us.

I had had my own fears as well, regarding evident tampering done with a particularly important sacred object that was created as part of my initiation; among other things, it contained various clippings from my body, taken during initiation rituals. Nora looked visibly annoyed when I asked for it back without prior notice, and waited while she went to fetch it from the temple. She took so long to return with it that I grew suspicious, and inspected its contents when I got home; it was empty.

So in addition to my profound grief over Victoria's rejection of me, sorrow lasting for months, and to a certain extent some years, I felt terror over what hold the spirit world might have over me as a consequence of Nora's tampering, despite the fact that I was innocent of any magic-making ever, whether for my benefit, or to affect another. In fairness to Victoria's change of heart towards me, it is true that I had increasingly wanted greater knowledge about Vodou mysteries, and to undergo the initiation of a *manbo*. I began asking more questions regarding rituals I witnessed. Victoria may have become apprehensive about my motives the way she had been with Alfred's, and fearful of the part of me she called "Zombie Activist," that could lead me to self-destruction. In losing Alfred, Victoria must have realized that intellectual prowess is insufficient, and that for all her cleverness and learnedness, she had no control over the lives of those she loved.

And in the end, I too grew to see how Vodou spirits repeatedly proved to be unruly, petulant, and never contented. The God I sought could not be in these spirits I witnessed—the God of love I desired could not be one to feast on testicles, and the blood of tortured animals.

For all of the fun, shame, and theatricality caused by Gede spirits parading in black or purple redingotes, wearing one-lens sunglasses, and zigzagging furiously all about the stage of an ongoing ceremony aglow with candlelight (the night air laden with the smell of Florida cologne, burning coal, charred meat, roasted tubers, spiced rum sprayed in fine mist from lips of possessed devotees as a form of revel or blessing), the true theatrical highlight of these Vodou days in my memory, as well as the final disillusionment, is of Jean, whose struggle was not with a Gede but with a warrior-spirit named Barbara.

And so, the greatest theatrical act surviving in my memory is that of Jean standing bare-footed and bare-breasted in the middle of a black bull's mutilated body. The Ogou warrior god, Barbara, demands a bull in sacrifice. This is a spirit who loves the brio of blood, the panache in standing upright inside an animal lying on its back, cut open from throat to tail, pulled apart enough for a man to march inside as conqueror, tramping proudly over the shivering disorder of organs ripped asunder, severed head misaligned, skin laid on the ground haphazardly like a discarded coat, cut away from ribs that resembled organ pipes unfolded around Jean the way a corolla would. Jean's white pants had turned red from the blood; his white *guayabera* shirt hung on a tree branch overhead, and gently floated in the breeze like a flag. The ground surrounding the carcass was stained with blood that ran in dense rivulets.

The silence from the roosters was noticeable in the hot afternoon. Their unusual quiet felt like a homage to the great black animal that had been led in with a rope the previous afternoon, its head bent low as if in deep understanding and resignation, and who became their comrade during that one night spent among them. Each of the roosters had a leg tied to the same needle-ridden *bayaron* tree that seemed like a dry menace looming over, but also stood as if in guard of them, while the speckled shade it cast over these flimsy creatures drew countless eyes of glaring light over the dusty ground on which they waited their turn.

    Jean emerged from the open torso of the beast like a reddening black lotus, gleefully singing aloud, knife in hand, unwilling to end the excitement of cutting pieces of meat and limbs from the bull's corpse. He distributed them to attendants who delighted in the generosity of this irrepressible god, reveling in open air while the sun warmed the earth, surrounded by speechless guests and devotees sitting a few feet away amidst Nora's delicate flowerbeds of pink and lavender.

5 The Pope in Port-au-Prince

1. The Way of a Pope

I must have wondered what to make of the pope when I was a child. He was a man vaguely familiar at best, but an old man, which to a child feels significant; an old man clad in priestly robes, sometimes red, sometimes white. I caught a glimpse of him now and then on the television, when he waved from an unreachable balcony affixed to the imposing façade of an antiquated building built in a city my father called Rome. The Pope's eyes would at other times be staring at me from a life-sized portrait hung high in a house where humorless crones lived, distant, lonely relations of my ours. These eyes also never failed to startle me when I'd come again face-to-face with a printed reproduction of the pope's benevolent visage left on a wall, as it seemed, to haunt the echoing cement couloir of a church presbytery. At each encounter, I felt the urge to bow.

The pope remained inscrutable even later in life. I saw in him an alien figure with claims to a mystifying heavenly heritage. I heard a detached voice using unintelligible words in a hidden microphone overly amplified through loud speakers, censuring a submissive crowd bound by a common muteness said to be devotion.

Religious piety in Vodou had seemed different than it was in the Catholic faith I knew. In Vodou, there was an actual relationship with the godhead, along with easy conversation that even included bargaining and feedback; it was an experience of intimacy one could often witness others having, and at times so personal that one would have both consciousness and body completely intermeshed with that of the god's. In Catholicism, there was reverence and true devotion, but God was always distant and mute. The Christian faith familiar to me was just that—faith—an impulse that does not rely on evidence. Church authorities and religious scholars have endlessly debated about the nature of Grace, and how it may impact one's capacity for faith. Regardless, apart from known miracles occuring in the course of history that attest to the existence of the spirit world, by and large, I have heard Catholics or Protestants more often say, "I believe that God exists," rather than "I know that God exists."

2. Politics and Church

To appease Pope John Paul II, and reduce world criticism of Haitian President-for-Life Baby Doc Duvalier's regime, son of the previous ghoul with the same self-proclaimed title, gave up the concordat signed between Pope Paul VI and his father. He was thereby renouncing power granted to the old dictator by the papacy in Rome, to appoint all church officials in Haiti, bishops and archbishops included.

Pope John XXIII was the pope of my childhood. His cherubim face hung above the bed of widows in a framed portrait under whose right side a dried strand of palm was precariously tucked, twisted in a loop, remnant of Palm Sunday, to serve as both relic and testimony. A wooden-bead rosary also hung beneath the holy face from a nail hammered at a slant, the cross pointing to the bed below, bed of nightmares and of much prayer—we were people living under constant curfews in the heart of the city. Only now do I realize how tired we all really were. Every Sunday in church, we prayed on our knees beneath life-size figures of saints who defied the politics of former times, their martyrdom portrayed in a rich array of flesh that was lacerated, gouged, skinned, quartered, disemboweled. And then of course there's decapitation and burning at the stake. Manifestly, Christians do not scare easily.

3. Welcoming the Pope

My father had settled in France with a new wife by the time Pope John Paul II came to Haiti in 1983. The pope came after Mardi Gras. Within a few days, crowds had gone from cheering loud carnival floats to hailing a noiseless pope-mobile, from laughing with a gyrating Mardi-Gras king in pink-sequined bikini to genuflecting at a sober prelate in white robes. A third of the 300,000 people who had come to watch the carnival celebrations a few days earlier had now come out of their nearby homes, or had walked barefoot over the slippery mud of steep rocky paths, crisscrossing mountains where marooned slaves once hid. Peasant women who had come down the mountains of Kenskoff added to the crowd gathered in the Champ de Mars gardens, in front of the glimmering presidential palace. They told television reporters who were covering the event that they had fasted to come see the pope; "but this was no hardship," they explained with defiant looks, "we are used to it. Our belly is empty more often than not." Haitians were lining the streets and sidewalks; they sat atop walls, crowded on balconies, while a multitude also waited at the airport.

The streets of Port-au-Prince had been strung with countless paper banderoles that bore the pope's colors, stretched from one side of the street to the other, hung between dilapidated colonial structures still used for commerce. Yellow, white, and sky blue hues fluttered in the air, ruffled by the disorderly, back and forth constant motion of *tap-tap*s, public transport buses that exhibited brightly painted coconut trees crowned by winged saints parading next to devils stoking hell's pits. Nuns waited in front of school gates displaying the pope's colors in torsade draperies, bougainvillea abundantly blooming high above the school's ochre walls. From thousands of rapidly fading leaflets plastered on every door and street lamps in town, a smiling image of the pope with open arms was asking Haitians in capital letters, "*MEN MWEN. KOTE NOU*—I AM HERE. WHERE ARE YOU?"

Nuns by the hundreds waited at the airport; the Sisters of Mercy were there; the Sisters of the Sacred Heart of Jesus were there. I too was there, alone, newly divorced, standing nearby nuns in blue, nuns in brown, nuns in rows squinting under the early afternoon March sun. They sweated under tight headscarves, holding little pastel-colored flags they hoped to be waving soon, once the pope had arrived, their small feet bound in airless shoes tucked under gray-metal folding-chairs. Uninterrupted rows of Madonna paper icons behind glass were propped on the ground, resting on the nuns' knees—the Virgin of La Caridad floating in a golden dress, light as clouds above an ultramarine ocean; the Virgin of the Immaculate Conception nested in her primeval grotto, from which water flows gently as soft a blue as the sash fastened to her waist; the scarred and stoic Black Madonna of Czestochowa; the lavishly bejeweled Lady of Perpetual Succor, archangels whispering on either side... no Virgin was left behind.

The presidential podium bore the black and red colors of the Duvalier revolution and flag—the blue stripe of the pre-Duvalier flag had long ago been switched. In that coal furnace of the Duvalier podium filled with dignitaries in somber suits, the pope's white and gold robes would surely be seen gleaming.

4. The Kiss

John Paul II had just landed in Port-au-Prince when he stood at the oval doorframe of a green-striped Alitalia plane, appraising the situation. He then slowly descended the wheeled-in metal stairs apposed to the plane, holding onto his round head-cap with one hand against the wind; he waved with the other in a measured gesture of recognition towards what could have been for him nothing but a featureless crowd; at the bottom of the stairs, John Paul II fell on his knees and kissed the earth. This might have made him feel gloomy, without his actually knowing why.

But what John Paul II actually kissed was the tar of Haiti's airport; a hard, purposeful, crusty layer that further sealed and silenced the blood-infused Haitian soil, suffocating since the Spaniards landed in 1492, dazzling the deep-rooted Taino Indians who greeted them. I might have wondered then, "Why do I suffer vultures?". And an inner voice could have answered, "You're helpless. The vulture moves in deep".

With his kiss, the pope bowed and acquiesced to the Haiti of both the forefathers who brought liberty, and present-day tyrants who brought oppression. The holy man brushed complying lips against land deeply seeped with extraordinary flavor—famine, epidemics, drought and fire, hurricanes, earthquakes and floods, pillaging, defilement, mass murder—the land about which Graham Greene wrote that, "we are nearer to the Europe of Nero and Tiberius than to the Africa of Nkrumah."

What was a pope's kiss on the earth meant to signify for these people? The whole thing looked senseless enough, but in its own way perfectly finished; a kiss over soil where 95% of the people lived with hunger, soil where the other 5% could grow imported roses fed by water preserved in private cisterns, drink imported milk refrigerated in glass bottles; this soil where no pope had ever come before; where at the time of John Paul II's visit, three quarters of the wealth of the country was shared among just forty families; John Paul II kissed it... good day noble gents and fair maidens!... under the watchful eyes of Jean-Claude Duvalier, surrounded by the quite unnatural odor of his dissolute court. The young despot boasted on television, "The son of a tiger is himself a tiger!" I imagine that the pope may have wondered if it was thoughtless of him to be calling on Duvalier now, but that this measured gesture would prove sufficient to spoil the objections of a protesting conscience..."

Having kissed the earth, the pope raised himself. His white robe flapped in the wind as he walked down a long red carpet to be greeted at the other end by the young black dictator and his mulatto wife; she, mother of two boys from a previous marriage discreetly annulled by papal decree so she could be married to the Haitian dictator in the cathedral refurbished for the occasion.

5. Fair Maiden of Papal Approval

The very way that she came in might have been indication enough. Had things not been as they have been since the beginning, with crowds not realizing what abuse they suffered, the young dictator-groom might have been well advised to build a moat around the Port-au-Prince Cathedral, and a drawbridge lowered to let only his bride in on their wedding day—she wore a priceless gown, designed for her in Paris; embroidered with pearls; a dress that made the mouths of ragged mothers drop, mothers who lined the way to the Cathedral's portal, holding half-starved children; generations of mendicants who would not fail to see in this fair-skinned bride, so unlike them, a living manifestation of the Holy Virgin, an earthly representation of heavenly splendor come to save them from their terrestrial malediction; for they never stopped believing that the roof of this wretched life, of which I now say so many hard things, would surely some day burst open, and all of us, shoulder to shoulder, will ascend.

We might however have done better to conjecture that the despot's wife would match him well: with much time on her hands, Madame President used it to have parties the likes of which had never been seen in Haiti since 1813, when King Henri Christophe lived in the Sans Souci Palace. Fur coat parties at the presidential palace became the rave. A special air-conditioned room was brought to sub-zero temperatures for the occasion. The First Lady delighted her guests, ones chosen from women she envied or feared in childhood, ones she could now lord over, and trample, including the wives of government officials, themselves being new at power and luxury. They were naturally subservient towards the President's wife, who helped them choose their own furs, and preserved them between parties in a special freezer room installed for this sole purpose. This slight-framed, pretty-doll First Lady bore two more sons, who thirty years after their family's forced exile in the middle of the night—angry mobs missing the chance to seize the pack of them within a hair's breath—returned to Haiti to plot the restoration of the Duvalier rule. Their mother had by then already divorced their father as soon as she saw him stripped of title and power, deprived of endless opportunities to plunder the nation's coffers.

Forgive my ranting; it is hard to not feel outraged.

Better I return to my cathedral story when the couple finally knelt at the altar, at eye level with the raised Host, indifferent to the effigies of saints looking down upon them. It is fair to assume, knowing who they were, that greater pleasure than the possible approval of saints would come to them from being endlessly placated, able each day to muzzle the multitude of obsequious government officials, sweating in suits meant for another climate, and whose overweight wives were presently suffocated in ruffled satin dresses cut too tight, discomfited by the heat, and the long wait for an event started unconscionably late, exhibiting widening rings of sweat under lush armpits within whose frizzy hair white body-powder had caked.

A multitude of the impoverished heirs of the much-acclaimed slave revolution were gathered outside, not allowed access—this was God's mansion, not at their disposal—elbowing and trampling each other to catch a glimpse of the regal couple, the white train of the bride that might have seemed, in their famished minds, a moist, satiated tongue that ran along the entire length of the cathedral's central aisle, whilst the bride, stunningly radiant in a pure white gown, faced with calculated chasteness in her gaze, the immaculate ring of the Holy Host presented to her from a gem-incrusted chalice of solid gold.

6. A Senseless Urge

I understand why it is said of planes that they resemble great birds—carried on wings as they are at a far enough distance in the air so as to make them imprecise and seemly alive; rubbing flanks with clouds; allowed to elongate arms and all finer extremities to feel the tips of heaven's touch. It is especially tempting to think that way when a plane holds someone dear—the plane becomes the bird, and almost feels like an extension of the cherished one sitting inside. The excitement alone causes us to identify with the warm-blooded, egg-laying-vertebrate lookalike now in the air; an immense flutter in the breast imitates within, the outer movement of real wings, whilst one's heart sinks and redresses repeatedly under the influence of air pressure; these sensations manifest a significant increase when we watch the plane actually circling in the air before reaching its decision to land. I saw the pope's plane that way; also how it hesitated; waffled above as if suddenly lacking in its previous breath and aplomb. But how the plane finally descended steadily with renewed firmness of conviction was the last I saw of this Italian machinery in action; the view I was afforded of the pope's exit from the plane, and the official welcome he received came from the next day's televised broadcast.

At the airport, I was brought to empathize with the kind of lives cattle have, roped off as I was then with a thousand others at a good distance behind the presidential podium. I wore a long white dress, thinking how people of a same family should dress alike to be immediately identified; perhaps an infantile, yet spiritual, part of me hoped that the pope might "find" me among strangers the way the Vodou god Anminan did. My hair hung loose to the middle of my back, a mistake the midday heat soon caused me to realize. It also finally dawned on me how I would see less of the pope than people lining the streets of Port-au-Prince would. Coming to the airport had been an error in judgment. My heart sank.

Shortly after the pope landed, and moved by instinct often seen in mammals, I edged my way towards the rope, only to find myself butting it, indecisive. Reaching the rope had required patience and obstinacy; working a passage for myself between people thus densely amalgamated seemed impossible to do, while their bare-arm perspiration rubbed on mine, mixing scents, exacerbating my innate, sensible repugnance. My hopes however lifted once I noticed how the roped area in which I was trapped, whilst only facing the back of the podium that blocked all view of the pope's situation, was actually only a hundred yards away from where the pope-mobile was parked, to the right, and itself also roped off. The hundred yards between the two roped areas, mine and the pope-mobile's, was a large cemented lot, one basically empty but for a dozen armed soldiers holding machine guns and sporting revolvers on their hips.

My remaining at the airport in spite of these discomforting circumstances attests to my stupidity; my father was usually more inclined to call this aspect of my character "mulishness"; the difference in animal metaphor here hardly matters except that one should refrain from putting the blame of human traits onto animals whose innocence in their natural drives and behaviors is obvious. I had nevertheless finally reached a point of vexation, wanting to leave, when I suddenly detected, walking at a casual pace among uniformed men, a figure in a white robe. My heart leapt.

Without thinking, I immediately ducked under the rope and started running towards the pope-mobile.

"STOP OR I'LL SHOOT!"

I must have heard these warnings countless times in the minute or so it took me to run across the empty lot; I heard them as if voices underwater. In retrospect, I do not understand why the soldiers didn't simply bar the way; that would have worked; it is also reasonable to think that a young woman, empty-handed in a long white dress, did not represent a convincing threat; it is likely that the heat weighed on the men's reflexes and thought. No one fired.

The pope reached his vehicle before I did. I had kept running until I found myself one foot away from him standing in the pope-mobile, and stopped.

I must have taken him by surprise. Short of breath, brazen heart thumping, I looked up to the pope, full of hope and fervor... and froze—his eyes were the coldest I had ever seen.

The pope and I stared in each other's eyes silently; in such moments, one learns how eternity is not an applicable human measure of time; John Paul II then slowly raised his right hand to bless me; without a word; without a touch; without a smile.

I was still standing in the same place when the pope-mobile began to move, gently at first; I had not heard the motor start. I might have stayed there a while, surrounded by people in frenzied motion, soldiers mostly, unconcerned with me now that the pope had gone. I have no memory of my return home; but it is a shallow door on an empty room that I closed that night before going to bed early at dusk, the sun sinking over the sea.

Haitian press and television would cut out most of the pope's speech at the airport; no one would know the difference anyhow; most of the people gathered heard nothing. What was learnt for that speech came from hearsay. Baby Doc however had been forced to be gracious, while ceremoniously chastised in front of his secret police and ministers by John Paul II, who delivered his speech in Haitian Kreyòl, declaring that "Jezi Kri vinn chache nou —Jesus Christ came to find you!" and also added, "But you must change your ways to deserve Him!"

6 Friends of my Spirit

A Foreign Spirit

1. Wool

Ali had a loom; eyes that took in everything; the tendency of pressing his hand to his forehead in thought. Tall and slim in an Arab robe during his afternoon promenade in our garden, he appeared to be a ghost collecting leaves, bending over the ground, touching trees, smelling bark, picking up husks, all the while mumbling to what he held in his hands, which he eventually took home in a bag. The virgin wool he later dyed in oversized cooking pots with matter he collected from the land would develop subtle hues that he could never reproduce exactly. Rugs he created from selections of these dyed wools, and wove within the structure of ancient Islamic patterns could be seen as singular expressions of his faith.

He brought the wool in a suitcase every three months from Casablanca. When he landed in Port-au-Prince for a six-week stay in the rented bungalow my father built, Ali's head was already filled with expectations of the diverse tints he would obtain from leaves and bark. He seemed like a man dreaming of making a personal rainbow; on this rainbow, arching within, he gladly leapt every afternoon during his stroll under tropical trees, and did so until he left for Morocco for another six weeks' absence.

Ali stored the dyed wool in a trunk he kept hidden from view, next to myrrh and frankincense. He took it out at dusk on days scheduled according to the cycles of the moon. From that trunk, and with the same respect given the anointed, he once showed me an assortment of balls of different sizes and textures, juxtaposing them with samples of leaves and bark from the garden. "Look! *This* peach-colored wool is begotten from *this* bark of the tamarind tree!" Ali's hands fluttered like marionettes in front of his face while he tried to convey the miracle of transformation effected in the wool by organic substances he claimed had transferred their healing power to it through the boiling process.

"Color moves us deeply and changes us," he explained, "organic hues resonate with our own organs and affect their vibratory qualities; when a tint pleases us intensely, it heals." As he spoke, his gaze became more defiant and his smile impish—he knew full well that some arguments rely solely on faith. "It is nothing like the harsh, chemical colors you see in mechanically mass-produced rugs!" he argued with surprising vehemence. "When you kneel on one of these rugs made from such wool, the hues themselves, as well as the patterns into which they are woven, send messages to your subconscious while your prayer addresses God." Listening to Ali speak of the effect on us of colors and patterns, I could not help think of the parallels with Vodou *vèvès* embroidered on flags or clothing, drawn on the ground with flour, painted on altars, and the emotional manner in which these abstractions act on the faithful's psyche. I also marveled at the consistency in the ways human beings of different cultures have made sense of, and communicated with the divine.

2. Silent Poet

Ali thus exhibited an unconventional grasp and appreciation of our exotic garden. Where and how he developed it is an enigma. He left his native Belgium at twenty, and it was some thirty more years until he first came to Haiti, having always wanted to set foot on what he called, "the mystic island." His feel for our land was not associated with familiar childhood tastes of fruits such as mangos and pomegranates, the Bouki and Malis games he played, or the toys he broke and buried under an avocado tree; it was not connected to the fragrance of vanilla plants growing along a serpentine brook sloping down verdant terraces; his emotions for the island, and his learning about the transience of life on earth, had never been connected with rotting corpses of grey-striped Mabouya lizards stumbled upon at the foot of a great breadfruit tree..And yet, this man felt and absorbed the unusual breath and essence of Haiti as if his soul had always been fed on it.

Once he had turned his back on his childhood home and Catholic religion, Ali never went back. "I didn't even know when my mother died," he said, on a day I found him in a confiding mood. It was an odd journey that led the young adventurer first to Paris, then to Morocco where he converted to Islam, and eventually, irresistibly, to Haiti. It was clear then, when he spoke of the mystic island with a strange glow in the eyes, that he was not referring to the charming exoticism of the place; he was speaking of sorcery, the supernatural, the occult, Vodou, all of which fascinated him. The man was an astrologer, a visionary, a silent poet who questioned the night sky at that odd hour when planets and stars come out of their shells. He was also the friend who slipped under my door at dawn, fragments of shy paper on which he would scribble quotes from the Quran. I kept one of them. "What is there to fear when you are with me?" There were other times when I found these bits of words on parchment paper, left under a stone beneath a tree where he had seen me sit the previous day, and felt I would surely return.

Trees were my friends; it took all of childhood for our love for each other to develop. The breadfruit tree was most loyal, as old as he was tall, trunk scarred, revealing dark lacerations, like marks left by a whip on a slave's back; his was a powerful body marred by the pressures of time, that still did not prevent it from expanding both in girth and in its high-reaching, vast-grasping of the skies. I lived near this tree during all the years Ali was my friend; the two are forever associated in my heart.

But it is *I* who deserted the trees when I sold our land after my father died; *I* who emptied all those river valley rooms my father had built for us to grow in; *I* who stood alone without my father in a foreign land when the breadfruit sensed, suffered, and survived the great earthquake in the company of others like him, all the mahogany, guava, coconut, palm, and frangipani, that were rooted yet somehow marooned when walls of our house crumbled, and fell all around.

3. Prayer Rug

At the time I befriended Ali, I had just gotten divorced for the second time. My then husband, Laurent, blamed this breakup on Vodou. I was thirty-one. I lived in our garden near him, my apartment was an oblong living space created underneath the pool terrace. I could hear lounge chairs being dragged above me by tenants as if over my own forehead; discern the trotting of dogs and the scuffing from their nails; catch conversations between people careless of my existence below. I felt I lived in a drum.

My father had subdivided our large house with its many floors into different apartments of various sizes, with the intention of renting them. Eventually therefore, foreigners came to live near, moved among us, making great noise and complaints. But when Ali strolled near my studio-apartment under the pool terrace, I heard his peaceful presence only because leaves would tell it with a distinguishably soft rustle meant to convey the undulant sway of a man ambling in a flowing robe beneath trees, the passing of a head of gray curls grown on a being enrobed in the silence of his thoughts about God.

"Five times a day that man unrolls that rug outside to yell 'Allah Akbar!'" my father protested before leaving for Paris to join his second wife, she, like him, like me, a divorcee. "It's a real nuisance! One would hope that he could pray inside, so he would not disturb the neighbors, but no, he says he 'likes to see the sky' when he prays. And when I complain, he argues that he pays rent, that it's *his* house, he can live and worship as he pleases. I am warning you, this no longer feels like home. I am happy I am leaving."

Ali's insolence inspired my father's admiration and interest as much as it offended him. Few people dared confront my father. Having grumbled that first time about Ali, he then shrugged his shoulders dismissively, adding with a smirk, "the bum makes nice rugs though. You ought to go see. I bought some."

But it was not for the rugs that I came to Ali. Instead, I was tempted by an astrological reading from a man consulted by politicians in two countries; a man who leaned forward as he walked, moved by great currents, yet was humble, his eyes always lowered; a man drawn by a magnet he alone felt and saw. During prayer he looked up to heaven, but when he "opened the sky" to read signs from the stars, he closed his eyes altogether so he might see inside the heavens like a blind man might. The white sheets of paper on which he drew numbers, diagrams, and planetary symbols, bore his name on the headings: Delta Acruz; *Ali* was the title he earned by making the pilgrimage to Mecca. That first time that I sat quietly with him, filled with thoughts about my recent divorce and loss of home—a growing accumulation of black marks—I heard him murmur, "Oh dear God… a broken bird has come before me."

Ali's birthdate was revealed to me unexpectedly on the rental documents my father left behind when he entrusted me with the management of his estate. My marriage had failed; I needed work and a home. His birthday was coming soon, I realized, this is my chance… he's been so kind to me… On my second visit, I brought him a cake; over the thick frosting, a sugar rainbow was arching. He took the cake from me, held it in silence, trembling; he slowly walked to the mahogany desk in front of which he sat down; he carefully put the cake on his desk; stared at it. After an awkward stretch of time, he said in a low voice, "No one has ever brought me a cake…" The short visit felt awkward; the cake was never cut and sliced in my presence; like something too sacred .

The man never talked about himself; he spoke of Allah instead. His pilgrimage to Mecca was an inextinguishable fire within, which he stoked with each recounting. "The Saudi Arabian's sky is filled with golden stars!" he said, marveling all anew. "Their brightness is fed by our faith. Fifteen million people flock each year to Mohammed's birthplace in Mecca to offer their souls. Pilgrims go around and around and round the great Kaaba stone—Islam's holy of holies. We are drunk, we whirl like Sufi dancers, magnificent planets in the vast brain of the universe! Once you have made the pilgrimage, you become Hajj, and only then can you be called 'Ali.'" My friend stopped talking suddenly, and gazed briefly into the distance with a growing frown. Then, with slight hesitation in the voice, he asked, "Would you want to be Hajj?"

"Yes!"

I learnt to pray in Arabic. He taught me patiently, standing on a prayer rug. I held on to his promise that he would take me to Mecca. He became a compass. Five times a day, there were now *two* people in the garden, crying, "Allah Akbar—God is the greatest! La ilaha illa Allah, Mohammad rasoulu Allah—there is no God but Allah, Mohammed is Allah's messenger."

The idea of a single God was not new to me since I was a Catholic. "Allah" would just be another name for the one God. I simply added Mohammed to the existing list of world prophets. It felt like the horizon had opened for me afresh.

It was not so for Ali. Soon after, the specter of death was carrying his luggage when my friend returned from Casablanca after a six-weeks' absence, and in one quick sweep, Bawon Samdi forever altered the composition and balance of my existence.

Ali opened a suitcase that no longer carried wool. On top of a few meager shirts, a yellow envelope was carefully laid; it contained new X-rays as well as a document attesting to the inscription of my Muslim name in Casablanca's great Mosque.

"What are the X-rays about?" I asked, ignoring the news of my new name.

Ali answered with a cursory gesture that imitated a hatchet coming down the back of his neck. Cancer had settled in his lungs.

Ali died a month later. He had refused all treatment, and accepted painkillers only. "I want to die whole," he said. His tone was harsh; this was not a point of discussion; his body was ailing, but not his will. "I am not going to leave pieces of me to decompose in a hospital's sanitized trash."

I tried staying with Ali on the night he died. But he was a proud man. His head was laid on the pillow like a fading bouquet his hands held at the throat. "I am afraid…" he finally said in a whisper, struggling to breathe, just before he asked me to go home with a gesture of the hand, and a smile.

With Ali's death, Islam was shut down for me.
I folded my prayer rug for good.
I lit a candle and howled under the swimming pool.

4. Resting Places

I buried Ali twice.

The first time I buried him was a temporary solution. I rented a grave at the Port-au-Prince cemetery for one year, time after which an unclaimed corpse would be thrown into a communal grave where souls turn into carcasses. I hoped that I would find his family in Belgium within that timeline, so they could take him home.

There were no mosques in Haiti then. I knew no one who might help me with a Muslim funeral. Ali had not wanted to be sent to a morgue. "Muslims are buried naked," he said. "The body is covered with white sugar, wrapped in a white cloth, laid bare into the earth."

This type of burial could not be done in Haiti unless it took place on your property. I could respect some of Ali's wishes, but not all. I found help at the morgue to strip him of his clothes, lay him on a white sheet, pour sugar over his face and limbs, and fold the sheet over. I did not see my friend naked. The man who would not have me see him die would not have wanted me to see him naked.

I fretted all year long about his anger at finding himself in a coffin, immured in the rented solitude of a nameless tomb. At year's end, no one had claimed Ali, so I went to dig him up with the help of a friend, Karl, who knew Ali and was devoted to both him and me. I knew that I would get caught in a maze of frantic bureaucratic mannerism if I raised the issue of legal right to claim a corpse, and thus left my enterprise to chance.

I drove into the Port-au-Prince cemetery with my little red car—Ali's old car. The watchman was gone, and the gate ajar. When I saw no one there to stop me, I took it as a sign. I closed my eyes: Ali was beckoning me with both hands, asking me to hurry.

At the grave, I stood at the place where I knew he waited, where he spread a handkerchief over the hollow in a worn step by his side, inviting me to sit.

"How are you to forgive me what you are about to see?" I asked, again closing my eyes, whereupon, I saw him step forward, take my hands, kiss them, wet them with tears.

A boy was crouched atop a nearby grave, picking at the scabs on his knees. I asked him for help, showing him the pickaxe and shovel Karl and I had brought. He eagerly slipped off the high place where he seemed to have existed outside of time. He worked with us as if he had dreamt of this work, and hoped all of his life for the chance to do it. Together, we loosened the bricks, widened the gap in the tomb's front wall, and pulled the coffin into the open air, resting it on weeds.

Again I saw Ali in my mind's eye. "How are you to forgive me what you are about to see?" But he came forward, and with his own hands, it seemed, opened the lid of the coffin.

Immediately, a soundless wave of gleam-corseted cockroaches scurried down the two sides of the coffin. They too had waited to be set free, and fast disappeared into the ordinary hundred, colorless cracks that permeate floors and walls of Caribbean cemeteries.

I looked inside, then reached for the yellowed sheet that appeared not to have rotted, and pulled it open. I thought that Ali would not object to my seeing this nakedness of a skeleton, as opposed to that of a corpse.

I startled: I was greeted by another face than the one I knew, but my friend was untouched—he seemed mummified, not decomposed—all body fat was gone, but the skin, now leather-like, had dried evenly over his face and body, the hair was long—he looked like people in the bog, whose idiosyncratic graves were also violated, their remains photographed and catalogued.

My car was small, and the trunk proportionate. I could not stretch Ali's body in a dignified manner inside, and take him out of the cemetery in the open. Whilst my intensions were pure, my actions were both illegal and sacrilegious, so I closed the sheet back over Ali's corpse; Karl held him at the head and I held the feet; the two of us folded him in two at the hips and put him in the trunk.

I thanked the boy, paid him a few gourds, and drove off. The gate was still ajar.

The Belgian Consulate in Haiti had contacted Ali's family at the time of his death. No one responded. I judged that no one missed him. So I brought Ali back home to me instead.

The home to which I brought Ali was a pink gingerbread house I rented in the mountains of Kenskoff. After Ali's death, I had left the apartment under the pool's terrace and moved into Ali's Bungalow.

"How can you stand it?" friends asked me, "living with Ali's ghost."

"I find it comforting," I said. "He was a man before he was a ghost. And this man loved me."

Not long after, I began longing for large vistas and brisk mountain air. Luck had it that I easily found a sweet pink house to rent, and moved to Kenskoff with my two female cats. They slept with me at night, the three of us indistinctly curled together in a single bed. I named my cats after a Haitian emperor and an Egyptian pharaoh, thinking the political might of their spirits would protect them. But, Soulouque first, and then Ramses, were eventually stolen for food by either one of my hungry neighbors, all of them poor farmers growing tubers out of plots too small to feed children in rags who sat on the doorsteps of mud huts.

I loved the mountain house, even though I soon had to mourn there all over again. The view over the mountains was stupendous when I opened the red shutters in the morning to see the land sloping all the way to the Port-au-Prince bay. I never lived in a house in Haiti that did not have a view of the bay. The bay has always embraced me, holding me close, bringing me home in deep, inexplicable ways. Yet that same bay once harbored Christopher Columbus, and allowed a brutal history to unfurl in its bosom. It was also this bay that my father pointed out to me in a large gesture the last time he and I were together.

So I brought Ali home to the house in Kenskoff for one night. I laid him on the bed in my guest room. I set wild mountain flowers in a vase on the nightstand. I lit myrrh and frankincense I saved from his wooden trunk once filled with dyed wool. I put on the Moroccan music he loved—indigenous drums and chants he played on nights of obscure longings when he wanted to dance, closing off doors and window shutters.

In the morning, pickaxe, shovel, and corpse were all that Karl and I were transporting in the rented jeep. Ali's remains were kept folded in the white sheet, making a small enough bundle to fit in the back of the four-wheel drive. His soul was the first for whom I would ever perform some sort of a rite for the dead. I chose a place cool enough for moss, quiet enough for angels, elevated enough for clouds to linger over during feast days. We were heading for the mountains of Seguin, above Kenskoff, to bury Ali again, this time in the earth, as he once wished, his kind of Haiti bog. The land was Karl's family property; but I doubt if he ever told his parents about the grave we dug there.

All along that journey, only the heartbreak was my own. The spirit of the place would have to intervene and assist me in this undertaking. The vehicle was chosen to be as light as possible for us to chance it across the mountains. I had to jump out of the car often, walk ahead, only Karl, as driver, staying inside.

Over the years, rain had continually washed away the topsoil over mountain ridges where forests had progressively been cut for fuel. Limestone rocks were now bared under the skies like jagged teeth. What were once already narrow bridges now resembled crumbling architecture, one stone at a time, leaning towards the valleys into whose engulfing womb the earth was pulled. Unpaved roads that had been cut into the flanks of a hill were dangerously eroded, and continuously narrowed down from constant landslides.

Karl and I yet made it safely to the mountaintop, and his family land. It was a misty day, but we still had a breathtaking view over the mountain ridges unfolding in the horizon. This was indeed Haiti—"land of mountains," according to the Taino word. Karl dug the grave alone. I waited next to Ali's body on a grassy patch a few feet away. No one came to ask questions, yet we both had a sense of being watched.

It was mid-afternoon when Karl dropped me off at the house before he drove back down to Port-au-Prince. I had the surprise of finding my ex-husband, Laurent, sitting in the living room, wearing a suit, holding a bouquet of red roses. He stood up, and apologized for coming unannounced, explaining that he convinced my house worker to let him in. He had taken a chance, in spite of the long drive from Port-au-Prince. "I did not want to risk you turning me down," he said. "I needed to talk to you. You were the best dream of my life. I miss you. I want us to try again."

I hesitated, but then sat down across from him, inviting him to sit as well. He looked relieved, but seeing him as a broken man was painful. "You miss your dream," I nevertheless said. "Not *me*."

No. It is *you* I miss."

"You have forgotten how intolerable it became… shall I remind you why…" I proceeded to recount my actions of the past two days—how I dug up the body of a friend at the downtown cemetery, lifted him out of the coffin, folded him in two, hid him in the trunk of my car, drove him up to the house, laid him on the bed in the guest bedroom, lit candles and incense. "I just come down from Seguin. I buried him for the second and final time…"

Laurent's face had paled. "Why do you do such things? Can't you see how awful…?"

"No. It is not awful. There is where we differ. I see it as a duty of friendship. To ensure that he had a place of true rest… a quiet eternity… save him from being dumped in a common grave…"

Laurent frowned, taking a deep breath. "Who was this man you loved so much?"

"A man unaccounted for."

As fate had it, I did not live in the Kenskoff house for long. In 1985, rebellions against Baby Doc's government were breaking out everywhere in the city and surrounding areas. Farmers near me lost no time in following the trend. They began setting fire at night to city dwellers' summer homes. Even though only a tenant, I represented the enemy. I soon was in fear for my life, and friends advised me to come back down to Port-au-Prince.

5. More Leaves

It had perhaps also been an unwittingly beneficent warning that I caught fire a couple of weeks prior to moving back to the hills of Bourdon, and the garden where Ali collected leaves.

Fire had seemed a recurrent theme in my life. I was not terribly surprised that it would be Anmınan, Vodou god of lightning, and no other who would declare his love for me. I burnt twice while growing up. My ears still resound from my mother's warnings. "You'll end up burning the house down some day! Stop lighting stolen candles from the kitchen at night!" But I loved the calm dance of a candle flame. Decades later, I still light a candle before sleep. But I had never actually *caught* fire; not until Kenskoff.

I had not seen Victoria in what felt like a long time. I stayed away from Vodou ceremonies, even though their vivid theatricality and the opportunity for singular interaction with odd divinities still held esthetic and spiritual attraction for me. The enhancement of community ties within a shared belief system expressed with specific foods, songs, and dances has unique beauty and power. But I had become leery of Vodou's deeper meaning and influence on human lives. What had initially been an intellectual endeavor had evolved into a potentially many-sided commitment I was not interested in making. I dismantled my initiation necklace, and threw its pieces at the crossroads.

But I missed divination and the divine. My mother and her French family excluded, I grew up in a business society whose preoccupations and rhythm of existence revolved around getting money, food, sex, and shelter. Never having to fight for, or lack any of it, I took life's bounty for granted, and concentrated on what I was missing. I enjoyed but did not sufficiently understand or value what privileges my family's concerns for material comfort, social status, and safety had brought me. Unlike 95% of the population that surrounded me in youth, I have never lacked food, proper clothing, a room of my own, medical care, schooling, or entertainment. But I shared with the economically disfavored people I met in Vodou ceremonies a yearning for the evidence and enjoyment of divinity's existence. I needed the company of people who not only believe in a larger realm of existence, but also in its pre-eminence over ours; people who believe in destiny, and therefore that human existence is somehow foreordained, given the use of a pre-determined array of options, moved by intelligent forces and meaningful purpose. Considering the observable intelligence and complexity in all forms of existence on the earth, or the mystifying astronomical order controlling the universe, it simply never made sense to me that human life could be reduced to matter defined as dead or alive.

I had my first astrological readings done in Berkeley while I was a student. Meeting the Gede and Ali had developed in me the taste for divination which itself fed into the concept of destiny and human accountability to a larger realm. With Ali dead, I lost access to an astrological perspective of my presence in the universe; and after the pope's cold stare, I was anything but reassured by the Christian faith I knew.

Graziela was a former Vodou priestess who made a living reading cards; she no longer was active in a temple, but still gave Vodou recipes for all manner of healing. In spite of her name, she had no physical grace, and was not Spanish. She came from peasant stock in the deep country of the Jacmel area, a province known for keeping alive its ancient Vodou traditions. She lived in the Pont-Morin neighborhood, where the Bourand Maternity Clinic had been, and where I was born. Her place was hard to find. You had to know about it, or been brought there by someone who knew. It was a small, plain cement house, built behind the back garage of another larger house, and accessed by a narrow, side alleyway where wastewater occasionally ran. The alley was also potholed; one had to be careful not to sprain an ankle.

I don't remember how I met Graziela, only how I went to her for help, asking for cleansing, horizon, and some happiness. Nothing unusual.

"I have *just* the thing!" she said without hesitation. "On ben chans—a luck bath. Very effective… easy… do it at midnight—the time when one day changes to another. You'll stand high up on a table, or chest, your feet in the bathwater." Graziela spoke calmly, but with authority, hands resting in her lap. Her voice was deep, her manner confident, while sitting down low, her plump body ensconced in a stiff wooden armchair, her short legs spread apart. She wore a nylon slip brought up above her breasts; she did not have a brassiere on, and her distractingly large nipples were pressing against the slip. She said, "Use a washbasin large enough so you can stand naked in it—like God made you. Pour seven perfumes. Choose what you like, but make sure you have Florida and Pompeïa. Add seven kinds of leaves, and seven kinds of flowers. Make sure you have basil and roses in the mix. If you don't know what good leaves to pick, ask the cook at your house; she'll know... You say there is a Monben tree in your garden? Take some... it's good. When you've got everything, put it all in the water, and rub it all well together... leaves and flowers must sweat their juices. You'll need twenty-one candles, the little white ones. Arrange them in a circle around the washbasin on the table. Before midnight, light the candles. Step into the bathwater. Midnight must find you praying the Lord's Prayer, rubbing yourself with the bathwater all over. Ask God what you want out loud. When you are done with the bath, let the candles burn out. Don't blow them off... One thing I can tell you, you're gonna smell really good!" Having spoken, Graziela chuckled, and got up.

Everything was ready at the appointed hour. The only high table I found was a rickety, narrow one on tall legs in my landlady's depot. I stood it in the shower stall, thinking that the mess of leaves from the bath would be easier to clean there. The washbasin was large enough for me to stand in, but I had to stick the candles very close around it, because the table was narrow. I used a chair to prop myself up on the table, and step into the washbasin. The fragrance filled the entire house. My cats would have enjoyed the commotion, had they still been alive, whiskers trembling, busy sorting out scents. The burning candles brought magic to the plainness of the bathroom. I chuckled like Graziela, wishing there'd be someone to see me.

Come midnight, my prayers started. I began rubbing the scented leaves all over my body.

It wasn't long until I began to feel uncomfortable, my legs particularly. Why do I feel so hot? I puzzled. I bent forward and looked down towards my feet. Ho! I am on fire!

In a flash, I understood how the candles were too close to the washbasin—the alcohol contained in the perfumes had caught fire... I was standing in the middle of a pool of flames... they already reached up to my breast... they'll catch in my hair any second... Get down right now!

Three hours later, I was shivering at my mother's gate.

She lived in Pétionville, divorced from my father who had settled in Paris with his second wife. My mother may never have been maternal in customary ways, but she was mostly kind. She might have pampered each of her many dogs more than she ever did me, but I could count on her to play the doctor, which made her feel close to her father, a surgeon, the love of her life. She kept his plaster-mold death mask hanging in her bedroom above the bed. There were times when she would take it down, and cradle it into her arms like an infant; she watched his deathly-white face with its closed eyelids, mourning him all over again.

"It's the middle of the night!" my mother complained with the broken voice of interrupted sleep. "What time is it?" She spoke from her upper floor bedroom window, facing the gate. "Can't this wait for morning?"

"I need help, Mother... I am burnt... I prayed driving all the way down from Kenskoff so I would not pass out from pain... I was sitting on my burns..."

"MON DIEU! I'll be right down..."

She was soon at the gate, fumbling through her jingling keys, looking for the padlock key. The dogs surrounded her, barking with excitement, tails wagging wildly, happy. One can count on a dog's joy.

"Okay... here...I have it... ah, shit! I dropped it... *shit!*"

It was a moonless night. She felt around on cement with her hands. The dogs got in the way, licking her bare arms, thinking it all a game.

"Damn it! Get off me..."

But it was not long until the gate was opened, and she wrapped her arms around me, warding off the dogs, leading me inside, treating me like a war casualty, giving orders.

"Sit down here."

"No—it hurts."

"Sit, I tell you! You're so stubborn—your father is right... You can't stand like this all night long."

"I know... but not now."

"Well, Let me have a look... lift up your kaftan!"

"I can't bear your looking yet."

"I am your mother!"

"There are large burnt patches everywhere, except on my face and head..."

"Thank God for that! Your face..."

"I fell..."

"Where?"

"From high up in the bathroom."

"The *Bathroom?* What on earth were you up to again?"

"I caught fire... but I immediately wrapped myself up in the bathroom rug...

"It's lucky you did!"

"Yes... it killed the flames... at first I did not feel the burns... I was just uncomfortably hot... and in shock... I could have died..."

"You're an idiot! Ah la la! What am I gonna do with you?"

"... and then the pain started... it woke me from the shock... the terrible burning made me look for cold... I made the mistake of getting under cold water... I knew I should not, but I could not resist... of course, the pain was unbearably worse when I got out of under the water..."

"You can thank God for being alive! Protected you from all that Vodou—the devil's work... Victoria! Ha! That one, I blame her for this. I warned you. You never listen. You think I'm jealous. But she's a witch. I know what I'm talking about..."

"I do thank God... I prayed nonstop. That's why I could drive down..."

Early next morning my mother took me to see Dr. Nollaw. He was already retired, but she had a filial tenderness for the old doctor. His gentle, affectionate manner caused her to miss her father. Dr. Nollaw was a revered Pétionville doctor, like my mother's father had been in his hometown of Sartrouville. It was a shock to the whole community when Dr. Nollaw announced he would shut his clinic down. No one understood why until the dementia started to show.

Dr. Nollaw opened his clinic for us in his grey-striped pajamas and bathrobe, holding a cup of coffee. He needed a shave, and parts of his breakfast lingered on the corners of his lips. He was delighted by our visit. He took a look at my legs and chuckled; they were heavy with large, water-filled blisters that made it difficult to walk. The water was sloshing around and I feared the skin would break; and it hurt. Dr Nollaw decided he'd pop the blisters with a needle, pierce the skin so the liquids would empty out. He pushed a few papers around, and had me sit on the edge of his desk. He brought a chair out and sat in front of me. His eyes were at the level of my knees. As Dr. Nollaw approached me slowly with a syringe, his hand started to shake; he stopped and adjusted his round spectacles; he drew closer and raised the syringe again; he then abruptly turned his attention to my mother.

"I have a joke you'll like," he said.

"Tell me," she said, rolling her eyes.

It was a dirty joke. My mother laughed wholeheartedly, and Dr. Nollaw was very flattered.

"I have another," he said again.

They both seemed to have forgotten me. "Dr. Nollaw?" I asked. "How about me?"

"Ah, yes…" He graciously turned around again, and raised the syringe to the level of my calves. His hand could not hold still. The closer he got to me, the worse it was. I began imagining that he was going to stab me instead of just prickling the surface of the skin. I suddenly grabbed the syringe from his hands. "Dr. Nollaw, forgive me. I'd rather pop my blisters myself."

"Aren't you afraid?"

"Not if *I* do it."

"All right then," my mother said, "Dr. Nollaw, leave her to it. Tell me that other joke."

Friars

6. Different Yet the Same

The massive popular riots against Baby Doc started in 1985 that made me fear for my life in Kenskoff had the intended effect on the government. Baby Doc and his family fled to France in early February 1986 aboard a U.S. Air Force craft. I had already come down from the mountains by then, and lived in the Bourdon apartment under the pool's terrace again.

My father also returned from Paris, but without his wife. He gave no explanation to anyone. I slowly realized that he was divorcing for the second time. His shame, regrets, solitude, and internal chaos were immeasurable and frightening. I thought of desperate souls in Dante's Inferno. He seemed like a man in quicksand attempting to grab unreachable sides of an engulfing pool. I also feared that his wounded spirit would swallow me. I yearned to escape.

It may be that the charmed-bath had a good effect, or that my prayers did. Perhaps God just took pity on his foolhardy daughter. In spring of that same year, through a series of good fortunes and the help of a new friend, I was accepted in the three-year Master of Fine Art's program at the University of Pennsylvania.

Why painting? Why would a former Berkeley anthropology graduate want to study art? One answer is that the Vodou chapter of my life was closed. A child also never truly abandons the hope of pleasing her parents. Had my mother been an acrobat I might have chanced learning the trapeze but, in Haiti, she had become a painter. Art was a form of acrobatics I could manage.

Philadelphia charmed me from the first. It snowed early that first year. I walked through the streets with my face lifted to the falling flakes, feeling like a prisoner set free. I could not have left Haiti without the financial support and blessing of my father, albeit given at the last minute, and after he tried everything to entice me to stay. He sadly made one more suicide attempt with sleeping pills that first year while I was away at school. My cousin William saved him; a spur-of-the-moment visit, and he found my father just in time to rush him to the hospital.

It is ten years later, in 1996 that my father died of a stroke in his car. I was forty-five. I am glad that I had had time to make him proud during these ten years in America, my second exile there. The first time that I had returned to Haiti from America, I was an anthropologist and young divorcee. When I left for America for the second time, I was again divorced. By the time my father died, I had become a successful painter and prize-winning poet. Pride was the closest feeling to happiness that he knew. He boasted so much about his daughter at parties that people whom I only first met at his funeral felt they already knew me. He loved my poems most.

My father's death interrupted my career as an American painter. I inherited the responsibility of managing his estate all over again, as I had when he left for France with his second wife, and I befriended Ali. I also inherited the responsibility of my mother and my brother, he who grew to be a man too fragile to ever truly blossom. I moved my mother back to her old home in Bourdon from which divorce had exiled her. In the next seven years, and until I finally sold the family property, I traveled back and forth between Haiti and the U.S. every two months, in much the same way that Ali had done between Haiti and Morocco. It is during those years that I befriended friars.

Father Lespinasse and Father Campion were Franciscan monks. The first time that I managed the family property had given me the opportunity to befriend Ali. This second time brought holy men to me as well.

A common friend introduced us: Guy first took me to lunch on a Sunday with Father Lespinasse at the Turgeau Seminary. These Sunday lunches with the friars became a weekly affair that sustained me through difficult years, a time when I put my life and career aside to take care of my family. I again felt about my life the way I did when I had gone to Graziela for help, and fled to Philadelphia.

The friars had been our next-door neighbors when I was the child seen standing at the Virgin of the Immaculate Conception's grotto. The proximity of holy men to our house should have been a blessing. However, monastery bells rung at regular times of the day resounded unpleasantly during my father's siesta time. He approached the friars with what he thought a reasonable offer.

"This will be a good solution to my discomfort," he explained. "The neighborhood will be quiet again. Everyone will be happy."

"No," is the answer he received. The brothers gently declined his proposition of installing electric alarms in place of the bells, albeit at his expense. My father saw it as a strange lack of conciliatory disposition exhibited by religious men. He truly believed their purpose would have been equally served by electric alarms as they were by ancient bells. Considering the man's temperament, it was inevitable that my father would resolve himself to another drastic measure. He sold our house and moved us to Bourdon for more land and fewer neighbors, careless about leaving behind the angel that stood above the children's pool,

Father Lespinasse's blue eyes were startling in a mulatto. The bird-like clarity, focus, and intensity of his gaze belied the heaviness in his shoulders, the white of his hair, the slow gentleness in his manner, the softness of his voice. Father Campion on the other hand, was a six-foot-six black man with black eyes. He walked towards visitors with immense flawless hands extended, his deep laughter heard echoing down the barren valley nearby the monastery.

The two men were the same man—God's men.

Father Lespinasse's students remember him as exacting but clement; unfailingly fair; expressing his political views with vehemence, albeit unpopular or dangerous, and especially if these were in support of the Bible; truth, like God, was indivisible. It turned out to be a great favor that Guy introduced me to Father Lespinasse and brought me to lunch with the friars on Sundays. Guy and Father Lespinasse had first been childhood friends, and then novices in a Port-au-Prince seminary at the same time. Guy's religious commitment eventually took him to a Dominican monastery in France. He was well embarked for an illustrious life in the church when he suddenly quit everything, after ten years. "I left the Dominicans because I lost the sense of God's eyes on me," he said. "I lost my faith."

Guy then left for India, became a Sanskrit scholar, and later married a Norwegian philosopher with whom he had a son. He taught philosophy in Norway for many years before his divorce, and final return to Haiti where I met him.

While Father Lespinasse shied away from public view, Father Campion drew crowds. He held exorcism Masses monthly at the Port-au-Prince Cathedral, escorted by strong assistants, walking up and down the central aisle, hunting for Satan.

"The devil is strong," he explained, one Sunday over lunch. "He produces unnatural force and violence even in the meekest and smallest of people. The demon gets angry with me and fights back. Someone possessed by Satan is wilder than any beast, they must be held down while I pray and administer holy water to help Jesus Christ and the archangels crush him. That's why I need strong men at the cathedral. But it is amazing to see, when I am done, how holy water no longer burns the flesh, how it no longer enrages a creature who only a moment before had squirmed desperately, torn all clothes, displayed sexual organs, and spurted obscene words in venomous fury, screeching resoundingly all over." Having said this, Father Campion smiled, observing my reaction. "You should come some day," he said again, "and see for yourself how people's eyes seem washed and translucent when the devil is gone. They glow, their entire face is enlivened like the desert after rainfall. Satan is ugly, he causes opacity and harshness on all he touches, while God only radiates. Never forget: Satan is real. The devil's greatest trick is to have us believe, and argue with each other, that he does not exist."

"Would you be willing to exorcize me, Father Campion?" I asked.

"Why would you think you need it?"

7. Friends of Circumstance

Lunch at the Turgeau seminary was simple and joyful. Its refectory had long tables set at mealtimes with plastic plates, metal dinnerware, paper napkins. Chairs were made of wooden frames and woven-straw seats. Hot dishes were brought out from the adjacent kitchen at a precise hour each day, then left on the tables with plastic-mesh covers to keep flies away. The insects remained near however, waiting for the opportunity to hover over one friar's or another's plateful of food, adroitly maneuvering their way between impatient hands shooing them away, or wanting to squash them; the flies always managed to briefly land heroically on the edge of a bean or a tomato instead. The monks came to the refectory at their leisure. They streamed in at various times during the two-hour lunch period, rarely speaking while they ate. The food had few variants; rice and red beans could be counted on, then chicken or beef cooked in an onion gravy, with plantain, yams, potatoes or carrots, mashed, fried or boiled. A few strands of lettuce and fresh tomatoes were rewards for those who came early. The food was cold by the end of the lunch period, an hour when most novices seemed almost to flock like hungry birds.

My mother came to lunch at the seminary a few times, and met Father Campion once. She was delighted; he was *just* her type—a Caribbean man, irresistibly handsome. It did not matter that he was a monk. When Guy whispered in her ear that he was an exorcist, she was beside herself with excitement. In spite of her advanced age, Mother was all rings and bangles and ruffles and lace and flower corsage and lipstick and black eyelashes fluttering away at Father Campion.

He remained unmoved.

Finally, she could no longer resist, and grabbed his hand. "Father Campion, I am going to read your palms. I am good at it. You're going to be astonished."

Father Campion smiled. He graciously relinquished his large hands into my mother's heavily bejeweled and arthritic fingers. As she spoke, telling him various things about his past, his temperament, and reasons for choices he made, he soon started to chuckle, then finally laughed out loud.

"I found you out, didn't I?" Mother said coquettishly. "Come on…Admit it!"

"Not completely," Father Campion replied, suddenly relaxed, his countenance not so stern. "But I admit that a lot of what you said is true."

"Now tell me, Father Campion… you don't mind that I call you Father do you? Well, Father, I am interested in exorcism. May I come watch you some day?"

"Of course. I do this at the Port-au-Prince cathedral. There is a set schedule."

Mother asked, "Can I have your phone number so I can call you about the next date? I'll give you mine too."

Father Campion and my mother exchanged phone numbers. He gave the general number for the seminary, and she gave her home number. He then excused himself.

Father Campion had hardly left when Mother turned to Father Lespinasse, who had been eating, but followed the conversation nonetheless, and said, "Father Lespinasse, forgive me for telling you this since you are a priest, but really, I find all men are the same—you make them feel handsome and interesting, and they melt in your hands."

"Is that so?" Father Lespinasse said with a sweet, amused smile. "I would not know dear lady. You see, I am not a man."

"'I am not a man?' What do you mean you are not a man?" She said with a chuckle, rolling her eyes.

"No… You see… I am a monk."

8. Orphanage for the Would-Be Dead

My last visits to the friars, in 2004, were two days apart—I saw Father Lespinasse first—just before my leaving Haiti for a kind of third, final exile. I had already become an American citizen during the ten years preceding my father's death. I came to say goodbye to Father Lespinasse and Father Campion with melancholy and gratitude. I had sold my family property to Michael and Sarah Miller who came from the U.S., and the proceeds divided in three shares.

"You are now as sinless as the day you were first baptized," Father Lespinasse said with a benevolent smile, after confessing and blessing me. "But if you want to marry again in the Catholic Church, you must get a papal annulment."

"Is it a complicated process… if one is not Baby Doc's fiancée…?"

Father Lespinasse giggled. "It takes time. When you go home, see a priest, and ask for help. He'll know what to advise. He'll probably want to interview you first, and analyze the circumstances of the marriage." The seriousness in the friar's eyes belied his smile. I was holding three bottles of holy water that he had just blessed for me after he received the complete confession of my life. "Sprinkle it in your living space once in a while," he last said. "Satan won't like it."

When I saw Father Campion, I confessed my experiences with Vodou with some malaise, and asked him again for an exorcism. He was reluctant. I knew his reputation as a strong opponent of Vodou. His impassioned public speeches from the pulpit were notorious. "I was not prepared for this request," he explained. "I don't have assistants with me to help in case some evil shows up." But, seeing my disappointment, he quickly said, "I'll give you a blessing. I'll go to my room, and get what I need."

Father Campion left me for only a few minutes, and came back with things necessary for a full exorcism. "While I was in my room," he said, "I had a feeling that it would be all right to do as you ask."

I sat calmly in a chair looking down at my feet, while Father Campion stood tall over me, holding holy water, an exorcist's book of prayers, a crucifix, and a Bible."

The exorcism took little time, and the water did not burn.

"All done?" I asked with some surprise.

"Yes."

"I am *exorcised*?"

"There was no evil around you. It seems that Vodou spirits have no hold on you. I blessed you as well. I wish you a good journey. We will miss seeing you on Sundays."

I was relieved to learn that I was free of influence from dark forces. Something had protected me in spite of my involvement with treacherous people who may have wished me harm. Victoria's warning that I might forever be beholden to forces whose attention I attracted or sought, had felt more like a threat. In perceiving Father Campion's relief that no evil was present, I recalled the Vodou priest who once told me about the various magical beings he encountered at night—werewolves who fed on children, or spirits as big as a house and eyes of fire. I asked him, "I grew up in Haiti hearing about all kinds of magical creatures. How come I never see any?"

"Innocence protects people," he said. "Those who mean no evil can see no evil."

When Father Lespinasse died seven years later during the 2010 earthquake in Haiti, I had not seem him again, but still had in my bedroom closet a bottle of the holy water he gave me. At the hour of his death, he had been getting dressed in his room to go teach when the earth's tremors started, and he was crushed under the walls of the Turgeau Seminary.

Father Lespinasse seemed like the sort of man who would endure like a biblical patriarch meant to feed generations of orphans. At the time when I met him, he had long been the sole inheritor of his childhood home. His many siblings, having become successful and wealthy, had no use for it when their parents died. He turned the old Victorian house into an orphanage that remained standing amidst the post-earthquake rubble of Pacot, one of the most devastated neighborhoods of Port-au-Prince.

Days after the earthquake, the orphanage echoed from cries of additional newborns left on its doorstep, swathed in soiled rags and shreds of cloth that testified to other tragedies than the earthquake alone. They were picked off the floor by leftover adolescent orphans who had missed all chances at being adopted, and still roamed the orphanage they could not outgrow. Disillusioned as they were, they helped Father Lespinasse and his assistant run the home that had become theirs; ghosts of the undead, aimless beings unaccounted for by an uncharitable elitist society that had not imagined a future for them, children wholly undesired, unloved except by Father Lespinasse.

Father Lespinasse's assistant was a childless woman who helped him raise innumerable orphans of the city. After the earthquake she, a gray-haired, overweight woman, made her solitary way up the steep and potholed road of the Turgeau hills that had become grim with debris, as most of Port-au-Prince had. She headed for the corner of the Immaculate Conception's grotto where she would veer left; she'd enter the small street leading to the seminary, treading on the same sidewalks I did in early childhood, until she finally passed by my old house with the bronze angel; soon after, she went through the gate of the seminary, where the road dead ends.

She sat on a pile of debris in the sun for four days until Father Lespinasse's remains were found. She waited each day until dusk fell, watching rescue teams search for survivors under the vast and deep rubble. The rope she brought each morning was to help pull him out if he was found alive, but trapped. The cloth was meant for privacy, to cover and protect him from an unavoidable form of indecency if he was found dead, and naked.

When our family moved to Bourdon, many decades earlier, to the land and garden where Ali wove rugs on a loom, my father had been running from the ringing bells of the Turgeau Seminary where Father Lespinasse died. Instead of holy friars as neighbors, we ended up with hungry slum dwellers, albeit living at the bottom of the valley, and on the other side of the small river that delineated our land. The 2010 earthquake would eventually make no distinctions between one side or the other; it would destroy all; the Turgeau seminary, the Bourdon slums, and the home my father built on several acres of land where fruits from my childhood hung on trees like ornaments of an inexhaustible Christmas. I was fond of stretching on home's alleyway to feel the sting of the sun on my bare legs; red ants would skirt around my tiny toes, causing me some alarm; the breeze ruffled through the small leaves of mahogany trees lining the alley, creating a calming hush sound; luminous clouds gathered above, and my eyes would follow them in their course, my whole being wishing to join them.

7 Losing the Garden

1. Promise Made Under Trees

Michael and Sarah Miller came to Haiti with pure hearts. I would learn from them about the Mormon Church.

    It remains a disquieting paradox that had I not staged a bit of fiction towards the end of their visit, the three of us might have been cheated out of a complex opportunity for spiritual development in doing charity; the lives of the neighborhood's poor would not have been dramatically improved, and the disinherited handicapped of Port-au-Prince would not have been offered prostheses that gave them a chance to take part in the active world.

    The problem arose when a possible crumbling of great dreams became suddenly manifest on Michael's last day in Haiti. Evil, the forever-scheming presence whose purpose is to hinder, hurt, or destroy, had become real in an instant. The alarm sounded in me powerfully. The threat I sensed to Michael and to me demanded that I devise a surprise stratagem on the spur of the moment in order to dismantle the devil's scheme, and outsmart him in the end.

Like a Medieval knight sent by his Lord, Michael first left Arizona to reconnoiter alone in Port-au-Prince.

    In those days, I walked in the garden under a wide-brim hat, and wore an ankle-length khaki skirt. I must have cut an odd figure to this American man looking to buy land and buildings that he meant to turn into a hospital for amputees. He came to the house, and introduced himself as an interested buyer; we decided right away to make a tour of the land. During that first, and all subsequent visits, I told him no lie. I was earnest in my will to sell the property, even whilst I knew how wrenching it would prove for me to separate from it, and even if it had already been seven years since my father died.

From the very beginning of my decision to sell, I struggled with a feeling of betrayal. My father had devoted his life's work to us, and his Sundays to the land. He would be seen standing firmly under the midday sun, a khaki cap covering his bald spot, planning and overseeing the placement of every stone in every wall, every tile, every wire, every window, every door, and every door handle used to enter the many rooms meant to protect us. The land represented my father. The land *was* my father. I was not just selling property, I was abandoning my ancestors to oblivion.

I knew nothing about Michael, Sarah, or the Mormon faith until that first walk in the garden during which we spoke of amputation and amputees. The unusual character of the couple's presence spoke of uncommon intelligence, educated sensitivity, and otherworldliness. Curiosity about their faith arose in me naturally. Their plans of a hospital aimed for charity helped me accept the coming loss of my roots, and the trees.

Dominant in memory were the rows of mahogany grown along both sides of the alleyway going through the land; they were the first of all trees that my father planted, having become synonymous with home for me. Then came numerous fruit-bearing trees: breadfruit, mango, avocado, cherry, tamarind, tangerine, coconut, lemon, sour orange and pomegranate, as well as decorative trees such as the calabash, frangipani and flamboyant; they all stood like immense bouquets set in celebration of our lives.

The trees had thrived with us. They grew tall and old as we did, until we no longer could clearly see from the balcony of the uppermost floors the blue brilliance of Port-au-Prince bay. In time, my father too had become an inseparable element of the land, buried as he was under the thick-leaved canopy of the tropical apricot tree grown near the narrow river.

My cousin William had warned me, "If you ever want to sell the estate, the tomb will be a problem. You'll regret burying your father there."

"I have no choice. He made this request long ago. His will is my command."

And then, I discovered how Mormons revere ancestors.

"We will respect and protect your father's grave," Michael promised. "We would very much like to hang a photo of him in the hospital's main hall. Your father is an important part of this land's history. Your mother and brother will also have a place here to stay. I understand their fragilities."

Oh…the wonder of having one's burden lifted by people of faith acting with great heart. I saw how I would no longer have to manage all the cleaning and repair staff: gardeners, housemaids, laundry maids, cooks and trash collectors, night watchmen, masons, carpenters, electricians and plumbers, as well as a collection of tenants who rented the apartments that my father built on the land, like Ali once did; but unlike Ali, they were foreigners, unable to handle life in countries that did not offer the modern comforts they were used to. I felt held hostage to an array of people who demanded each day that I listen, explain, console, exchange, repair, satisfy and provide for their needs.

It was a wonder then that just six years after Michael and Sarah bought the land, in 2004, Port-au-Prince suffered the 2010 earthquake. In far greater numbers than before the earthquake, men, women, and children all too recently mauled, hardly recovered from the trauma, filed each day in uneven lines to the hospital, crowding in what had been my family home, to be made whole again. The time had also begun when no one would care any longer that my father's gravesite might progressively become a convenient dumping ground. Attention quickly shifted from maintaining what existed, to rebuilding what fell. Devotion went to uncovering the rubble-buried dead, rather than catering to old remains cushioned in proper coffins under marble tombstones.

2. Face of a Slum

Visit after visit, I stood with Michael in the shade of magnificent fruit-bearing trees, strolled on grassy terraces, walked up soft-curving garden stairways that led to white-walled buildings or a pink-domed villa; but time and again, Michael had turned and paused, quietly scrutinizing the slum dwellings creeping up the slopes of the Protestant Church's property opposite ours; the two properties, the Protestant Church's and my father's, were laid out like cheeks of a giant in a face bisected by a river instead of a nose.

When my father bought his land and first rented tractors on Sundays until he had moved enough earth and leveled terraces, the Protestant land was covered only with wild bush, the river shallow enough to wade through. That wild area soon became my running ground in the company of my devoted Trotinette, a low-to-the-ground mutt, unafraid of thorns.

Small cornfields eventually appeared in irregular patches along the river, preceding the emergence of a couple of shacks built by the very people who had first planted the corn, testing reactions. The church tolerated both corn and shacks, so both grew in scope and number. By the time the church cared about evidence that they were losing their property, it was impossible to throw people out. The slum community then continued to mushroom on the face of the land, indiscriminately gray, without design or harmony, each new growth instantly incorporated to the whole as if with organic instinct.

The contrasting "developments" on either side of the river—my family's few gleaming white buildings opposite sprawling muddy slums—oddly reflected and symbolized the country's unattended, ongoing socio-economic illness.

Each side was forced to tolerate the other every day. Each had to ignore this continuing insult to human rights, namely the right to live in a God-given lush environment with common dignity, order, and love.

Each side suppressed renewed upsurges of ancestral anger: People of the slums stifled their anger at being invisible, abandoned, forgotten, used for cheap labor, abused, existing to serve and meriting no reward, and this going from one generation to the next since the slave revolution of 1804. On the side of the wealthy people, the anger was rooted in guilt over the plight of the disinherited from whose poverty they benefitted and therefore perpetrated; their anger is mixed with irritation at their own dependency on a servant-class they despise for being a nearly sub-human social category with whom they must nevertheless associate themselves, and bring into the privacy of their homes to use as servant labor.

As a child, I was spared.

I saw the slums as a foreign country through which I traveled with curiosity and wonder. Slum people looked different, but were friendly. My innocence was protected. I was welcomed. From the shadowed corners of windowless shacks, old men fetched weary drums, and astonished me with the sounds and joyful rhythms they could create.

3. The Jahr House

In time, the growth of the slums was stopped by the construction of an asphalt road and a wall made of stones brought down from the mountains of La Boule. The road could be seen as a social-class divider that mimicked the river below. It was accessed from other roads that led to the side of the hill, and built like a belt around it, some two-thirds of the way up from the river. It was to be known as the Jahr house road.

It began at a tall iron gate, then softly swirled around the hill, leading to the very top where Lebanese settlers built a three-story mansion as long as a city block. This home was meant to accommodate three generations of their continually growing family, the Jahr family, members of an immigrant merchant population that was increasingly successful in Haiti. The size of the house spoke of assembly. It must have been a great expatriate's dream, this desire to keep one's extended family together in a foreign land under the leadership of a patriarch, much as Old Testament people had when they followed Moses.

The general rectangular shape and modern massiveness of that house constructed in cement blocks and concrete, was however neither successfully softened by cream-colored arches on every floor, nor enlivened by the coral color the walls eventually came to be painted. Built on the hilltop overlooking the slums, but also with a view on the opposite green hill of trees my father created, the Jahr house looked huge no matter from how far you observed it. It became a landmark for maps and directions to the Bourdon and Canapé-Vert hills areas, much as the presidential palace served for directions to and around downtown Port-au-Prince. It was an eyesore.

During the time when the Jahr house was being built, I no longer roamed the slums alone, and joined my brother and his friends who used the construction site as a playground. Trotinette came along. Her tongue would hang to the side when she got thirsty or tired, but she never gave up following me. When an area proved too difficult for her to manage crossing or climbing over with short legs, I carried her. I tremble now to think of the risks my brother and I took, climbing scaffoldings, hiding in narrow spaces not easily accessible, and chasing each other on unfinished stairways leading to a plunging void. We did this until the construction was finished, and the Jahrs' extended family moved in.

At dusk, my family would sit on a green garden bench to watch the sunset. The four of us sat in silence, each lost in thought. From where we sat, the completed Jahr house loomed like a geometric god safeguarding his children in a hilltop nest, head profiled against the darkening sky in which my brother and I competed to identify stars.

One of those nights, the Jahr house went up in flames. We were all in bed and asleep. The sudden, massive fire took the lives of men, women, and children, grandparents too old to run, and heavily pregnant women too slow in gathering toddlers. The tragedy affected everyone, even the envious and the poor. No one outside the closed Lebanese community had known the Jahr family, but after having seen their house tower over us each day, they had become part of our lives, part of the Port-au-Prince community, even if only through gossip.

Survivors of the tragedy abandoned the house. They spread in other wealthy areas of the city, and began to integrate themselves. The house remained a part of their history, a limb they would not reshape or sever, a standing ruin they could neither face nor level, a ghost on the hill, left as a reminder of human futility or damnation. The town's gaze became accustomed to the effort of avoiding it.

4. We The People

"So, what's the story behind that burnt house?" Michael asked.

Michael asked this question during our last stroll on his last day in Haiti. Sarah had not come for this trip. He would be leaving for Arizona the next morning, and deciding within the coming weeks whether or not to buy the estate.

"What burnt house?" I chuckled, in a derisive attempt to deny this persistent evidence of trauma, this charred, hollowed mansion frozen in timeless contemplation of gray slum dwellings inching upward towards it, like hands reaching out from the pits of hell.

However exclusive the location and size of my land in the hills, and above the bay of Port-au-Prince, the fact remained that, owing to the trees grown very tall all around, the slums and the burnt house above it were its only view remaining.

"How long has it been like that?" Michael asked again.

Desecration happens over inexplicable time, I wanted to say. The house has been damaged for as long as we have, and stands in reflection of us. Satan's sickness-bearers are clever and patient. A subtle step is made initially, the alterations to our inner selves start imperceptibly, yet are finite. By the time we are aware of what we have become, we are used to the absence of music.

"Is it noisy here at night?"

I still did not answer his question—my mind was traveling—I was strangely, and vividly engaged in my thoughts, filled with a vague sense and vision of things to come soon, wondering about images from a dream I recently had, and temporarily forgotten: I saw how clothes had been hung over the line where all things dry, in a land whose people sip water from rivulets running on the edges of city streets. I stood on a barren, stony land overbuilt with mud shacks, making an offer to the strongman of these slums, its *kazèk*. His face was pockmarked and sweaty under a worn straw hat. We spoke opposite each other, surrounded by children of his family who looked up to him with fear, while he looked at me with doubt. "Help? Feast?" He asked, incredulous. "Nothing good has ever been offered to me…"

My mind then made a sudden jump back to the present, and I remembered Michael's question, also growing aware of the increasing unease caused by my silence.

"Noisy?" I repeated out loud. "No. Why?"

When Michael asked the question, we stood right above the pink-domed villa that had charmed him from the first. My father had been very proud of this house he built; the dome particularly, being the roof of the main bedroom. Michael had been toying with the idea of keeping this house as Sarah's and his private residence during the regular visits to Haiti they would be making in future years; the couple intended to help manage the hospital, while continuing its funding.

"Are you sure?" Michael asked again.

"About what?"

"That it's not noisy here at night?"

"Usually not,." I noticed that Michael was looking right at the slums. "Tenants never complain about that."

Just as we were speaking, I examined the layout of the land and constructions ahead of us as if with Michael's eyes: Aligned almost in a straight row before us were, first the villa right beneath the terrace where we stood; then farther down from the villa came my father's grave stretched under the apricot tree; then I could see the undulating gray line of the river beyond the grave, while across the river stood the slums starting at the bottom of the hill opposite us; and finally, way up above the slums was the Jahr house. So I said, "Why don't you come tonight and judge for yourself?"

"I'll come after dinner."

"Good idea," I said, masking my alarm, eyes focused on the cross above my father's tomb, small and alone.

It was only after my father died that people of the slums became a cohesive otherness I observed with apprehension and experienced with disenchantment, as they too came to relate to me that way. Until then, I thought I had friends there. The wanderings of childhood had led me to sit with them inside their shacks, enjoy the simplicity and warmth within their walls, and feel the mystery of their existence.

Gracilia lived in the slums. She crossed the river twice a week to do our laundry after she had done hers. I often crouched close by in the early morning hours, and watched her squat at the river's edge while she did her laundry, keeping her skirts gathered up between her large thighs. Using a rock, she first pounded flat and molded a long bar of Rosita soap into a ball. She then vigorously rubbed the soap onto her meager bed sheets, or the flimsy, faded dresses of her many little girls. Once she had finished scrubbing the clothes with her hands and piled them one on top of the other, she rinsed them one by one into the river. I watched the river turn milky. After she had wrung and spread all the garments to dry in the sun all day over scrawny bushes and piles of rocks, she headed up to our house. She picked her clothes up later at the end of her workday with us, having finished ironing our clothes with the heavy coal iron, even my cotton underwear.

Saint-Ayus lived in the slums during my childhood as well. He was only seventeen at the time he was hired to do odd jobs in the house, duties that included watching over my brother and me during those nights when our parents were out late. He played card games with us, and taught me how to cheat. He was fired many times for laziness or theft, but forgiven and re-hired the next day. We attended the Catholic baptism of the first of his five children. Cake and assorted milk sweets were laid on a carefully ironed tablecloth spread over a narrow, rickety table. Saint Ayus stayed with us many years until he left without notice. He boarded a precarious boat for the Bahamas, hoping for a better life. Enduring new servitude in luxury hotels catering to wealthy people other than his countrymen, he sent money to pay passage for his children so they could join him there, one at a time. But when his wife's turn came, she refused to go.

I remember her delicate prettiness but not her name. She must have preferred to hang her dreams on pillars of the shack she knew, and in whose darkness she kept memories of love shared there. The thatch and mud walls had been the backdrop of all her children's laughter; like all children do, hers had had the secret for disregarding poverty, feeling the irrelevance of its short span within the enormity of existence, even if they were seen too often to tremble within it. Saint-Ayus's wife stayed in Haiti; she had a name there, even if it was among the nameless, the invisibles of society. Her neighbors knew her.

Gracilia and Saint-Ayus's wife came to my father's burial ceremony near the river, and so did the gardeners, masons and carpenters who had worked for him through the years of planting and building our great home. Octavio was one of those who worked as a mason; he started as an apprentice since he was a young man; but Octavio drank too much, ate too little for too many years, and lost his teeth early, still preferring to spend his meager salary on drinking *kleren* than at the dentist. Dental care is a luxury that poor people can't afford; teeth usually decay until they have to be pulled out, and *kleren* is again useful as painkiller. At the close of the burial ceremony, Octavio was drunk and swayed dangerously. He stood on the wide metal structure woven a few feet above the hole with the coffin laid at the bottom. The metal crossbars on which he was perched were meant to hold the layer of cement concrete and gravel that was going to be poured into the hole, filling it all around and above the coffin. My plan was to create a definite, hard fortification that would protect my father's remains from grave robbers and sorcerers living nearby, and who would be sure to steal into the night, aiming for the fresh tomb. When the cement was poured down, it crushed the countless fresh flower wreaths that covered the mahogany coffin, hiding it from view. Octavio sang and danced the lewd dances of the Gede spirits of the dead, deaf to the protestations of the Catholic Priest, who had said prayers at the church funeral service, and also stood at the grave to bless it. Octavio gyrated his hips wildly, naked but for checkered briefs, drenched in rum and cement water, reveling in the portent of a life's ending.

My father's burial was the pivotal event of our family on this earth. It was also part of a continuum in the history of our land in which Michael showed interest and respect.

Yet, that day of the funeral and subsequent burial, it was obvious that the land of whose history my father was a part did not stop at the river's edge; it went beyond, it embraced the slums, it crawled up the hill all the way to the Jahr house, went down and further, encompassing all the stories, all the people's misery, all of Haiti. My father's was a family story, a Haitian story, in all its untranslatable beauty and cruelty.

But it was also at the time of my father's burial that people of the slums receded further from my life, less because of how I saw them than how they came to perceive me. More than inheriting property, I inherited a persona, one established with power over them, power of money, power to pay, hire, loan, give, relieve, help, or not.

In their eyes, I had lost my humanity. My power parted us, and it did so mainly because it was not as great as they imagined. It wasn't that I wouldn't transform their lives, it was that I couldn't; the money and power were insufficient. I became a foreigner at home, and thus lost all sense of having a home there.

I could no longer sit with the gardener and ask about the names of spirits in plants. Nènè, the young man who swept leaves from the terraces at dawn, and had also stood at the burial site, no longer came by to chat in the afternoons and tell me of his child's progress at school—the son he had once asked me to name.

"Alexander!" I told him—"a great name of a great man who conquered many lands!"

5. Middle Man

And so, homeless at home, I trembled, thinking of Michael. Power was now in *his* hands. I feared that the night would bring doom. Some noisy devilry would be sure to happen just when he came by for the night-visit I had suggested. Normally, it never did; but the Prince of Hell would do all in his might to frighten Michael away, make sure that people of that land, at that time, would miss out on charity, and that I, now a foreigner in my own country, would fritter my life away in isolation and fruitlessness.

"Get me Boss Michel right away," I said to my accountant in our basement office as soon as Michael had left. It was a white, bare, damp room, furnished with two mahogany desks made from trees of the garden. A plastic clock hung too high was adding boredom minute by minute. Three straw chairs lined up along the wall closest to the door waited for workers to be able to sit when they came by.

Boss Michel was a young man when he started to work for my father. He was first an apprentice running errands for masons on the estate who allowed him to watch their work. Then he became a mason himself, then a carpenter, a site supervisor, and a work organizer. He joined President Baby Doc Duvalier's private militia just so he could have a gun bouncing on his hip; he liked the social status he gained from wearing it in poor neighborhoods, and the unease it caused; everyone laughed at his jokes now. When his hair started to gray, he took to wearing the same army-green cap my father did.

But Boss Michel's power ended in 1986 with Jean-Claude Duvalier's exile, at the same time when I left the pink house in the mountains of Kenskoff, and came back down to Bourdon.

There had been riots in the streets of Port-au-Prince and in the provinces. Once the president was gone, politicians were murdered in their villas, and slum gangs hunted down Duvalier partisans living in their midst; these included especially those people enrolled in the private militia like Boss Michel was and who had, for years, threatened, abused, robbed, raped and imprisoned their neighbors, albeit poor people like them. Enraged crowds chased after men as they did after rats in the slums, until the terrified creature was cornered in a piss-and-trash hole, bloodshot eyes gleaming from tears and fright. The crowd would hold the human beast down while a car tire was hung around his neck, and set on fire. The avengers laughed, taunted, and pointed while their target howled in agony, and until they were satisfied to see that a man could burn down like any mansion.

But Boss Michel had only wanted the aura of the uniform. He had not hurt anyone. He only strutted. He had been an illiterate country boy who yearned for respect, had looked around the slums to see who yielded power there, and seeing that those men were Vodou priests or gun-bearers, he aligned himself with both. He got the gunpower from the militia he joined, and the protection of Vodou priests and gods by making a pact with Ogou, the Vodou divinity of war and warriors, whose colors, red and blue, had been those of the Haitian flag since the slave revolution, and until Papa Doc Duvalier took away the blue stripe to replace it with a black one. The pact with Ogou was sealed under the skin of Boss Michel's shoulders with the insertion of several sewing needles that stayed there permanently. The man felt self-important afterwards, and gained an unshakable confidence that he was divinely protected at all times.

Status and privilege can be had even in the slums. Boss Michel lived in the neighborhood of the Christ-Roi Church, a higher-status slum than the one across from our land. His house had several rooms, even if only built with bare-bone cement blocks covered with corrugated-iron roofing.

When the manhunt started in his neighborhood, Boss Michel came to hide on our estate. By day he would sleep in a depot room. By night he would roam the property, startled by every noise, waiting for his wife to bring him food and change of clothes. Even after the troubles quieted, and the manhunt had stopped, Boss Michel stayed on. He never moved out, and turned into our permanent night watchman instead. The depot room was emptied of stuff kept in storage, painted white like the rest, and became *his* room. Furniture that disappeared from the apartments reappeared there. We ignored it, just as we had over the years ignored ongoing disappearances of blocks and cement sacks from my father's construction sites. During the manhunt, Boss Michel developed a rage that never left him. The fact that he had a gun and would love to use it was well known in the neighborhood, and sufficiently alarming to keep thieves away, even after it became evident to us that he was fast asleep in the bushes and under the stars before midnight,.

Thieves are a constant threat in a country where a small minority holds all the wealth. Yet, as a child, they were to me as magical as mythical creatures in fairy tales. When a house had been robbed, the details were recounted all over town; a thief stealing in the night, stark naked, black skin shining from coconut oil rubbed all over, making it slippery and impossible to grab onto. But those had been the days when nobody had guns except the army. It is a different world in Haiti now where doors and windows are barred with wrought iron painted black, and the tops of property walls are lined with barbed wire. A wealthy man's house is guarded like a U.S. military base in a foreign country, and an armed watchman is a necessity.

6. Staging Reality

After I sent for Boss Michel, it wasn't long until I heard a slight knock on the office door followed by his greeting, "La Madam, kouman ou ye—The Missus, how are you?"

"I have a problem, Boss Michel—Mr. Miller is coming here tonight after dinner to visit the place one last time before he goes back to the U.S. He wants to check if people who live by the river across from us in the valley are noisy at night. I can't take a chance that they might suddenly decide to have a once-in-a lifetime neighborhood party or a Vodou ceremony with drums going wild. Too much is at stake for all of us. I don't know what time 'after dinner' means for Mr. Miller, so I need the whole neighborhood quiet the whole night."

Boss Michel was grinning, jiggling with idle fingers the large set of keys he kept on a ring, forever hanging on the hip opposite from the gun's. He lifted his green cap, brushed his head with one hand then put the cap back down. He visibly could not contain the mounting excitement he felt—Boss Michel loved to be the man of the moment—he saw the power in it, sensing how he was an instrumental part of its machinery, if not at its center. Finally, he plopped himself down with a deep groan into one of the three straw chairs, asking, "Ki sa ou vle m fè—what do you want me to do?"

"I want you to go to the people living across the river and talk to the man who is big boss down there."

"You mean the kazèk?"

"Yes, the kazèk."

"Okay. And then what?"

"Then you tell him this story: that I have a white American living in an apartment right across from them down by the river, and the man is deathly ill."

Boss Michel's chest started trembling from a mounting yet contained chuckle. "What's the man's big illness?' he asked.

"Tell him the American has a problem with his head. Any bit of sound gives him terrible pain. He needs silence."

Boss Michel nodded his head several times with what I took for growing admiration. "Wè—I see… Wè…" he mumbled with a smile.

"Explain to the kazèk that the sick man is flying early in the morning to go to an emergency hospital in Miami, but that he needs to survive the night. And then you ask the kazèk what it would take for me to make an agreement with everybody down there so that no radio, no music, no argument, no screaming pig, dog, donkey or mad rooster is heard at all through the entire night—I want the valley to be as calm as it always is. And I want this agreement to be from 6:00 pm tonight to 6:00 am tomorrow."

Boss Michel sprang up to his feet, keys jingling. "I'll be right back! Don't worry!" he blurted, rushing out the door.

When Boss Michel came back, he was all sweaty. With an officious look, he again plopped himself down in the same straw chair he had left an hour earlier, removing his cap to fan his face, and with both legs stretched ahead and sprawled wide open, he said, "That kazèk is no fool!"

"Why?"

"Tande—listen: the minute I got down there and asked for him, he has some assistant tell me he is busy and I must wait. Then he gets all arrogant and asks, 'Eske ou gen randevou—did you make an appointment?'

"I tell him, 'No, I didn't.'

"He pretends to be annoyed. 'Man… you can't come in here without an appointment!'

"I try smiling. 'You are right, but…"

"He cuts me short. 'This is not some bus station, and you just show up for the bus.'

"So I pretend to cower and show respect. 'Okay, okay… but this is an emergency, I come for the Missus in the white buildings across the river…' And before I even finish my sentence, now all of a sudden the kazèk himself enters the room! Fòk se koute li t ap koute nou bò pòt la—he must have been listening to us by the door!

"The kazèk looks at me like I am a worm. 'What do I care about your Missus and her emergency! Can *I* go see *her* when *I* have a problem?'

"So I behave the same I did with the assistant—all smooth and small. 'Okay, okay... I know what you mean...'

"'No, you don't!'

"'Yes, I do,' I am holding my ground because I can see he is getting curious, and I know he smells that an opportunity has come his way. The kazèk then pretends he is losing patience with me so he does not lose face by showing he is actually interested.

"So he shouts one last time, 'No you don't!' and then asks, 'Do I know you?'

"Yes, you do. I am Boss Michel. Ask around... Come on, I am for real. Don't give me a hard time.'

"'What is it you want?'

"'There is a white man up there who is about to die. The Missus is responsible for him. You can help and she is willing to pay. You have authority here. Ou gen vre pouvwa—You have real power.'

"Now I can see the kazèk is relaxing. He tells me, 'well, now... it costs me a lot to have authority, and all the people in the valley depend on me, and they listen to me...'

"'I know, I know... that is exactly why I come to you. Here is the thing: the white man is ill in the head and in the ears—he needs to hear no noise all night, or his head might explode. Li pa ka tolere oken ti bri—He can't suffer any little sound. The missus wants no radio, no drum, no music, no talking loud, no party, and no arguments all night. She wants it starting at 6:00 tonight and going until 6:00 tomorrow morning. Can you arrange that?'

"'Yes... I can arrange that,' the kazèk tells me. And now he is showing me all his teeth in a wide grin. 'But it will cost you a lot,' he says. 'It so happens there was a neighborhood party planned just for tonight. People already bought the sodas and the rum, the pig is already killed, musicians already hired and paid. What you are asking for is gonna cause real loss, and lots of waste for us. Plus the disappointment.'"

At this point, Boss Michel could no longer contain his laughter, and neither could I. "So, how much does he want?" I asked.

"3000.00 Gourdes!"

"That's quite a lot, Boss Michel!"

"Yep! But you won't hear 'beep' from 6:00 at night to 6:00 in the morning. He wants half now, and the other half tomorrow."

"Okay. It's lucky someone just paid the rent and I have the cash. Here, you go give him half of the money now, and tell him to come get the other half tomorrow in this office. Tell him I want to thank him personally. I have got to meet this kazèk!"

Filled with anxiety and a kind of shame, I too left at 6:00 pm to visit Guy, my friend with whom I lunched on Sundays at the Turgeau seminary with Father Lespinasse, and without whose affection and advice I might not have survived those challenging years and family duties that befell me after my father's death. I had no secrets for Guy; he welcomed me at any hour and for whatever length of time I needed. Instead of making me feel I was ever a burden to him in the slightest way, he smiled with real joy each time I came to visit, and I never had to call first. "Nous avons une relation privilégiée—We have a privileged relationship," he said while embracing me at a time when I was apologizing for coming late, and unannounced.

I left Guy and came back home at 1:00 a.m. to find Boss Michel waiting for me at the gate with unusual agitation. I had hardly parked in the garage when he opened my car door with a wide grin. "Bonswa, La Madam—good evening Maam!"

"Good evening to you too, Boss Michel! How did it go?"

Boss Michel suddenly broke into a little Indian dance of his own—making small rhythmic steps, going in a circle, bending torso forward, then straightening, hopping here, hopping there, jiggling keys.

Could he have seen an old movie about Cow-Boys and Indians on TV? I wondered. I stood in smiling amazement until he finally calmed down, stood straight, and said all in one breath, "Misye Miller did not come until 11:30 pm! You *just* missed him! He came in a big

SUV with a bunch of people. They all came out of the car, and went straight to the pink house. They were all talking a lot. They were having a good time. I kept quiet as if I wasn't there, and they already owned the place. Not that I want to see you go The Missus... but I want to help..."

"Oh... thank you, Boss Michel!"

"... So they stayed a while near the pink house. They went quiet too. They were listening. Then all of them walked down all the way to your father's grave. I followed them, but they never knew I did. They stayed there for a while too, and were looking at the houses of the people across the river. Not a sound the whole time. The whole valley was as dead as your father in his grave. Like it always is. But tonight I became aware of it for the first time—I guess I had never thought about it. Not a single bit of light. Pa menm on grenn tète mèch—not even a single burning candle. Nothing. Then Misye Miller and his friends walked all over the property, making a large circle until they came back to their car. Man... that kazèk has real authority! You got to give him that—the valley was so quiet the whole time that the quiet must have got to Misye Miller and his friends too, and they were very quiet when they got back into their big SUV, and drove away. I tell you, you *just* missed them."

8 The Great Earthquake

1. The Earthquake in the News

The yearly ruination of the walls he built were a lifelong struggle for my father. As far back as my memory goes, my vision of him is of a man burdened. He was not one to raise his fist to the sky however. His mother taught him too much respect for the unknown; he could never allow himself such a gesture of incapacitation. He did not blame his family either, but suffering came to us as we watched his distress.

It is unnatural that so vital a substance as water is—albeit in mad, swelling rivers that sap, loosen, and steal away the foundation walls of our house, or in hurricane rainfalls that hammer into our roofs—that is should also be destiny's tool for obliteration, to the extent that one might wonder where vengeance or forgiveness might be fitted into the larger scheme of events.

And yet it was the same water, pouring down from the same heavens, that were the fundamental elements of my gentlest and most liberatingly joyful childhood memories; rainwater that announced itself with the rhythmic pounding over tin roofs, ordering me to undress quickly, and run naked in the garden under the porous umbrellas of coconut fronds, each time surprised by the cool touch of rain in a country otherwise searing.

Regardless of claims to the contrary, natural disasters are beyond our immediate emotional grasp. Such was the January 12, 2010 earthquake in Haiti. Scientists and newscast reporters alarm and intimidate us with precision in numbers. But does it help a condemned man to anticipate what caliber of gun, riffles, or bullets will be used to kill him? To give details about numbers and scientific calculation to people affected by the earthquake, is like talking about billions of dollars of profit made in the gun industry to a man whose world comprises his donkey, his goat, and his food dish. Common mortals might almost feel they stand accused as well, being at fault in their ignorance of the elaborate predictions and warnings offered long ago about such coming calamities; they might sense their heart abnormally pierced anew with all the 'I told you so' that haunt every childhood.

Haitians were therefore advised that the collapse of homes and buildings would be a consequence of Haiti's lack of building codes; without adequate reinforcements, the buildings could disintegrate under the force of the quake.

Had neglect developed into a habit? A 2007 earthquake hazard study concluded that a worst case forecast would involve an earthquake with a magnitude of 7.2; further measurements presented to the 18th Caribbean Geologic conference in March 2008 already recommended high priority studies due to the elevated risk of major seismic activity in Port-au-Prince.

Vocabulary used to speak about the earthquake relies on words such as *blame*, *shattering*, and devastation of the earth due to a system of *faults*. The word *sin* does not seem to lag far behind. Is "fault" comprised in the making of the earth and of its destiny? Events and people conspire daily in reminding men of their imperfections. Human beings are forcibly living under great weight.

Were he not already dead by the time of the January 12, 2010 earthquake in Haiti, my father would have collapsed with his house, his work and his city. To think of all the years he spent dreading hellish occurrences from above, coming down on us in diluvial rain, tropical cyclones, and hurricanes, he never found himself doubting the earth he counted on. Even the Taino god of the storm, Hurakàn, might have argued that for a country beset by hunger in an already strained infrastructure, the earthquake seemed like a highly unreasonable act of nature.

I must however wonder if the meticulous accuracy of news reports really means to convey the inscrutable monstrousness of ungodly events? Is the reductive aspect of facts even able to comfort us in the least? It may at times be tempting to align oneself with natural man, and believe the sun can be placated. True, we have seen and learnt to appreciate the peculiarities of many people; we would not be likely to take offense at them, but be grateful instead. The voice for which we hunger feeds us with educated detachment; and so we heard with stunned listlessness in January 2010 how "A large-scale earthquake occurred on the West Indian island of Hispaniola, which comprises the countries of Haiti and the Dominican Republic.

"The earthquake hit at 4:53 p.m. some fifteen miles southwest of the Haitian capital of Port-au-Prince. The initial shock registered a magnitude of 7.0, and was soon followed by two aftershocks of magnitude 5.9 and 5.5. Most severely affected was Haiti, occupying the western third of the island.

"Geologists initially blamed the earthquake on the movement of the Caribbean tectonic plate eastward along the Enriquilo-Plantain Garden fault system. This fault system constitutes a transform boundary that separates the Gonâve microplate (fragment of the North American Plate upon which Haiti is positioned) from the Caribbean plate. The earthquake was produced by contractional deformation along the Léogâne fault, discovered underneath the city of Léogâne. This hidden fault descends northward at an oblique angle from the Enriquillo-Plantain Garden fault system. A number of geologists argue that the earthquake was a consequence of the slippage of rock upward across its plane of fracture.

"Occurring at a depth of 8.1 miles, the tremor was fairly shallow, a phenomenon that increased the intensity of shaking at the earth's surface. The densely populated region around Port-au-Prince, located on the gulf of Gonâve, was among those most devastatingly affected; the city of Léogâne was essentially leveled. The power system failed. Communication lines were lost."

2. The Earthquake in Mystics' Views

Mystics around the world hold their own views on what real forces affect our lives and the movements of the earth. Considering the amount of people filing into Vodou temples, as well as in Masonic, Rosicrucian, or Martinist lodges, it is evident that Haiti can boast no shortage of mystics. Astrologers and diviners also adhere to mystical interpretations of the laws of the universe. It seems to be their belief that karma influences reward or retribution, and stands as a major factor impacting human and world destinies.

Having pondered over this, I admit to wondering if there was a spiritual and karmic explanation as to why the Church of St. Louis King of France that my family built with stone and cement long ago, and in which my father served as altar boy, completely crumbled during the earthquake, whilst Father Lespinasse's orphanage run in his shaky old family home now enduring in near-rotted wood, remained untouched.

World geologists were busy with complex scientific calculations, and repeatedly warned about increasing risks of significant seismic activity in Port-au-Prince, decades before the earthquake finally happened. During those same years, Haitian mystics were claiming that the economic, social and political havoc in the country had a spiritual origin instead. They believed the island's problems to be repercussions of the Indian genocide, the unrest of ghosts, the anger of their god Yúcahu, and the revenge of disappointed Vodou spirits with whom Boukman made a pact sealed in blood during the Bois Caïman ceremony at the start of the slave revolution. Mystics warned that Haiti has been paying a price for not keeping promises made to the gods, whoever these may be.

Within a day or so after the earthquake, I received a photo then wildly disseminated on the Internet; it showed two large, gray hands looming in a sky claimed to be over Haiti the day of the earthquake. The interpretation of dark forces at play in the catastrophe was obvious. Regardless of the fact that many protested the photo was a fake, invoking montage and photo-shop manipulations, it had already made a sensible impression on its worldwide, intended audience.

The concept of punishment for sin has circulated for centuries in the history of humanity, whether Christians or not; while it may play a role in Christian-influenced Vodou and other cultures, non-scientific interpretations of the seism in Haiti is not restricted to Haitian opinion. In the United States, Pat Robertson, the Evangelical Christian who once suggested that God was punishing Americans with Hurricane Katrina, said that Haitians made a pact with the devil to be freed from their French colonizers in the 18th century. As far as Robertson was concerned, the fault was not in the ground; it's in the Haitians.

Vodou worshippers appear in agreement with ideas expounded by mystics in various lodges. It is not rare to find Vodou priests who are members of one or all Port-au-Prince lodges. It is possibly also the case in areas of the world where Haitian immigrants live. But in Port-au-Prince, there are feast days when members of the Masonic Lodges will parade through the streets of Port-au-Prince in full regalia; the other lodges have their parade days too; no one seems surprised that many of the same faces reappear in all.

In Haiti, mystics inspire awe, as do Vodou priests and priestesses; both are seen as persons possessing a kind of spiritual power that appears to influence or alter the material world. As I see it, their advantage over Vodou priests and the gods they serve, might be that adherence to the lodge only requires loyalty and secrecy in order for one to benefit from the support of the members, whilst Vodou priests and the spirits they serve require continuous bounty and sacrifice in exchange for help.

I believe that this commitment to making continuous offerings to the gods, even at high costs to a family's welfare, is the main reason why so many people nowadays flee from Vodou, and flock to the various Protestant Churches that compete for Haitian souls, offering Christ's unbounded protection and forgiveness, along with free material support.

Mystics I met, Ali included, all were at some point in their lives, students of the Kabbalah—the ancient Jewish tradition of mystical interpretation of the Bible—and of Papus, founder of the Martinist order. Theirs was a higher form of mysticism; one not focused on manipulating forces in the universe for one's benefit, but on achieving purity of the soul wherefrom one derives the deeper knowledge of everything.

In his study "The Path of the Heart," Papus wrote that, "There are humble people without academic qualifications and medical experience to whom heaven is so accessible that the sick are healed at their request... Joan of Arc had never read a treatise on strategy nor seen a battlefield, but she defeated at her first attempt the greatest tacticians of her time. How could this be? It is quite simple: because she surrendered completely to the Divine Will and did not question the invisible... the adepts of the intellectual plane cannot understand mystics because they attempt to measure universal faculties with the limited capacities of their brains. Because he cannot understand him, the critic insults the mystic and holds him in contempt whilst the mystic prays for his tormentor and carries on with his labor of love."

3. The Earthquake in my Heart

I was a child who gazed at the sky. Each time we drove past the Church of the Sacred Heart of Jesus in Port-au-Prince, my eyes met with Christ. I never missed the chance, as we passed the church, to look up, contemplate the immense Christ who stood on top of the steeple, weightless, lifted on a cloudless sky, graceful and white against the blue, blue, forever blue vastness, there for all time, arms opened wide, extended like branches of a tree on which we would all rest.

Yet, on January twelfth 2010, the Port-au-Prince sky let go of its Christ. The roof over all saints who long ago presided over my First Communion vows at Sacred Heart, collapsed in on itself. God's son now lies face down, open arms embracing dirt.

All roofs over all saints protecting the whole city collapsed onto us all. The roof over the Cathedral with the stained glass angels collapsed onto the Archbishop of God, its rose window now deserted like the bloodied eye of a Cyclops. The roof of Saint Anne's Church collapsed onto maimed creatures who clustered at the parvis, begging for alms. The roof of the Church of Saint Trinity collapsed onto empty pews, dropping its mural of the Nativity and the company of heaven. Gone are the angels, gone the colors, silent all trumpeters and men. All hearts bleed as one heart.

The roofs of all of Port-au-Prince collapsed onto the people they sheltered; they buckled, cracked, contorted, sagged, crumpled, slumped, and caved in. Limbs of churches lie with limbs of people, dried, splintered, brittle and oddly disassembled like limbs of a crustacean carelessly crushed under a murderous foot. Humans, severed and suffocated, lie among broken statues of wingless martyrs and angels. The sun pulls moisture from souls trapped alive. A hard white dust covers the city.

All manner of self-maimed beggars, the armless, the legless who daily assemble, fret and sigh on the city's sidewalks and compete for alms at the crossroads where cars stop at red lights, all the self-mutilated beings sitting on the remaining stumps they spared themselves, all the crippled are left whole and untouched—there were no roofs to fall on the marginal, carbon-monoxide-poisoned sidewalk nether regions where they have lived with rodents, scuttering like insects. People think these beggars suffered from an act of God. They did not. They amputated themselves to become visible. They believed the human condition is the act of God, all the while they were crawling along streets called Good Faith and Miracles that now have crumpled six feet high from the exacting pressure of an unbridled earth.

All beggars watch with bloodshot eyes walls of an unreachable world of wealth

collapsed around them, their mutilated flesh realizing that hell only now has arrived. All the buried and the detained, ghosts and gangsters walled in graves or prison cells at the penitentiary, are set loose, while free men are trapped under ruins where their screams endlessly echo.

The dead at the cemetery are not indifferent to being disinterred. My grandmother's soul sits pensively on the debris of the family tomb, watching her husband's bones exposed to the sun.

The dead and the crippled are endowed with odd vision. They shudder as they see a formless black cloud, like a flock of distant birds, quiver and float over the disemboweled city—it is the restless souls of people buried alive at the crossroads during black magic ceremonies, who now have been stirred out of their improper graves by an uncanny hunger. They search to learn the fate of those who murdered them; tied them up, and pitched them in a pit, to be buried alive. They want to watch them die a similar death—suffocating under the rubble of Vodou temples, heart pumping a cannibal's blood.

The dead and the crippled tremble when they perceive at the margin of this woeful cloud, like grim lace of a more delicate nature, vacillating and unsure, souls of the stolen newborns bled and crushed in sacrificial offerings in a night when cocks crowed, mocking dawn. It is a free-for-all in this stricken land where only the laughter of orphans flown out in cargo planes, may rest on clouds and resonate in heaven.

And me, childless mother of dreams, I pray; Prayer is here; Prayer has come for us. I pray for my mother; it is through our own flesh that we perceive, feel, and understand the world. I think of her red lips, her mirrors, her bare breast, and the blemished shield of her hands over her face when she cries. I pray she is not crushed under the collapse of her roof, her dear brittle bones cracked, piercing her like self-inflicted daggers, entombed like a Pharaoh with her dogs, barking their way through the underworld. So I gaze at the white hopeful sky. Looking up, I beseech Him, "Please, God, do not punish her for greed, vanity, and folly. *You* made her imperfect. Dear God, forgive all! Just forgive…"

II

Choice

9 Claiming Holy Ground

1. All Good Sons

My childhood friend was dying of A.I.D.S. in a Miami hospice. "What now?" he asked me, immobile and blind between soiled, damp sheets. This sort of ending was all that he had feared might happen to him, as it did to many of our friends, the blindness particularly. The sky was untypically overcast in this otherwise predictably sunny American state; grey clouds hung like lumps; heavy, moist air came in from the open windows above him. "What are you going to do?" he said again, "and what about God?"

"Don't know," was all I could mumble, my throat feeling tight, my eyes averting his entreating gaze after having been forced to see and assess the swollen mound of rubble his face had become; and yet a face so beautiful once, green eyes on a man tall and elegant, continually in demand as a model for men's fashion magazines in New York.

"Keep looking... giving God up is not in your nature..." he wheezed out, his left hand slowly lifting; he was pulling it out silently from under the colorless sheets where it had lain close to an exposed hip bone sunk like a worn sea vessel. Released in the open, his fingers stretched as if to touch the air in a delicate quiver; the hand then turned and moved towards the place out of which he heard my voice coming, seemingly searching for me; it suddenly stopped, like a chess pawn momentarily suspended, before descending slowly to alight onto its likeness, my own hand laid on my lap. "Something will turn up..."

he said in a bright effort, while all that remained of his life and of his work were there, on either side of the bed railing—the emaciated stack of his body's cellular mass abandoned alongside the bars on the one side, and his paintings on paper propped up on the other, gathered in an artist's black cardboard folder, ready for me to take away; layer after layer of subhuman creatures rendered in a fluorescent medium on large sheets of thick watercolor paper. "You keep them now…" he said with difficulty. "No one else cares… make them glow again… under the right light… it's all I have left…"

God will have answered him before I could. Now I imagine them espying me together: "Look at that one coming near her," God says, pointing towards a man on the earth below, the two of them comfortably stretched on a cumulus cloud. God then also confides: "Among my sons, I am greatly pleased with that one. I have given him all that is needed for a man to be carried above others, to live like a bird among beasts. A man pure and unflinching. But these traits that I find endearing might inspire him to trust in those who mean to destroy him. So I keep watch. Still, he has no equal in his capacity to persuade men to come along on a journey where the unlikely is commonplace.

"'We are in this world, and not of this world,' this man reminds himself each day at dawn. He burns to make things right in the world, and suffers from those who feel an urge to lie. His expansive nature, when frustrated, becomes at times like poison in the brain, and turns into an appetite so extreme and diverse it could ruin him; it is also how his indefatigable enthusiasm for the ultimate goodness in the souls of all people might become lodged at the base of his spine like the mound of an improper delta, and he will turn to me so I can calm him, and then rouse him anew with divine rage."

This is the way I like to think that God brought me a new friend, this son he loves and watches from above, Michael and Sarah's son-in-law who, unlike them, was a convert to the Church of Jesus Christ of Latter-day Saints, and not born into it.

My new friend was upright and guarded like a formidable cactus of the Arizona desert, too restless and taut to fold and sit for long.

Like his father before him, he fathered many sons. He named the first boy after him: Roland. Among men of biblical temperament, there are men who father men; other men are meant to raise daughters who are then meant to mother. Parenting is a divine office.

Roland's wife was given a significant name, Eve. Her siblings were grown and gone when I first came to her parents' home in the Arizona desert, except for nine-year-old Ruby who bore her jewel-name well. She taught me all she knew about scorpions. It is likely that she sensed how, being without a home, an insect life awaited me.

But almost seven years after selling my home, the devastation of Port-au-Prince in January 2010 immensely eased my conscience. My father's lifework crumbled on its own, enough for me to have wondered if, like us, the inanimate world has karma and destinies imparted from the start. I realized that I had been spared loss and ruin. Such were the thoughts, however futile by then, and in my present condition, going through my head, as I received news of the earthquake.

The enduring personal trauma would however soon sink in. The earthquake has become a large metaphor in my life. Tremors would never fully come to an end. The world of my beginnings all but collapsed, and with it seemingly all ties to the island from which I constructed and derived my identity. My childhood had been deleted. I would never return to familiar places where I could feel the untranslatable sense of comfort and belonging afforded by places where one grew up; places where one may sit, and just be.

No more lyrical potholed sidewalks going to the Virgin of the Immaculate grotto; no more family home with mahogany paneling; no more *kaka zombie* on private family paths that zigzagged through the neighborhood where my cousins and I played hide and seek; no more Paramount movie theater, or Champs de Mars gardens; no more Miracle Street where the PHIPPS & Co. offices stood, right next to the Bank of Nova Scotia, and across from Stark's where we bought Rum-Raisin ice-cream; no more family insurance company and butter factory, where father, uncle, and grandfather spent the best years of their adult lives. They each sat in front of imposing mahogany desks on which they kept calendars displaying photographs of European landscapes and plazas. During all of the forty years my father worked for the family business, I saw preserved under glass on his desktop a large image of a multicolored field of tulips that slowly faded and blued. There would also be no more Port-au-Prince waterfront with illuminated fountains, one minute green, the next blue, then red, on whose curving edges lounged several magnificently large-breasted bronze mermaids whose tails held magic, and around whom I frivolously roller-skated in a pink organza dress; no more 4:00 pm outings with grandparents, both grandmother and the chauffeur wearing white gloves, but hers in crochet, the four of us sitting in the car at the wharf, watching the sparkling water hitting the metal flanks of an ocean liner out of which American tourists filed in bright flowered shirts and fuchsia pink plastic sunglasses; each of these foreign visitors' steps were accompanied by the music of debonair folk musicians playing on goat-skin drums and homemade tin guitars, singing about mermaids, whales, a panama hat that fell in the sea, the girl Angelica who should stay put at home, and the *Haiti Chérie* song praising an incomparable country, the island one must leave in order to understand how longing and weight set in the heart.

As Haiti was reevaluating itself, as Port-au-Prince was redrawing its maps, adding rubbles on its strata, I found myself challenged to do the same. Now God would be sitting like Rodin's statue of The Thinker, waiting to see what I would do. In my own geological history, I could trace my ancestry back to the beginnings of Haiti, a revolutionaries' island—people engaged in challenging and restructuring an established order.

What was James Phipps leaving behind in 1805? What were those things and people he would never feel or see again? In which ways did he imagine he would be recreating himself when he chose this unruly island as his own, and allowed Jean-Jacques Dessalines to naturalize him? Two centuries later, I find myself hoping that I will do honor to my ancestor's boldness, match his courage, even if puzzled as to which way I might do that.

For many years prior to the earthquake, a successful writer friend of mine kept admonishing me to make a better effort at getting my collection of short stories published. "You need to find a serious

New York agent. You can't expect to get anywhere by sending your work to competitions once in a rare while."

"That's the best I can do for now," I said. "When God wants this work published, He'll help me."

As it happened, my collection, "The Company of Heaven: Stories from Haiti," won the Iowa Short Fiction Award the day the earthquake did a tabula rasa over my life. Some of the lives that got buried under the collapse of the city would forever be recounted in my book.

It was four days after the earthquake that I learnt my mother and brother had survived. Roland forwarded to me a series of photos of the Miller's hospital that he had seen on Facebook. About one of the photos he wrote, "Is this your brother?"

Yes, it was. It was my very own Gaëtan, standing up, yet leaning forward towards the mound of broken debris our home had become, his mouth gaping, his fingers I imagined to be crumpled as they were stuck inside pockets of pants that looked loose at the waist. It was indeed my brother, alive and facing the final waste of all of his father's life, a man once elected unanimously as President of the Port-au-Prince Chamber of Commerce. What were my brother's thoughts then, I wonder, when he saw the living symbol of our family's history, social status, and pride leveled miserably in front of him, he who was repeatedly demeaned for his incompetence in business, his inability to hold a job, build the smallest amount of anything tangible and worldly, and live up to the family's and society's expectations of one of his most favored sons, a developing country's most fortunate offspring? What did he feel about his own childhood being eradicated in a few seconds of the earth's tremor? Did he resort just for once to swallowing pills to ease his pain, he who valued clarity of mind foremost, he who never smoked, took drugs or alcohol of any sort? "I don't like it when my head spins," he said. Where did he go for comfort, a poet at heart, a selfless man devoid of any vanity who seemed colorblind when it came to human skin, never thought of people in terms of profit, or class distinctions? When Gaëtan went to the slums, a dozen runny-nosed, swollen-bellied children poured out of dark, one-room mud huts, flocking to him in glee.

As for me, winning the literary prize, and having my stories published by a renowned university press, helped me overcome some of the sense of loss incurred from the earthquake; it gave me the feeling that I was going through a meaningful, personal evolutionary process within an otherwise senseless human catastrophe. Having to make the manuscript ready with a professional editor kept me distracted and focused on another realm.

Roland turned out to be both a rescuer from my past, and preparer for a journey ahead. I simply had to allow the unknown to happen. We had a business relationship at first. Our monthly phone conversations ran over my investments, the world's economic instability and the United States' president. Yet these topics were by no means sufficient to allow meaningful growth of a friendship. Progressively, we included God, savagery in childhood, and the Mormon Plan of Salvation, itself the basis of his new faith.

At times, Roland read scriptural passages relating to physical death that kept me interested in resurrection. I was informed as amply as I wished, but Roland tended not to repeat explanations. He preferred to send me books about Mormon beliefs that I was able to ponder at leisure; we discussed these new ideas I was discovering during our next conversations; he also recommended favorite scriptures of his, and emailed articles about those scriptures. He was preparing the way for angels, and he knew it.

2. Another Chance

It nevertheless took ten years after our initial meeting in Arizona for Roland and I to drop eyes on each other again. It did not entail great expense. The sky had shifted. It was as Chairman of the Arizona Republican Party that Roland invited my husband and me to a fundraising gala evening he was hosting in Boston.

I had recently married an English pianist, orchestral conductor, and opera coach. Fate arguably showed a sense of humor in choosing for Roderick a wife who can't read music. Shortly before meeting him, fate had nevertheless been instrumental in helping me seek, and obtain, a papal annulment for my first marriage; I hoped this would be the only thing I would have in common with Baby Doc Duvalier's wife. I was nineteen at the time, and the ceremony was held at St. Peter's in Pétionville. It wouldn't be too many months after the wedding that, as a new student in anthropology, I'd find myself sitting in classrooms at the University of California in Berkeley.

But I shall never forget my father's heavy step, shoulders, and brow, that day of my first wedding. As he walked me down the aisle, the faces of my cousins, aunts and uncles, and of all Haitian high society, had turned to see me enter the church in white. My brother wore a bow tie and looked princely. My mother had just recovered from a long illness that nearly left her paralyzed; she wore a sequined, wine-colored gown that emphasized her dark beauty, but hid the legs that would need much rehabilitative therapy until she could walk again without help. I would always remember my father's grief when he gave me away in church; it was therefore not a surprise, albeit another sadness, that he later declined the opportunity to attend my second marriage to Laurent, a divorced architect with three small daughters, who each wore a crown of white daisies all day that day.

The papal annulment had been a two-year process that brought a lot of upset to family members involved, and to me. I had to write an extensive essay about my childhood and the circumstances in and around the marriage. Three witnesses of my choice also had to write essays about their knowledge and vision of that relationship. My ex-husband secretly contested some of the claims developed in my essay; I found out about it when the ecclesiastical tribunal ordered that I meet with a psychoanalyst meant to verify the truth of my story, and evaluate my emotional health. He had a sense of humor, and gave me advice for a lifetime, also reminding me of Rousseau's Candide's words, "All is well in the best possible world."

My musical taste has included opera as far back as I remember, and I thought it fortuitous that I would now be sharing my life with a man who devoted much of his to this high art.

"What would you like for a birthday gift?" my father asked when I turned fifteen.

"Go to the Paris opera."

They were playing Carmen. A story ending with the flighty heroine's death was not much of a birthday symbol; we ignored it. We were living in France then, and Father took the whole family to the opera, including my six-foot tall French grandmother who wore her ankle-length mink coat. She was regal, and bored stiff; my mother too; she had grown from singing opera, to preferring Edith Piaf; she and I would cry while listening together to overwrought songs about never regretting the past, being indifferent to the sky falling over, or the earth collapsing, as long as love was true. Carmen was an Edith Piaf sort of character. My mother nevertheless found Chagall's famous ceiling at the opera more interesting than Carmen's heartbreak.

"A good painter, no doubt, " she said on the way home, "but everybody flying all over, donkeys and goats alike, it's tiresome."

When I eventually announced to my mother over the phone that I had married an English concert pianist, she said, "English? Suit yourself... but Englishmen are like the French, they have no lips for kissing. I prefer black men."

I ignored her comment and said again, "Not only is he a pianist, but he is an opera coach as well. You have some things in common."

She grew silent; when she spoke, it was to tell me about a stray cat she had just adopted. "You know I hate cats, but this ugly creature persisted in wanting my affection. I gave in. What else could I do? I like animals better than men."

Roderick was playing Chopin's Nocturne in c# minor when we met. He was at the piano in the Massachusetts house of a friend of mine, in Concord. The living room was hung with portraits of herself as a child painted by her mother. A physicist whose passion was the piano, her husband was eager to host Roderick when organizers of a conference on Transcendentalism asked the favor. Roderick would be speaking on music's relationship to spirituality.

"I loved him immediately," I told Roland.

It had become a ritual before dinner that my friends would ask me to read a poem. So I had come prepared. Roderick admitted thinking mockingly, "Ah... a little verse before dinner... how elegant..."

If my poetry moved him before I did, his musicianship did too. I soon wrote poetry for him, describing him as a man who tended to the easing of souls, weaving sounds like cloth meant to cloak and carry us. His large back was bent over the piano that first night, his chest swelling at times, his eyelids closed like a priest at the altar. It was as if I had waited all my life for music that would announce the one I longed to know. All mute prayers were answered when he came. His face took the place of all landscape, stars made me laugh like never I could. We were married within two months.

"Save me from a life without you," I wrote, "angels without songs, flowers without color, your voice just a memory my body rescues from the frost. Forbid me peace where you are no more, entering worlds with thought rather than touch, masquerading with ideas, and Silence the only friend. Hold my hand while I draw from my love of you, so nothing is in vain, and all that courses returns to you."

Before the wedding ceremony, I sought a fatherly blessing from my friend from Mombai, who owned an Indian import shop on Mount Auburn Street, close to the St John the Evangelist monastery.

"Your life is going to have a great soundtrack!" he said.

I wore a crown of white calla lilies, and stood amidst all manner of Buddhas, Cosmic Shivas, and delicately inlaid boxes, one of which I took home to store my dreams. I opened it the following morning to insert a secret. I found already hidden inside a miniature rosewood carving of an elephant, trunk upturned, for good luck. I smiled, remembering the words my friend whispered in my ears when he handed me the box, "Your father sees you. He is pleased."

3. Plan of Salvation

Roland urged Roderick and me to attend the fundraising gala. Preparations for the event were made in a luxurious hotel of the downtown Boston area where all streets and highways collude to alienate an already stressed population of discourteous drivers. Coming from Cambridge, it would only take the crossing of the Charles River for us to be in Boston. Yet we left home early and nevertheless arrived late. Had this been going on in a huge fairground, the event would have been easy to spot from a distance. As things stood, we found ourselves relieved to find an empty space in an all-gray concrete, multileveled, underground parking garage.

Once in the hotel building, interminable hallways that I tackled on high heels offered many avenues for speeding in the wrong direction. We eventually managed successfully to locate the event, entering a muted, vast, glass-and-steel, impersonal carpeted room filled with people crowding the bar area. Mirror paneling all around the room reflected the crowd from one wall to the other. This was certainly a studied effect meant to increase the sense of being in a lively, full room; it was also useful in helping one keep track of people and faces in the room without having to turn around at the risk of offending one's interlocutor while losing thread of the conversation.

We hardly found time to talk with Roland in the course of the evening. In the end, it hardly mattered. Due to our monthly phone conversations, I had come to know my friend the way the blind might. My body was like walls of a drum in which he was lodged, and remembered as resonance. I saw his face again that day as if startled with newfound sight. I also felt some melancholy watching him charming strangers in the large hall. His eyes fell on me at times, lonely.

In the meantime, Roland's assistant grew curious. He came to sit with Roderick and me, setting his orange soda down on the table we shared with tweed-wearing Bostonians, drinking California wine. "Hi! I'm Charles."

I chuckled. "There is a river named after you around here… Many bridges stretch across it!"

"No kidding? I'll have to cross over tomorrow."

"Without fail! Is the soda because you are a Mormon?"

"Yes. No alcohol. Are you a Mormon too?"

"I am not, but I am well-impressed with Mormon theology."

"How's that?"

"Oh… you don't want to hear it. You know it all!"

He chuckled. "Of course I want to hear! In fact, I am holding my breath!"

"You'll need to!" I joked to hide the fact that I really did not feel like making the effort of having a serious conversation when I came to relax and be invisible in a crowd.

"Please..." he insisted.

I took a deep breath. "Well... keep in mind that what I know is from conversations with Roland, and from books he sent me. I could have gotten it all wrong."

"I doubt it. Come on... I am not going to let you wiggle out of it."

"Okay. To begin with, let's say that what impresses me with Mormon theology is foremost the way it has built an entire structure of beliefs on the basis that human beings carry the substance of divinity."

Charles's pale blue eyes widened. "I have never heard it explained quite so succinctly," he said. "Can you expand?"

"Well... the way I see it... *first* in the Mormon theological structure, comes your belief in a time of existence near God that precedes human birth."

"Ah...we call it Pre-Existence."

"*Second,* is the *freedom of choice* given to human beings. It involved both leaving heaven, and then being sole masters of our actions on earth. My intuition tells me that we agreed to this with the understanding that mortal life is a gift, but also a burden."

Charles was grinning. "That's right!"

"It could however be the Haitian Catholic in me that's influencing what I call intuition."

"How about non-Catholic Haitians?" Charles asked. "What's their take on mortal life?"

"Non-Catholic Haitians and Vodou worshippers are all under the influence of one or the other Christian belief systems," I said. "That's just part of growing up in Haiti. But my impression of Vodou worshippers is that they have a constant feeling of burden, and not a *gift* of choice as such. I think they feel powerless under the command and the whims of the gods. I don't have the sense they believe themselves to be in control of their spiritual destinies—their only option is to continuously sacrifice to please the gods." Charles looked thoughtful. I said, "Mind you, while it's clear that much of Mormon theology is based on beliefs shared by all Christians, I find that the specific structure Mormons have built around these principles is unique."

"Unique in which way?"

"It's abstract, invisible yet solid, and… in my opinion, quite believable!"

Charles took a sip of soda, and said, "Don't know about how *solid* it all is! … It's solid for me, but what does *solid* mean for you?"

I wanted to run. What had I gotten myself into? I believed I was coming to a mindless evening to meet an old friend, sit cross-legged in a giant plate of Southwestern hors d'oeuvres, aloof in the midst of wealthy people harassed by ambitious schemes, and here I found myself in front of a Mormon Inquisition. Yet, this blond, long-legged, affable fellow with a soft oval face, earnest gaze and full lips meant well. It was obvious that he loved theology. I had to make an effort. I said, "Solid is the word that came to mind, but it is perhaps not the best. There are so many words we say thoughtlessly, not knowing we'll be challenged for them."

Charles chuckled. "Come on… don't evade me like that."

"Alright… The word *solid*, in reference to a theological structure, might evoke the idea of a firm base… unadulterated material… something genuine… reasonable… plausible… protective… all of which is needed to endure in this world."

"I cannot disagree with any of this," Charles said, scratching his neck.

His good humor helped me relax. "*Solid* connotes of something strong," I said, "and confident enough to encompasses or occupy bold, unknown areas. A structure unshakable enough as to willingly allow new currents of thought to challenge what forces that up to now belonged to the world of pure faith." I stopped talking and observed Charles. I laughed like a child cornered and confronted with certain disaster. "How am I doing so far? Am I incomprehensible enough to sound impressive?"

"Definitely! Just great! I am completely lost, and yet I am with you all the way!"

"Hey, where are you going?" Roderick said playfully. "Are you taking me along?"

I said, "My love, you are indispensable for my journey to be successful."

"Oh now... I was not asking that much... But I am eager to see what landscape you are going to paint for us here."

"Me too!" Charles said. He sounded truly joyous. "But on *solid* ground?"

I sang, "Ab-so-lu-te-ly!" and said, "You men are too clever! So I propose a new angle to the issues of theology and faith—I move to venture that nowadays *solid* is more likely to apply to science than to faith—science has been the tangible god to whom the world has bowed."

"The world?" Roderick asked. "Do you think that all of the human population has been educated well enough to be able to understand science, let alone 'bow'?"

"I think so. Even the less educated among us are affected by scientific discoveries and ensuing technology. All of us are taken along in the stream of changes. But see where it has gotten us to require that all reality be *visible* and *measurable*?"

"And where is that?" Charles asked.

I shifted in my seat. "Look around... it has gotten us to more science of course... But fortunately, many scientists nowadays, and philosophers too, have slowly given up pride and confidence on the certainties of science."

"Like who?" Roderick asked.

I felt some alarm. "Well... for example," I said after some hesitation, "Lewis Thomas published an essay in a 1980 edition of the *Harvard Magazine* that I read some time ago. I think it was titled, 'On the Uncertainty of Science.' He built an interesting case for valuing better our human talent for ambiguity and language... he advised that we should admit, and be concerned about, how little we understand as small a creature as a flea... and much less about the making of a thought."

"A single man's essay written some 35 years ago!" Roderick said. "What's the strength of that argument? And where would the modern world be without the advancement of science since 1980, if we had paid heed to his warnings and put limits on research?"

I wondered when my husband had become such a champion of science. I knew him to be passionate about music and poetry, a Freemason very knowledgeable about various expressions of mysticism throughout the world. But was he just egging me on to stimulate the conversation? "It is indeed just one man, but not *any* man!" I said. "And take also Alton Chase—in a forum at BYU... 1985 I think... he gave a stupendous account of what the world has lost since the Renaissance, a period of history, in his view, when we started revering knowledge over faith and virtue."

Charles and Roderick both seemed disconcerted and became silent. I took this advantage to make an additional remark, albeit bitterly. "Chase described how this attitude was evidenced with the Nazis, those superbly educated and intelligent people who expanded through science their capacity to do evil, instead of their power to avoid it, and ameliorate the human quality of life in the world."

Roderick leaned towards me. "My darling, it seems vastly unfair to utilize such a heinous yet singular sample of Western history to make a case against science over religion."

"*Singular?*" I asked, appalled. "Horrors committed by Nazi scientists were not a *singular* happening. What about the nuclear bombing at Hiroshima... and modern warfare weapons said to pulverize bodies at a distance—a whole squadron is made to disappear in front of your eyes—pfft... dissolved... And what about genetic experimentation? And industrial pollution that is destroying the environment, whole populations of living organisms... How about carcinogens in processed foods that are affecting our health every day that goes by... All of these things are the products of human ingenuity and unlimited desire, choices made by people whose minds and thinking processes are unchecked by the wisdom and higher morality of a larger faith."

Charles raised an arm as if to vote. "I am with you there!" he said. "Roderick, you've got to admit..."

I was emboldened by Charles's support. "In all of history," I said, "this complete letting loose of reason and ego is unparalleled. It can't be what God hoped for! Nothing in the Christian Bible, the Muslim Koran, the Indian Upanishads, and nothing in religious oral traditions I know, such as Vodou, ever suggest that God does not want us to limit earthly impulses and greed, preferring that we put compassion for mankind first, become self-aware moral beings... In Vodou, there is the belief in the Granmèt, the Great Master, the power above all other gods. He too wants us not to harm others."

"My darling, it seems that this argument has been brewing inside you for a while... but would you then rather have all scientific progress banned?"

"No. But you must understand that to praise one thing is not to condemn another..."

"True enough, dear wife..."

"And, *dear* husband, let's also agree that the methods of science deal primarily with things of the material world, but they do not necessarily exclude... or disprove... the existence of a world of spirit..."

"Okay... I'll agree to that..."

"And also, I am rather inclined to think that the material and the spiritual worlds represent together the *totality* of reality, the whole face of existence... I would argue that Faith can be said to be the hope for things which are not seen, but are nevertheless true..."

Charles touched my hand. His eyes were glowing. "It may be," he said, "that the principal evidence for the existence of spirit is within ourselves... Others have witnessed miracles, or attest that they had spiritual experiences of real significance... prophets throughout the ages, modern-day Mormon prophets as well, have testified how they had conversations with God face-to-face. I believe them wholeheartedly. But none of these have as much evidential weight for me as do my own experiences of the workings of my own unconscious... We Mormons believe in personal revelations given to us directly from the divine world, call it God, Jesus, or the Holy Ghost, it is the heavenly world addressing us. They have a responsibility towards us. In coming to earth, we made a kind of contractual agreement. There are obligations on both sides. These revelations, sometimes mere promptings, can come as answers to prayers or questions, or when we need it... The Eureka moments that give us answers to problems are not the product of human cleverness or chance. As Latter-day Saints, we believe that it is the heavenly realm acting to inspire and help us. There are real mysteries in the world... we'll never truly know everything while we are down here."

Charles then fell silent. He looked absentmindedly at the crowded room. Just as I was wondering if he might be wondering about Roland, his eyes fell back on me with a slight frown. "Sorry... I didn't mean to make a long tirade," he said, winking at Roderick. "These are issues dear to my heart, but tell me what you think about the Christian freedom of choice you first mentioned before your husband here decided to play the devil's advocate?"

Roderick laughed. "What? Does the devil exist? He needs an advocate?"

I sighed. "It's been said that the devil's greatest trick is to have us believe that he does not exist."

"We believe that because we hope it's true," Roderick said.

I was wondering how I had gotten into this conversation? I would have much preferred to be listening to others than arguing a point in which I have long lost interest. But I made a brave face. "I think that I will let go of the devil's tail for now," I said, "and answer Charles about freedom of choice."

"Good choice!" Charles said, looking pleased.

"Yes Charles... What interests me in freedom of choice is what it reveals about our relationship with divinity. I see God acting both as *trusting,* and *trusted,* father... First, the fact that He is spoken of as *our* father, and we as His *children*, implies that we come from Him, and thus we partake of His divinity, it is inherent."

"Absolutely!" Charles cried out.

"Then, I am interested in God's role as *trusting* father. I like that He trust us, that He believes we will live up to His challenge, *trusts* that we will be obedient to divine laws... that we will remain loyal to our original parents."

"Awesome!" You're right. Mormons do believe in a heavenly father *and* a heavenly mother."

I smiled. "Well, 'awesome' is a bit inflated for what I said. But it is awesome, if true, that we should have heavenly parents. And awesome that we should deserve this trust because of those family ties."

"How about the 'trusted father' part of this?" Roderick asked, "What do you make of that?"

"What I make is that I find it significant, that we did trust God as well. We trusted His estimate of us, and His decision to give us freedom of choice."

"You've got it!" Charles said enthusiastically. His eyes grew moist, and he kept repeating, "Yeah…you've got it! Yeah…"

What a dear man! I thought. How invested in his faith! "I am glad you think that 'I've got it!'" I said. "You see, I admire this Mormon vision that reveals a high regard for human beings. My impression from my Catholic upbringing is that the emphasis is on our being sinners, not on our divinity… We are made 'in the image of God,' but more as a *reflection* of that image, and not from being of the *same* substance… the spark of divinity is in us, but just a spark."

I expected at that point that I would have gotten a chuckle from Charles or Roderick, but both looked grave. "Then there is the added difficulty in the notion that Grace cannot be earned," I said. "It can only be given. This belief makes God appear somewhat capricious, fearsome even. But with Mormons, the initial trust that involved freedom of choice enables us to work and earn Grace."

"Yes!" Charles agreed brightly. "The Mormon view is that with freedom of choice there is an implicit trust in our capacity for maturity. We are able to choose what may be harder."

"Yes, Charles… I am moved…" I said softly, "by this profound instance when God trusted, and did not impose. He took a risk on us…"

"Could you also say that we took a risk on God as well?" Roderick asked.

I did not look at Roderick's face, so I could not tell if he was joking. My own mood had been made a bit solemn by the topic, so I answered him half in jest. "You could say that, but not without being irreverent, and even sacrilegious in suggesting that God could be a risk factor."

"In reality," Roderick asked, "can there be something intrinsically so holy that we can actually be sacrilegious to it?"

"Of course," Charles said. "The notion of moral imperatives is intrinsically linked to the notion of something sacred and holy… the two are essentially connected…"

"I don't see that, Charles, something moral is not necessarily holy."

"I disagree. I am referring to high levels of understanding either notion. A high level of morality implies a high level of purity and holiness... if you betray or desecrate that high level of morality, whether it is an idea or a being, you are acting in a sacrilegious manner... profane... irreverent... unholy... The antonym of 'holy' is 'sinful.'"

"Charles, my friend, Sin has fat feet, for sure!"

Charles was not distracted by Roderick's joke. "In the Book of Mormon," he argued, "in section 2 Nephi, the prophet Nephi speaks of the necessity of opposition in all things... If you remove the notion of holy, you must remove the idea of sin as well... But Nephi also explains how the world would be in a dead state, no motion of any kind, if opposition in all things did not exist—there'd be neither life nor death, no corruption or incorruptibility, no happiness or misery, no sensitivity or insensitivity..."

"Sounds like the Cosmic Shiva of the Hindu religion," I said.

"Hey, you're right!" Roderick said, delighted. "It's the idea of destruction and creation being necessary to each other. No creation without destruction, and therefore no movement. Shiva's cosmic dance happening in the universe, and inside of us, is the continuous interplay of creation and destruction..."

"Of course!" Charles said. "And there again comes in the notion of *freedom of choice*. The choices we make create the rhythms of that dance. Adam had to fall so the dance would start, so mankind could begin."

"But Eve was the brave one here! She made the bold choice. Not Adam..."

"Oh... watch out for the Evolutionists here, dear wife... they'll have your head on the issue of the birth of humanity!"

"Dear husband... let them fight with the Cosmic Shiva, or old Bawon Samdi, and not with insignificant me! There is more to the universe than they or we know about! There *has* to be..."

Charles laughed, but quickly sobered. "Nephi agrees that there would not have been any meaning to God's Creation if His wisdom had not been challenged, or outright destroyed... he writes that if you say there is no holy, there is then no sin... if you say there is no sin, meaning everything goes, then there is no justice... if there is no justice, everything is bound to be a mess, and so there is no happiness... and if there is no justice or happiness, there is no punishment and unhappiness... Nephi goes so far as to argue that if these things do not matter, then there is no God, and if God does not exist, neither do we, nor does the earth, and anything that moves in the universe."

"We're back to square one then," Roderick said.

"What do you mean?" I asked.

Roderick grinned. "Faith—The issue of God's existence."

"Oh clever guy!"

But Charles wished to discuss further. "No," he said. "We are back to the notion of *holy*. If there is no God, then nothing is holy, and if nothing is holy, then there is no God. One breathes with the other. And I am led to wonder how human beings thought up the idea of holy in the first place—something so singular and precious that it needs immeasurable protection and regard? How did we even invent concepts such as *sacrilegious*, and create words for them? And how did we communicate these notions to each other well enough that we agreed on a few sounds meant to signify that singular idea? How was that thought generated in the first place?"

"I'd say it's all social and linguistic evolution!" Roderick said as if in a roar. "You're sneaking back to Lewis Thomas and science's ignorance regarding the making of a thought. Yet our ignorance at how thoughts are generated does not necessarily serve as evidence that they come from God, or even prove His existence, does it?"

"Sacrilegious husband!"

"Have we really invented anything?" Charles said, ignoring my outburst, raising his brows. "Or did we just progressively discover what was moving inside of us, and merely waiting, so we could finally begin utilizing what God installed in us and in the universe? We are amazed by our capacity for thought, but how about our capacity for language... and in such diversity... putting words together in an order and grammar that has its own internal logic? Even the seemingly dumbest human being has that capacity, and learns how to speak. So I ask you this, Could we really imagine God if he was not inside of us already?"

"Talk about *risk* factor!" Roderick said.

The three of us then guffawed a little nervously. Speaking of God in a flippant manner was unsettling. Yet Charles's whole heart was in this conversation. These were the politics he cared about, not the fundraising. He could not end with a joke. "The risk that God and we took on each other is a deep issue," he said. "Trust is a deep issue. It lies at the basis of all relationships. There is no growth without trust. We have to take a risk in others the way God did in us. It's hard at times… really hard…"

Hearing this, I sobered up too. "I also think that one implication of freedom of choice and the divine trust put in us," I said, "is that we have an innate sense of, and need for law."

"Law?" Roderick looked both perplexed and excited. The conversation was picking up new wind.

"Yes, Roderick. Law in terms of order and balance… an innate sensibility to it that would come from our divine origins. It could be argued that this innate sense of order implies a sense of harmony as well, both of which are manifested on earth as moral beauty."

"For sure, my Love! Yet I suppose that you are not just talking about *moral* beauty, but beauty manifested in the creative arts as well… a strong sense of order is absolutely necessary in composing or playing music… and, as you well know, in organizing an image on canvas… or writing a sentence."

"But of course! In speaking of moral beauty, I include all manner of esthetics. Moral beauty is a form of esthetics that is perforce involved in our law-making… we are capable of seeing law, divine or earthly law, not as something that restricts and impedes us, but as something spiritual and wise."

Charles looked ecstatic. He murmured, "Beautiful…"

"But here I have to close the circle we opened earlier," I said, "by mentioning the *third* aspect in Mormon theology that I see organized on the belief that we carry the substance of divinity in us."

"Wow… you haven't lost the thread, have you?" Roderick said

with an admiring whistle, and stroking my hand. "And what is that third aspect?"

"It is the fact that this whole journey to which we consent, is all about our being able to return where we started."

"*Return?* Return where?"

"To heaven, of course!"

"Heavens!" Roderick gasped, rolling his eyes. "Life is a two-way ticket then?"

"Yep!" Charles said. "Heaven—where we aim to return with honor so we can again be in the company of our divine parents... But we are not returning the same as when we left."

"That's for sure, Charles! Whoever left this place unscathed?"

"Here is my trickster husband again!"

"No, but seriously," Roderick insisted, "Charles, the notion that we come back changed can be said of any trip. Besides, that 'drawing-a-circle-and-return-to-where-we-started' idea is not new..."

"Mormons are Christians, Roderick!" Charles said, trying to appear light-hearted, but visibly provoked. "There is a reason why The Book of Mormon is called *Another* Testimony of Jesus Christ—we don't present it as a different belief system—we are in support of Christianity, not a challenge to it."

Roderick shook his head. "Charles, I was only referring to Eastern philosophies, and Western poets such as T.S. Elliot who have elaborated about this return to the source, and how we draw a circle with our lives."

"Hey Charles! Get ready. My husband here is going to tell you about Elliot's Four Quartets!"

And without even the slightest hesitation, Roderick started reciting, "...Words move, music moves... but that which is only living can only die... can words or music reach the stillness... while the note lasts...or say that the end precedes the beginning... and the end and the beginning were always there... before the beginning and after the end...and all is always now..." Charles and I were moved, but then Roderick only scoffed at himself, "These are just the few disjointed sentences of the poem that I remember. I once set myself to memorizing it... it's mostly gone now... the poem is very long."

"It had to be the part about music that you'd remember," I said.

Roderick shrugged his shoulders, nevertheless looking pleased. "It also makes me think of William Carlos Williams's famous quote about poetry. It goes like this, 'It is difficult to get the news from poems, yet men die miserably every day for lack of what is found there.'"

"Lovely!" Charles exclaimed, joining his hands as if in prayer. "And to pick up on the idea that this return journey is not a new idea… the difference I wish to mention is that for us Mormons, that return is part of our daily concerns, all our efforts and sacrifices, all that we ultimately aim for."

"How exhausting!" Roderick said, laughing.

I agreed. "Yes, our life is in our hands. That is what I understand of Mormon theology, and why I am, as I said earlier, 'well-impressed' by it."

Charles's face, and entire being, relaxed. "You have gone right to the center of it all… what you talked about is what we call the Plan of Salvation."

"I know…"

"Of course you do… and it is indeed crucial to our beliefs."

"I know… and I find it thrilling that at the root of this theology is the understanding that every action determines a reaction, and that the sum total of all the reactions in our lives will be whether we do return to living near God or not, in what manner, and in what realm…"

"I am afraid so…" Charles said, shaking his head.

"On a lighter note," I said, winking at Roderick, hoping to break the seriousness of this conversation, "I admit that while the idea of heaven as a real place where we live for all eternity is enchanting, it is also attractive to a claustrophobe like me—I can look forward to space incalculably multiplied compared to what I have on earth… even if greedy politicians 'die miserably every day' for dominion over that minute piece of cake!"

"You're too much!" Charles cried out, eyes shining.

I smiled at the compliment, but it stood to reason that Charles should feel delighted that I speak of his faith in such flattering terms. I said, "would you agree that freedom of choice gives us control over our quality of life *before* death, and also *after* death? And that we can *shape* eternity then?"

"Absolutely!"

"But I have to tell you this… I am not that excited by the idea of a stratified heaven into three realms."

"What realms?" Roderick asked.

"Celestial, Terrestrial, and Telestial."

"Sounds complicated…"

"It's not. But stratification implies classifying, which implies differentiating, which implies high, medium, and low… I would obviously want to get into the higher realm… stratification on earth is brutal enough, I'd prefer heaven without it.."

Roderick chuckled. "Ah… my wife! Just a minute ago you said you were looking forward to all that space? Now you're going to be picky about which eternity you'll get?"

"Why not?"

"Ah, but one could argue…" Charles said, "that striving to get to the Celestial Realm will make a better person out of each one of us. Besides, heaven can't be a hodge-podge of everyone. That's unpleasant enough on earth… People vary in their levels of commitment, and in their ideas of what is heavenly, or plain fun. It should stand to reason that we should have freedom of choice about heaven too."

I giggled. "Charles, you're the one who is 'too much' at this table!"

Roderick had been observing Charles's and my exchanges with obvious amusement, but at that point, he shook his head in mock disbelief. "I'm amazed how you got my wife to talk so much, Charles," he said. "Usually, she sits back and lets me do all the talking. Her mind likes flight. It's like she looks for a window behind every interlocutor." Roderick then raised both hands as if shuffling marionettes. "She looks for the kind of window out of which she might hop and dive into a blue ocean, swim with beings with three hearts, nine brains, eight arms, an intelligence based on touch, and touch that can taste, boneless water creatures, striped with excitement…"

Charles looked confused.

"...Octopuses!" Roderick explained, "I am talking about octopuses!" He laughed so wholeheartedly that Charles joined in, I took the opportunity of this diversion to ask, "Well Charles, have I answered you?"

"Awesomely!" he said, still giggling about the octopuses.

"I'll be right back!" Roderick suddenly announced, getting up. "I'll get us some hors-d'oeuvres!"

"Great!" I said, and then turned to Charles. "Listen... I almost forgot... and it's not a *fourth* aspect per se, but one profoundly connected to the second one—the freedom of choice. I really like Mormon rejection of the notion of original sin. I grew up with that shame—being a woman—and the blame put on Eve."

Charles said nothing, but the sparkle in his eyes was engaging. I felt encouraged to continue. "I agree that people are accountable for their own sins... we can either damn or redeem ourselves... I love that Mormon don't-pass-the-buck, and don't-hide-behind-Jesus's-atonement position... The Mormon Church doesn't protect its adulterers, thieves, sex-offenders, or any wrongdoers—you do it, you pay for it... your church doesn't look the other way—it excommunicates them right off... and I also like that people always have a chance to redeem themselves through service actions, and reintegrate the church.."

"Wow! Is it Roland who's behind what you know of our church?"

"Yes... but I read quite a bit about it too... I told you that earlier..."

"Yes, but it seems so precise in your mind... well-digested... How do you do it?"

"Old school habits.. I take notes... draw diagrams... but I discussed things with Roland too."

"How come you're not a Mormon yet?"

"No need... It's one thing to admire a theology and its followers, and another matter to create a revolution in one's life. It takes energy... humility... fearlessness."

"It takes plain courage!" Charles said, brushing his hair back with one hand, uncrossing one leg, and crossing the other. "So then, what church do you belong to?" he asked.

"I don't belong to a church, Charles. I belong to God."

"I walked straight into that pole, didn't I!"

"What pole is that?" we heard suddenly. Roderick had just returned with a plateful of assorted Southwestern finger-foods that he placed on the table. The display of red, green, and cheesy appetizers with scents already tingling my nose, provided great diversion. I began tasting morsels.

"I used to attend a monastery chapel's services," I said, chewing on a miniature quesadilla. "I revered the monks. Now, they no longer seem holy, but men kept safely apart from the struggles of economic survival, and the duties of family life... Christian leaders profess responsibility for my timeless soul, while they open wide the doors of their church once a week, at a small appointed hour."

Charles responded immediately. "There is no religious career or paid position in the Mormon Church. It's maintained by voluntary service only. Members of the church earn their livelihood outside the church. It's an instrument for spreading Christ's gospel, and develop our own relationship to God, not a place to hide in heavenly bliss like a monk. Mormons are active doers."

"I know all that," I said. "But they are not the only good Christians doing good in the world, even if I agree that the Mormon Church offers what seems to me the best way to establish a direct relationship to God."

"You must mean how to receive personal revelations," Charles said. "And yes, revelations are afforded to us if we seek them... and I know that you know that, but my speech is actually aiming at Roderick."

"Why me? I am not even in the running here!"

"I know... but all of us are actually 'in the running' when it comes to matters of divinity... you'd be such a strong man for the church... the bishop at my church told me that it's easier to find strong women to rely on in the church than strong men. It's three to one."

"Why is that?"

4. Angels Come

Allow yourself for a moment to believe that angels exist. Imagine that they are in the flesh, their wings a metaphor for the flight of mind they offer, one from which we may not return unchanged, so unusually beautiful and bold are perspectives with which they present us.

It was towards evening that angels landed with both feet in my heart. Who were they? Children at play between heaven and earth? A dream? Wayfarers? A singular constellation of only two stars suddenly alighted on the hard cement of a twenty-first century pavement in Massachusetts? They held a small plate of truffles identical to those sold at the chocolate house on Brattle Street out of which I had just emerged, oblivious to the vulgarity and waning of an ordinary business day. My first glance fell on their nametags. I was startled. "Elders? … You must be Mormons!" I cried out, "Oh… I love Mormons!"

They beamed.

They stood like brave weathervanes clad with unpretentious grey suits neatly buttoned over slight frames, brightly colored ties lying flat on late-adolescent chests. "Why do you love us?" They asked in unison, and with what I thought some disbelief.

At first I hesitated, I admit frankly, but with a certain degree of pleasure. Feeling some conceit, I advised myself to show what I am made of anyway. It was good that I decided there and then to renounce old habits, and cease giving way to vague dreams. It appeared that my destiny had come to meet me, so I gave the elders a prolonged look.

Elder Fenn's eyes reminded me of jewels mysteriously hardened from garden moss spreading freely under ferns, but shaped like tender leaves of a homegrown begonia. Elder Langford's eyes on the other hand, seemed to gaze with the quiver seen over pools born to reflect the calm of a vast sky where winds learnt to dissipate the resolve of clouds. He does not lower his glance, never breaks off a conversation; perhaps that very glance is his way of questioning.

Presenting myself as a poet was doubtless a form of brazenness. Only God may define and introduce the poet, His shaman, a Greek Orpheus. The matter of poetry is resolved only in revelation. Any self-named poet is a poseur. Sensitivity is not an occupation displayed on business cards. Having already allowed myself audacity however, it was an easy stretch to think this chance meeting of some significance to the elders' lives, and not in mine.

"Can we come visit you?" they asked. "Or would you rather come see us at church?"

There need not always be real reasons for disruptions in one's life; still, I felt it was really no time for paying calls. I thought wrongly that they could never reach me by any road stretching through the darkness of ages, even if I have not been perfectly satisfied with my own company. Such ideas were undoubtedly due to the influence of gloomy habits.

Fortunately, a fresh sense of trust had insinuated itself between us. What was there to prevent me from believing that some people are destined for each other? I was clamped onto clay I did not know to be already crumbling. I could have remained quietly with familiar Christians, and even Catholics. Yet I could no longer wait. Depending on the outcome, vanity can prove to be of service to oneself—I thought I'd favor them with a visit.

We met at church. Elder Fenn noted my questions on a pad; he seemed to delay and defer; but he had the cautiousness of shy persons inclined to measure their answers; he was like a treasurer in charge of a chest of rare gems he would loot bit by bit to lay at my feet. He taught me how, long before we are born, the trapeze is already set for us on earth—we are acrobats of character; all the doors leading to the stage are progressively flung wide open; the timing of it all has divine perfection beyond our understanding. God is patient.

Elder Langford's approach to conversation was more intimate, charged with a sense of urgency. "I started on my mission with a broken heart," he confided at the start. "I had turned eighteen. My parents announced their divorce just before I left on my two-year mission. Maybe it was good it happened then. I had to focus on other things, on other people, on Christ, on being a successful missionary. I am lucky that I was sent here to Cambridge. This is perfect for me! Some missions are hardship missions. Haiti would be one."

My worst trouble came from fear; sensing evil's interference in my life whilst I only wanted to solve the enigma of my being.

For that, the elders had answers, including an endless stretch of days devoted to helping me find my purpose. I was at first more interested in their spiritual being than in their "Mormonism," but grew increasingly charmed by the level of insights we shared.

"Does it feel different to be you now that you're missionaries?" I asked.

"Of course!" Elder Langford said. "Thinking of the Lord living in us makes us feel large. We need Him because while we are missionaries, we are constantly reminded of our limitations. People can be harsh when we approach them, sometimes violent, even if they can see that we are motivated only by the best of intentions. It's like this little boy, the son of a friend. He put a superman cape on, and ran around the house, completely naked underneath. He jumped on his parents' bed, going up and down with his arms wide open, yelling, 'I am superman, I am the strongest, nothing can beat me!' And then suddenly, he saw himself in the mirror across from the bed, and his arms flapped down. He saw how naked and puny he was—a little worm. He tore the cape off, ran to his room, and shut the door."

I never thought that God would use charm to transform someone. It became however obvious how the elders were charmed beings with knowledge whose spell I was slowly surrendering to during the two months' time when we met twice a week.

"My mission is coming to a close," Elder Langford said one afternoon. From a towering ship, sadness sunk its anchor in the depths. I am a native of the Caribbean coast, I thought derisively. For the story of my capture, I will depend on the evidence of Mormons. A hunting expedition was sent out and overtook me on this journey in a foreign land. I had come down for chocolate among foreign troops at dusk, and I got caught. I was musing along these lines when the second shot hit me in the chest: "Will you be baptized by us before I go?"

There was real candor here.

I could not refuse the elders. Still, it would require a leap of faith. Many questions remained. Spiritual growth is an aquatic tree, I thought. It is unclear where and how it will grow. The underwater territory is imprecise, and highly personal. Only broad lines might be drawn in advance while the real beauty of the habitat hides in delicate lines of maturation. Like a spider's web, it must not be touched, only observed. A leap of faith was required of me now. I laughed aloud as if I were about to do something unnatural, and asked, "Explain why I should be baptized when I already am? Has my godfather not had any real significance? Am I not already a Christian?"

Elder Langford shook his head while Elder Fenn brushed his hair with one evasive hand. This was a moment when a hostess coming in with golden meringues on a silver salver would have been a deliciously magical interruption; blood seemed to have been drawn instead; yet Elder Langford began to speak soberly. "We all know the similarities between our and other Christian churches. The differences are what matters most. I can list them now if you like?"

I said, "I know how we have talked enough about this, but the information is scattered throughout our many conversations. I would benefit from a summary."

Elder Langford nodded. He said, "The first point is the restoration of priesthood power through the actions of Joseph Smith. This had been lost after all the apostles died, and politics of religion took over. Our church is modeled after Jesus Christ's first church." He spoke solemnly, eyes cast down, as if looking inwardly. "The second issue is that we have a living prophet and a continuous quorum of twelve apostles. No other Christian Church has that. Third is the issue of return—we make specific covenants with the Lord, covenants that help us return to Him in heaven. A fourth point is that we believe families are bound together for eternity. We perform sealing ordinances to ensure that. A fifth difference relates to the temple. While our churches are open to all on Sundays, we have a temple strictly reserved for God. This is His house. No unclean thing may enter there and be in His presence. And then last but not least are the ordinances for the dead done by proxy. Baptisms for the dead were done at the time of Christ. There are scriptural evidences of that. One mention is in Paul's letter to the Corinthians… And that's it, I think, I covered all the differences between our church and other Christian Churches."

"You will be a terrible friend to lose," I said. "I should have listened to my mother—she warned me that I'd set fire to the house if I kept playing with matches."

Elder Langford looked up with tears in his eyes. "Whether you convert or not, you too will be a terrible friend to part with."

I chuckled. "Don't worry about that. You're not going to lose me. I agree to be baptized."

"Elder Fenn and I are really excited about your baptism!" Elder Langford wrote a few days later. "It will be the best memory of my mission days!"

A continuous flow of short emails kept coming from the elders; the computer had become their umbilical cord to me. "Bishop Johnson has already spoken about you to the Haitians in church! There is an Eloi family with two little girls."

"That's a real Haitian name!" I wrote back. "I know of a Saint Eloi painter who produces unsettling paintings on Vodou themes."

Then I read again, "It will be so wonderful to meet Roland. It's a great thing to have a friend fly from Arizona to come baptize you. And you say that Adam is going to sing?"

"Yes, Adam will sing Panis Angelicus. Have you heard him? What a tenor!"

"Yes! We hear him sing in church sometimes. Remember it was Adam who gave us the plate of chocolates when we met you, and he was still working at Burdick's? It really was destiny that we met that day!"

"Just as I thought—angels are made of chocolate!"

"You're funny! If you want my opinion, I think it will be really special to have your husband play the piano at your baptism."

"He intends to play as long as we swear not to get him in the water!"

"Ha! Ha! Ha!"

5. Wildlife Sanctuary

The Wednesday when Roderick and I discovered the Ipswich River Wildlife Sanctuary a few miles from our new home was also the day I wrote to Bishop Johnson telling him that I had accepted the missionaries' invitation to be baptized. I started my letter, "It is not without much trepidation..." and Bishop Johnson readily replied, "Your wise decision fills me with joy!" I paused on the word "wise."

We saw many deer during our walk in the woods but they noticed us first, becoming still, ears up. Wildlife listens well; they didn't shuffle joyous feet like we did through the new carpet of brown leaves; they didn't scoff like we did, at the sudden appearance and rapid fleeing of red-tailed squirrels zigzagging across the path.

Human beings have an instinctual understanding of sanctuary for wildlife and the necessity of creating holy ground—a sacred place where all that is delicate and vital may live.

Baptism acknowledges wildlife in us, and its need for peace. The Holy Spirit seems an eternal surveyor of spiritual worthiness. He comes to the call of each convert, a call made as if from the conch shell the 1804 African slaves in Haiti used for rallying in their fight against an evil system. Boukman and the first marooned slaves declared the mountains holy ground. They invoked the gods watching from the great expanse of the Caribbean sky sparkling above each day; they took the sun as witness; they called out to the clouds; they lit a great fire in their assembly place; they cried out to the moon, and counted the stars; they prayed for liberation from all that ensnared and constricted them, vowing to sacrifice all for the deliverance from abomination in their lives; then they set fires in the houses of all those who put shackles around their feet, their lives, and souls.

As Roderick and I walked the serpentine path along the river, the lowering sun of the coming dusk fired many colors on the surface of the water, reminding us of its constant promise, of night to be followed by dawn, of death to be followed by a different birth.

I thought of my adolescence in France. I recalled walks I took alone in the forest of Maisons-Laffitte, near Paris, where I lived with my mother. These were the years of Duvalier dictatorship in Haiti, when my father had sent us away to safety in France. What lonely years! I banged my head to sleep on my pillow every night until I saw stars. My mother told me that I would die of brain cancer, so I made myself a cloth doll to hold in bed. She had large blue buttons for eyes, like Elder Langford's. While clutching the doll to resist the urge of banging my head, I mourned my father's absence and the island of my birth. I mourned my wish for a coming home; a return to deep and far-reaching roots in a place where my father and my grandfather would have taken me for walks during which I would have heard stories about their own fathers and grandfathers. I thought of Bishop Johnson's letter that said the Holy Ghost would thereafter accompany me. Roderick held my hand. He stood straight in spite of the voluminous backpack he bore, rejuvenated by this New England landscape reminiscent of his native England. He said, "I hope to take you home some day and show you the Marlow River near the house where I grew up. My father built a great door for our house."

"We will," I answered, thinking of my childhood's river valley instead. "We will go back home some day. We will leave this place."

10—Forgiveness

1. Clayton and Me

"I am here because Christ could not be here in person," said a smiling six-foot-six Clayton Christensen wearing a suit and tie, bending his head as he walked through the doorway to his living room. Elders Fenn and Langford had described him as an old man slowed by damaging illness, but the man I saw was no older than me, and his dark hair previously affected by chemo therapy had grown back. He gave me his hand in welcome, then led me with great simplicity to the cream leather couch where he suggested I sit. He then stepped a little to the side, folded his long limbs carefully, and settled soundlessly into a plush armchair. He had not kept me waiting.

A date for my baptism had been set. While interviews before baptism are customarily scheduled with either young missionary who taught the convert, the problem of my age and complex life experiences presented itself. Church authorities are careful not to burden young missionaries with listening to life stories they would not comprehend, or are inappropriate for them to be processing and counseling on. With two days remaining before the baptism ceremony, Elders Fenn and Langford were hard pressed to find someone suitable at a time when all bishops and Mission President counselors serving the area happened to be absent, or committed elsewhere. I thought it my good fortune then that a Harvard professor normally overburdened with duty, was the only one able to meet with me. At the time of our appointment, Clayton Christensen was, besides a full-time professor, also serving as First Counselor in the Cambridge Mission Presidency of the Church of Jesus Christ of Latter-day Saints.

It was nearly ten years since I sold the family property where I grew up, and three years since the 2010 earthquake devastated the country of my birth. But there comes a time in life when we become our own country. We understand that exile is the basic human condition, and accept how people we counted as part of our personal nation have died, gone astray, or betrayed the trust. Either way, we reach a point when we survey the land—our inner self—with new eyes; we redefine its character and future. The many outside influences we believed part of our essential structure turn out to have been a wild horde. The realm we face is vast, but the path is slim. We collect meaning on the way like bark and leaves that eventually stain, dreams fallen at our feet that seep into the ground, and become part of the personal domain on which we stand.

    I was feeling some alarm that evening of the interview, sitting on the front edge of the sofa, seeking comfort from geometric designs of the Persian rug at my feet, when Clayton Christensen suddenly got up. "Excuse me. I forgot to bring the Book of Mormon and other documents. I'll be right back."

    During the brief time that my host left me alone, my anxiety intensified. I brooded over the fact that the Mormon Church might define this particular meeting as an interview, but the Catholic in me anticipated more of a confession. Childhood memories and related emotions were crowding in my mind. I remembered the insecurity I felt kneeling in front of priests who held an indefinable power over my destiny, and could deny me God's blessing. Now I would again have to divulge private events of my life to a stranger. I thought that even if he is viewed as a holy man, and therefore kind, it was a disquieting situation to find myself in. I kept shifting on my seat; I fiddled with the brass nails on the edge of the couch's armrest; I repeatedly told myself that he is just a man, but an inner voice answered me instantly with an "Oh yes… a man, but not *any* man—and don't forget what you read on the Internet." Then, I began imagining Clayton Christensen overhearing my thoughts and responding to them. He might have argued that it is unfortunate to rely on the Internet for information about him, because a list of facts about a man's work says nothing about his spirit. To this, I might have answered , all the while thinking myself clever, that facts referring to the tangible world can also have meaning in the intangible one. "How so?" He'd question. "Simple," I'd say—"for example, the Internet informs that you served as an Area Seventy from 2002 to 2009…"

Hearing that, I know he would not have failed to interrupt me, asking, "Have you bothered to look up the meaning of 'Area Seventy'?"

"Yes Sir! Most certainly!. I read that it is a priesthood office. The Area Seventy is a traveling minister, a special witness of Jesus Christ charged with the mission of preaching the gospel to the entire world under the guidance of the twelve apostles of the Mormon Church… Therefore, all this told me *clearly* about the spiritual man you are. To illustrate that, I can even quote Saint Matthew from the Bible saying, "by their fruits you will recognize them."

My mind nevertheless played further tricks on me—it began showing that Clayton Christensen was not impressed by my answers. "I did serve," he admitted. "But the Internet cannot reveal the ways in which the experience transformed me… *transformation*, and not a *position* of service in the church is what I am about the man in the moment, sitting here, now."

"Indeed a good argument," I must have conceded. But I tend towards bravado, so I challenged him. "The *position*," I might have said, "is given only to a certain type of men. That in itself is telling enough. And the Internet also explains how the Area Seventy are men equal in priesthood authority with the Quorum of the Twelve Apostles, and this certainly suggests much about the man you were at the time, as well as the holier man it was trusted you would *transform* into—that transformed man is the one sitting here with me."

Right then, I would have thought I had him. I am sure I sniggered.

"Transformation is a vague term," he might have nonetheless replied… but I cut him short—"Oh… regardless! All I've read is quite enough to make me feel ordinary and small... Forbes magazine called you 'one of the most influential business theorists of the last 50 years'... and you were ranked *twice* as number one in the Thinkers 50."

"Stop! That 's enough."—This humble man would have certainly been blushing by then, asking if the Internet tells how "*just* a man" he felt when he was diagnosed with lymphoma, and suffered a stroke, both things in 2010? The year of the Haiti earthquake actually...

I groaned, for sure... "Oh, nice try... But you still managed to publish two books the very next year."

I think that at that point I would be sure to have felt him resting his hand on mine, saying softly, "It seems this interview is making you anxious... there is no need to... but is anxiety also the reason you watched that barbarous movie about forgiveness last night?

Thunder!

"*Forgiveness*? You mean the story about the Hatfield and the McCoy's family blood feud started right after the American Civil War ended?"

2. Blood Feud

The movie about that family blood feud was inspired by true events, and the names were not changed. In the beginning, Hatfield deserts his company just before the men were killed in battle. Every soldier in the company died except for his good friend McCoy, who ended up being the only survivor of the massacre, and never forgave Hatfield for his desertion. In fact, McCoy lived to regret not shooting Hatfield in the back, whilst he watched him stealing away on his horse in the dark to reunite with his wife and children,.

"I am choosing to do my duty towards *them* and protect *them* rather than die pointlessly here with all of you," Hatfield argued. "You'd do the same and come with me if you had any sense."

"And where would be the honor of that, if every man here decided to abandon the others to suit himself? We swore an oath, Hatfield, remember?"

"I see no oath here, McCoy, no law, no God that makes sense..."

At war's ending, the family feud began between the West-Virginia Hatfields and the Kentucky McCoys. The movie presented the story of a several-years blood shed during which the god-fearing, self-righteous, vindictive, and unforgiving McCoy never failed to trust that God was on his side; even after the deaths of his four sons, two daughters, one brother, and a number of nephews and nieces, either of which were stabbed, shot, executed, or mutilated by the proud, fool-hardy, family-conscious Hatfields, acting in retaliation for their own loss of sons, brothers, nephews and cousins. Mothers then seemed able to produce a continuous supply of children, allowing their slaughter in support of the stubborn pride of aged husbands.

A miraculous interlude happened: love between a Hatfield and a McCoy in what could be described as a post civil war, short-lived, version of the classic Romeo and Juliet story. But not quite. Johnse Hatfield failed to defy paternal authority, and risk losing home and family for the love of Roseanne, even whilst she had abandoned hers for him. Johnse let Roseanne be kicked out of *his* house by his father, and later did nothing to intervene upon learning that she was disowned by her own father, the god-loving McCoy. While Johnse went and married her cousin, the pregnant Roseanne took refuge at the house of a kindly old aunt in whose arms she soon died of a broken-heart, and the ill health it had fostered.

At the end of this true American family saga, albeit perhaps overplayed, in which mothers appeared to have no value other than to produce strings of sons given as rifle-fodder and daughters meant to help rear younger siblings, Mrs. McCoy finally goes insane. It is at this point, after the loss of *all* his sons and the collapse of his wife, that McCoy abandons God, and replaces Him with a bottle of whiskey.

As for Hatfield, he had two sons left alive and still free, while other sons, nephews, and a brother—himself a US court judge—were in jail awaiting for justice (a justice that turned into a mockery: organizing the public hanging of the only innocent Hatfield, a half-wit who barely knew what to do with the rifle forced into his hands, and once stopped in the middle of a disorderly shooting to save a rabbit, gently shooing it away). It is at that point that Hatfield sent a formal letter to the newspapers saying that the feud had lost meaning for him, and he wished for peace.

3. Aftermath

"Devil Anse" Hatfield who had no care for God throughout his life whilst he murdered men and youths alike, finds Him in the end. He repents for sins committed in the eyes of the Lord, and is baptized in the waters of a river.

"Ole Ran'l" McCoy who had his mind fixed on God throughout all the violence he executed and suffered, finally loses Him completely and dies in the flames of his house that he had accidentally set on fire, lying in a drunken stupor.

I sat a long while in silence after the movie ended, and dreamt of snakes during the night: heinous reptiles invaded my room; I managed to kill a long, dark one with a stick; harder to kill was an opalescent, double-bodied, double-headed snake, a reptilian form of Siamese twins joined at the tails instead of the hip, a free-formed, yin-yang, good and evil arabesque, yet a potential uroboros; I was only able to smash one head of this twinned creature. Upon waking, I understood that ridding my house of the snake had been a job half done.

But what did the snake represent? The devil serpent in Genesis? A symbolic representation of my involvement with Vodou and its snake-god Dambala? Or was it a timely recall of the only childhood dream that I remember, pursued as I was by a snake all night long, running through the neighborhood paths where kaka zombie grew?

The following day, and all the while preparing for my interview with Clayton Christensen, I mulled over the movie. I observed how three McCoy sons had been tied to a Pawpaw tree before being executed by a Hatfield vigilante platoon, with a total of 50 shots fired on their bodies. Similarly tied to twinned posts in front of the Port-au-Prince cemetery, my cousin Guslé's rebel companions, Louis Drouin and Marcel Numa, had been put before a firing squad by Duvalier in a

1964 televised, public display attended by school children. I saw the video of the execution on television when I was a child; it was broadcast for a week. When I saw it as an adult on the Internet, the years in between vanished, and I felt like a child again. Emotional distance is not an issue of time. The older I become, the more these twenty-year-old men look like children butchered in a live theater. They were the remainders of my cousin's original company of twelve; they had been caught a few days prior to the final battle where the last three men fought against the whole of Duvalier's army in the mountains of L'Asile, and where Guslé was the last to die.

The two captured companions had been imprisoned for questioning; they were also tortured, reviled, and kept alive so their execution could be a tool for further political intimidation. A rumor spread that Marcel Numa's father had been brought to the prison to meet his son before the execution. "I see no son of mine here." Those were the last words Marcel Numa heard from his father. One hopes that father and son had a deeper understanding of the moment—a patriarch having to disown his child in order to protect the rest of his family. The Numa were the only family who did not suffer from the Jeremy massacre where all family members of the Jeune Haiti rebels were exterminated. Marcel Numa was notably the only black man in the group. Duvalier was a black country doctor whose campaign had rested on the support of the black peasantry. People like the Numa family had been *his* people.

While continuing to ponder parallels between lives of people in the movie and those of my family, I found myself comparing emotional damage done by the murder of their sons to Mrs. McCoy and to my aunt Nicole, Guslé's mother. While it took the killing of seven of her children for Mrs. McCoy to finally lose her sanity, I concluded that the rage and paranoia manifest in my aunt's lucid mind until she died at 93, had been harm done to her sanity and emotional structure as well. My aunt's mourning was never softened by the idea that her son had become immortal as a consequence of the gift of his life he made to his countrymen, as some people tried to make her believe. It was instead as if the goodness born from her body of a son who made exceptional choices, had boomeranged, and returned to her flesh as an everlasting wound.

Perhaps my aunt had been at a disadvantage. Mrs. Hatfield and Mrs. McCoy were civil war mothers. During the four years that left 750,000 dead, they had perhaps become accustomed, resigned, or even numbed, to the mercilessness of wars where sons die before their fathers, and women lose both. My aunt's own wound came from the sudden blow she received while opening a newspaper, and she recognized the decapitated head held up by the hair in a front page photograph celebrating the demise of the rebel's leader. She had received no news of him since learning about his plans to overthrow the Duvalier government, and liberate Haiti.

In an effort to understand the psychology and endurance of these civil war mothers, it may be helpful to view the Hatfield/McCoy family feud itself as an excrescence of the blood-thirst started in the nation during the early 1860s; it may also be understood as a dissident prolongation of a barbaric craving that had become so monstrously familiar as to seem acceptable, a situation and disorder to which human beings may become addicted, and to an extent that modern psychological studies of the effect of war on the psyche still find hard to evaluate fully.

My cousin's *Jeune Haiti* rebel movement was a similar outgrowth of a civil-war, a Caribbean one, developed at a time when Haitian civilians were killed at random by Haitian police, when Haitian rebel youths shot back at Haitian army youths, simple people of the peasantry uninterested in rifles and battle, like the innocent Hatfield, men who enrolled in the army for lack of work options, unable to foresee that bloodshed between people of a nation is a close relative of family feuds.

What fitting irony, I told myself, having noticed in the Christensen's living room a row of miniature pumpkins lined up, platoon-like, on the fireplace's mantle piece, that the time of my baptism interview, combined with my watching the movie about a blood feud, is actually Halloween, the time of year on the Christian calendar where much of the world population is making ready for rowdy celebrations of the dead.

4. The Issue of Satan

"I am here only because Christ could not be here in person..."—Hearing this, I wondered about the man whom Christ saw fit to represent him.

I found that he was indeed kind. He asked no pointed question, as I feared he might. He treated me instead like a friend with whom he was sharing his thoughts and some stories of his life. Forgiveness was the starting point of our conversation. "When you repent with all sincerity, you are forgiven," he said. "What is forgiven is instantly forgotten. Christ will no longer remember your sins, and you should not remember them either. Erase them from your consciousness."

My heart was beating fast; my sense of humor had vanished; my mouth felt dry. Clayton Christensen however looked relaxed. His voice had a muffled quality, like sound coming from another room... or was it the effect of dusk? His forcefulness showed in his gaze. His eyes never looked down when he spoke. He warned, "Be aware that Satan and the Savior stand in full contrast to each other in their behavior towards sin—before sin, the Savior is inflexible about your obeying His commandments, and only because He wants you spared the scars to your psyche that come as a consequence to sinning. After you have sinned, he is immensely flexible and compassionate." Just as I felt a growing calm from hearing these words, Clayton Christensen suddenly gripped his knees, leaned forward, raising his eyebrows, and said, "This is where you must be vigilant! Satan's behavior is the direct opposite of the Savior's—he is flexible before sin, and inflexible after. At first, he makes light of all considerations other than the pleasures he swears you need and deserve, and with complete disregard for the consequences of your acts on others. Yet, after you have sinned, he refuses to let go—Satan wants you feeling endlessly guilty, shamed, remorseful, unable to forgive yourself."

My mind then began to wander; past moments for which I still felt shame came crowding in. "Don't worry..." I heard. "We're all sick people..." I looked up with embarrassment. Clayton Christensen's eyes were filled with tenderness, as he seemed to have read my thoughts. "Let me tell you when I first realized we are all sick people," he said. "I was already married and a father when I was at the university studying for my Ph.D., and they asked me to serve as bishop of the University Ward in Cambridge. 'Bishop of a *ward*?' a fellow student asked me. 'Are you going to be some kind of priest in a hospital?' 'Not at all.' I said. 'I am a Mormon. A ward refers to a congregation of our church.' My fellow student was stunned. But then his confusion showed me something that I had not realized before, namely that we are all sick people." Clayton Christensen chuckled, then leaned back into his armchair. "A hospital and a Mormon ward both have people suffering in varying degrees of ill-health, in the body or in the mind. The way I see it, in the church we are both staff and patients. The difference with hospitals is that Mormons take care of each other for free."

I was taken aback by what I had just heard, and charmed. Clayton Christensen was smiling. Silence settled briefly between us, as if to cushion us better. But, it wasn't long until it was gently broken. "Now tell me your story, in your words, how you see it. Where did you grow up? How was life in your family? What was your life like, then and after?"

He never asked me about sin, and appeared to trust that I would tell him what mattered. It is then that I began to love him. So, did I describe to him the daily display of my mother's nipples through her low-cut décolleté dress? Did I betray my manic-depressive father's unconscionable insensitivity towards his fragile son? Did I denounce the ongoing internal strife in a family of four, choked by jealousies, failures, and shame, people loving and hating each other, bound by duty and need? Did I admit to divorce and remarriage, and the eventual papal annulment granted much later? Did I decry the kinds of thefts, small crimes, and destruction happening within each relationship I had? Did I report on raising other people's children who easily forgot me because I was not of their blood? Did I reveal a life lived in fear of not disproving my tearless mother's prediction that I would "end up like my father," me, a woman urged forward only by sheer animal instinct, my choices and behavior most often mere carbon copies of those of others I watched when growing up, and which had become so familiar that I did not realize their absurdity or question their distastefulness? Did I tell him about the peculiar interference within my body of Vodou forces hard to qualify or name? Of course, I did. And nothing I said appeared to perturb this man in the least. I felt his admiration rather than his judgment. I left the house uplifted that evening.

Our conversation lasted twice the time scheduled for, and ended with Clayton Christensen expressing his regrets that we had to stop. We got up and walked to another large room where other people had been waiting. I was introduced to Mrs. Christensen and the friends in glorious terms. "This was the most articulate, sensitive exchange I have ever had in an interview; and she speaks better English than we do."

I wish that my own mother had treated me with a fraction of that kind of respect when I told her about my conversion. But perhaps she was unwittingly making me pay in advance for what I would reveal about her during that interview. "Quoi! Tu es FOLLE—What! Are you NUTS?" she said. "You're telling me that you've joined a cult? A CULT! Good GOD! My daughter is insane! Fit-to-be-tied!"

"Mother... it's not a *cult*..."

"YES IT IS... First it's Vodou, now it's *Mormons*! When will you LEARN? This has got to stop!"

"Oh Mother... can't you show a little interest in my search for God... and what it is I commit to?"

"'*Commit*' is the right word—you ought to be *committed!*"

"How about having some respect for what I value... or just love me how I am?"

"Respect? What do you mean *respect*? You change religion as often as you do husbands!"

5. A Lucid People

Clayton Christensen spoke in parables. "Let me tell you a story," he said. "My colleagues at the Harvard Business School know me as a religious man. One colleague said to me one day, 'Clayton, you are one of six Mormons I have ever met in my entire life of a scholar. You are all highly educated, and you all seem very lucid people. So, how is it you can believe in all that stuff about Joseph Smith?' I smiled, of course, and said to my colleague, 'Imagine that a man dies and goes to heaven. There he meets God, but finds Him in a huge storeroom, looking at endless rows and stacks of files. Imagine that you realize that this is where God stores the world's knowledge, all the wisdom ever to be learnt. 'Why does God hoard it all?' You might ask. 'Why not give it all to mankind *before* anyone can make a mistake, and have to suffer from sin?' Sins are mistakes in choice of action, mind you, that is all. Sins are not items on a list of behaviors likely to entrap human beings. 'Then, why do scriptures speak of punishment?' you might ask, 'if sins are just mistakes?' And that's when I'll tell you that punishment is in the *consequences* of these actions, and not in any vengeful act of God. God wants you happy, and therefore free of sin." Clayton Christensen stopped speaking, stared into space, his right hand frozen in an open gesture. Then his eyes shifted back towards me. "Going back to my story… I told my colleague, 'Imagine again that God no longer wants to hoard all that wisdom and the answers to all questions. He'll give it away now! Mankind needs answers, God is impatient for Man to be happy and wise. So God opens all the files. He makes paper airplanes with each sheet of paper containing a specific wisdom, or an answer. God starts sending these paper airplanes down to earth, and catch it who can, unawares, unprepared! Here it is! And imagine people—family, friends, *everybody*—going about their business in the streets… at the dinner table… lying in bed… some even in deep mourning and, ouch! This one is hit by one plane, and ouch! That one is hit by another. They pick up the paper, puzzled, and unfold it. They read what is inside. What is this about? What is this answer to a question they had not asked, and not even thought of? What are they to do with a message for which they had not made ready? Where are they to store it? Inevitably, they end up making a paper ball, and throwing it in the wastebasket…" Clayton Christensen stopped suddenly, observing me. "I see you smile… do you know why you smile?"

"I smile because I am wondering where you are going with this… and for the playfulness of it all."

"I see… what I mean to say with this little tale is that any answer is useless to one who has not formulated the question for it."

"In France, your story would be called an *argument par l'absurde*. A literal translation might be, 'argument built on absurd premises.'"

Clayton Christensen chuckled. "I grant you that my story uses outlandish premises to illustrate a point. I am however not *arguing* a point."

"Translation is a problem. The French word, '*argument*' might be better served by English words like 'reasoning' or 'discourse,' while '*absurde*' and 'absurd' may be what we used to call 'false-friends' in my English language classes."

"I grant you that my story requires a playful mind, if not an outright leap of faith. But how else to talk about God?"

"That very leap is what made me smile," I said. "And it is such a leap that I am taking in converting."

"My colleagues do not understand this faith we have in Joseph Smith as the Lord's first modern-day prophet because they have not wondered about him. That's the point I made with the '*absurde*' story. They should start by asking, 'Who was he? What were his concerns? What motivated him? What actions did he take that led him to become who we know him to be? What answers was he sent, what revelations, and in which way were they given to him?' But, you see, my colleagues have not asked, so they have not received, and so they do not understand how I can believe in 'all that stuff about Joseph Smith'." Clayton Christensen took a pause. His eyes enveloped me with warmth I had never experienced; him a stranger to me, suddenly seemed a close friend... I also saw how discreetly he looked at his watch.

"Oh... I have taken too much of your time! But there are just a couple more things..." He picked up the Book of Mormon on the coffee table in front of him, and seemed to be searching for a quote when he looked up again. "Never cease to ask questions," he said, "so that you prepare yourself for communication and revelation from God. You can have your own answers to all your questions of faith." I knew these were parting words. I felt sad, thinking how this was not a friend I could count on seeing again any time soon. But he still had some last advice to give. "After your baptism, you will be cleansed of the past. If you sin again, and we do—we are human—you must confess directly to God. Ask forgiveness for yourself. Remember the injunction, 'ask and ye shall receive. Knock and it shall be opened unto you.' I felt I was a child again in this man's presence, thrilled with the charm of being in a world where the marvelous still existed. "I am not here in judgment of you," he said again, "I am here because Christ could not be here in person, and I offer you, with my presence, someone to talk to. That is all I am. It is Christ who hears you right now, and forgives you. It is He who accepts your gesture today, and welcomes you."

11 Fervor

1. The Andromeda Galaxy

The Andromeda galaxy with its finely textured dust lanes adroitly spirals across my computer screen on an artificial-blue infinite studded with stars. Its diameter spans 75,000 light years but is reduced to a few inches before my eyes as I sit down to write each day, unwittingly reminded of my insignificance, while I nevertheless feel supreme urgency and importance in deciding on every word that will carry my meaning and proof of existence.

How will I harmonize God and the Big Bang scientific theory? How to reconcile the human mind's vision of a divine realm with this irrefutable, observable universe that swirls black holes at different poles of intergalactic space, and where the sun each day is seen to rise—its diameter a hundred times larger than that of the earth and one million times its volume, a mass possessing 300,000 time more total matter than the earth, center of our solar system, with 700 times as much mass as all of the planets of our solar system combined, comets and asteroids included?

And yet, here I stand, believing in God. Here I stand, me, a trifling microcosm engaged in the continuous assertion that its presence in the universe is not inconsequential, a picayune creature engrossed with the belief that she does have a future, that this future is of importance, and enough so that all can, and should, be done on earth for me to draw an upward, glorious curve towards the heavens, thus allowing me in the end to find, enter, and forever dwell in God's presence.

Intuition continually pushes and bears me like a strong wind. I find myself standing in new places of the mind that hold me for a while until I am again transported elsewhere, creatively engaged in making eternal sense of the dislocated trajectory of my being, my heart clasped at its galactic center.

2. A Pot of Gold

While I stood in the baptismal waters, waiting to be plunged backward and immersed, hearing "Juliette Simone Marilène…in the name of Jesus-Christ…" I looked for my husband's face through the glass fence-protection. Roderick sat directly across from me in the row of chairs lined up near the basin's edge, but behind the string of children who seemed like ants before a pool of syrup, they too come to watch, gathered and kneeling close to each other, filled with expectation. My husband at that moment appeared old and sad and sunken. He was probably more aware than I was of the portent of the baptismal ritual in which I was involved, standing as I was in water up to my waist, my hands resting on my friend Roland's left hand and wrist, his right hand opened wide ready to support my back, both of us wearing white. Perhaps Roderick felt the death implied in the moment more than I did. Perhaps his anxiety for my wellbeing explains why he asked so many times during the afternoon, and still the next morning, "Are you happy?"

Everyone remarked on how I glowed. But when I found myself alone in front of a cold bathroom mirror afterwards, I only noticed how old and sad and sunken I too looked. It was as if I were seeing myself from the inside only, bearing the fatigue of the preceding weeks, the vast years past—the restless, dream-filled nights, mind filling up differently by day—but now slowly absorbing new possibilities of vision and meaning of self in the world and the heavens, struggling to remain grounded while yearning to join an otherworldly space.

In that post-baptism moment, my inner vision began first with a desire to tell how there really is a pot of gold at one end of the rainbow. It rests in a pasture where I want to sleep while stars fill me with their lyrics. The bishop speaks of the Holy Ghost who will accompany me in the future, but the Holy Ghost was there already, weighing on my face as I fell irresistibly backward in the water. I feel how goodness wants to be restored. Johan Sebastian Bach's preludes linger from minor to major on the piano where my husband sits with the pallor of ghosts. Friends, many friends are here, shoulder pressing shoulder. All the sweetness of the earth with the bread of angels has been spread on tables, the fragrance of lychees, persimmons, mangoes, oranges, while golden almonds nest in a high cake set in the midst of all the silver and gold chocolate coins of my childhood's desires. It is indeed a fair of the spirits! My hair is wet. A butterfly carved in amber is pinned at my breast. Ah…wonder is born anew while an echo persists along clean walls, wanting to know, "Are you happy?"

3. Oliver's People

Religious fervor runs in my family. My maternal grandmother, Simone, claimed Saint Oliver Plunkett as part of her ancestry, and recounted tales of his martyrdom. He was born on All Saints Day in the year 1625, and only 55 years old when as archbishop of Armargh and Primate of All Ireland, he was found guilty of high treason for promoting the Roman faith.

It was a time when persecution against Catholics was renewed. But Oliver is said to have confirmed 48,655 Catholics over a four-year period following the beginning of his apostolate in Armagh in 1670; he was 45 years old. Despite the ban on public practice of Roman Catholicism and the persecution started after Cromwell's conquest of Ireland in 1649, then renewed in 1673, Oliver Plunkett never forsook his flock. He refused to go into exile and protect himself; he went into hiding instead. In order to bring the sacrament within the reach of the suffering faithful, he underwent the severest hardships, seeking out their abodes in the mountains and in the woods, enduring cold and extreme hunger. When the end of his life grew near, when all that God may have required of him was accomplished, and he stood in the English court hearing his guilty verdict returned by the jury along with a death sentence, he replied, "Deo Gratias—Thanks be to God!"

And then, the Chief Justice addressed Oliver Plunkett, saying, "Your condemnation is for setting up your false religion.".

Joseph Smith was killed in Illinois for similar reasons 164 years later, in 1844.

Numerous pleas for mercy had been made to save Oliver Plunkett's life, even by Louis XIV, king of France. Oliver was nevertheless hanged, drawn, and quartered at Tyburn on July 1st 1681, the last Roman Catholic martyr to die in England.

His body was initially buried in two tin boxes. The remains were then exhumed two years later, in 1683, and moved to Germany. The head was brought to Rome, then to Armagh, eventually to Drogheda in 1921, where seventy years later, I was able to see him. When I stood inside St Peter's of Drogheda looking at my family saint's head that does not decompose, his face a distinctive face, resting inside a sealed glass box, I saw how his eyes, closed and desiccated, expressed fervor still.

By then, several members of my family in France had already traveled to attend Oliver Plunkett's canonization in 1975; among them my uncle Jean-Claude and his son Frederic, who later was sworn in as a Knight of Malta. Oliver then became the first new Irish saint in almost 700 years.

It was nearly twenty-five years later, on the evening of March 8th 2014, that I found myself speaking to a microphone in front of hundreds of people at a Massachusetts Mormon stake conference, declaring, "It is the eyes of Mormons that have brought me here."

Having said this, I felt a stir in the air, standing as I was in a red jacket, a new convert to the Church of Jesus Christ of Latter-day Saints. The room was brightly lit. I spoke again, explaining how, "the truth in Mormon faith is revealed in eyes of people with a feel for miracles. Purity in them appears like innocence." I stopped a moment, and looked up from my paper. I saw many puzzled faces. I lowered my eyes again to continue reading. "But Mormon innocence is not like a child's inability for cunning. It is a reflection of intent. It is a *choice*, and a choice developed in a heart honed with clarity and otherworldly concerns. Theirs are the eyes of passion, they are the eyes of saints."

I held my breath. I was like a swimmer who started with élan; then a jump up and a dive; and once in the water, with little time to rally, must swim to the far end of the pool.

"Tell your conversion story—" I read further, "that is what I was asked to do here today. But I cannot explain why I have joined this church. Conversion stories cannot be explained by events unfolding within just weeks or months prior to baptism. They come from a lifetime process of interconnected moments, all too vast to be properly analyzed, too subtle to be perceived fully. Grace does not fall upon an unsuspecting being suddenly. Grace has been there all along. Grace has lurked, watched, and followed you throughout life, leaving a token down on the spot it knows you will happen to pass through. One day, you actually notice it, and wonder: shall I pick it up, finally?

"If you choose *not* to pick it up, Grace takes the token again, and puts it down further, staying near, camouflaged. The one time that you finally decide to pick up the token is when it appears that Grace has intervened. But it did not: Grace is continually active. Each day after conversion we are converted anew, because each day we choose anew. My conversion story might take a whole book for me to tell it—a book that follows a single thread—a book that uncovers the signs of my need for God from the beginning, and reveals its manifestations throughout my life.

"Perhaps my conversion started with the sound of the monastery bells in Turgeau when I was a child? And though my father ran from them, and took us far away to live on new grounds, it may be that I have been trying to get back to the rallying sounds of heaven's bells ever since? I am therefore not converted at all—I did not change religion—I was always a Christian. I am still a Christian. I belong to my ancestor Saint Oliver Plunkett's people, a family of Christians. I joined a church whose doctrines and ordinances are the closest of any present-day church to what they were in biblical times."

At this point of my talk, I glanced at faces in the front row. A woman was readjusting a blue scarf around her shoulders. I read again as if addressing her: "We are people each day converting anew, people thereby committed to act on the gift of metamorphosis. So, should we move about as if people alone with our own demons while a thousand worlds are waiting to burst out of our heads? Should we live like absent-minded window-gazers, and not with vision and coherence? Yes, I was born an innocent child, guilty of no single evil, a gymnast who thereafter trained herself in performing feats of balance in the unending stream of traffic. And then my father died in a car crash, and I was on my own. Fate packed me off to America, like so many immigrants. We looked for freedom, the opportunity to shape one's own narrative in the vastness of space, sky, and teeming cities, declaring, 'I am my newfound land!'

"Within each one of us waits a great fire in which to die and rise again. We have no other option but to transform. It is a high-minded urge to keep oneself under good management in the quiet lamplight. Very little points the way. The whole enterprise looks senseless enough, close scrutiny is impossible, yet we cannot afford to be caught unawares, disrespecting truth, renouncing dreams of wholeness and belonging, claiming it had all gone by too fast, the experience was thin in too many ways, we did not know how to deepen it."

All of a sudden, I realized how my voice was almost breaking. I narrowed my gaze to find a point of rest. The man I saw was chewing gum. I interpreted his frowning as distaste for my lack of simplicity in the way I spoke, but no matter "I recognize my insignificance without self-pity," I said with final vigor. "I nevertheless must acknowledge being in the hands of a master who must have taken some pride in what he might do with me. In choosing this baptism, I simply did what had to be done."

12 Apostasy Revisited

1. The Great Gathering

Rise up! All of you—the dead, disappeared, and disowned—souls scattered in the infinite, army unbound, faceless and famished; time has come for us to assemble on sand strips poured from God's hourglass! "It is good to die..." I was stupefied to realize how my thoughts were filled with words from the Haitian National Anthem in the early morning hours following my baptism. *"Pour le pays pour les ancêtres, mourir est beau... marchons unis*—It is good to die for country and ancestors... Let us march together as one." These words of The Dessalinièné anthem were perhaps arguably fitting, as words appealing to inordinate élans of the human heart. Conversion comes from such élan. It is also true that the anthem is part of the Haitian unconscious. We sang it every morning in school, standing in rows, grouped by age and grade.

I found myself in a different school almost every year because of my father's concern that his children receive the finest education. This continued even during my adolescent years in France, new schools bringing new friends, none lasting beyond the season. But in Haitian schools, the Dessalinièné was a constant. It was every Haitian youth's morning alarm call.

Of all my early school years in Haiti, it is the year that I spent in the Lerom School that I remember most. The unsubstantiated but veritable hatred its spinster director felt for me was memorable. She never missed a chance to punish me for trifles in the harshest way.

I trembled at her approach from behind while we sang the national anthem. I recognized her scent with singular alarm, slight as I was, wanting to either blot her or be blotted on the spot, an eight year old standing in the soft, uneven line of little girls whose greater height reached below the school's director's shallow breast. All the while I was experiencing this escalating panic, graves of ancestors were invoked in the Dessalinièneè vividly enough to seem incomprehensibly strewn about an infinite landscape.

Oldest among my cousins, Guslé was only ten when he held me with skinny arms at the baptismal fonts. A fading photograph in many yellowing shades of grey taken by the angel water basin attests to that day's festivities: my face and eyes emerge out of an abundance of intricate lace that surrounds my head, and embellish the embroidered white linen dress whose ruffled skirt cascades amply, fanning wide all the way down to Guslé's legs standing straight and spindly.

He too must have sung the Dessalinièneè each day at the boy's school of Saint Louis de Gonzague. He was twenty-four the year he died for his country and countrymen. It is hard to think of him now as an *ancestor*, spying on us from the roots of rainfall. I once heard his mother reproach, "My son died for the country, while he should have lived for his family."

2. A Phone Conversation

"Louise?"

"Hey…"

"How are you?"

"Okay… Happy to hear from you… What's up?"

"I wanted to tell you that I joined the Mormon Church—I got baptized and everything…"

"Really… when?"

"Two or three months ago…"

"And you're telling me *now*?"

"I didn't tell anybody… Only Roderick obviously…"

"Why not?"

"I wanted it between God and me... not worry about pleasing or displeasing anyone..."

"And what's changed that you're telling me now?"

"I have a request... your brother has come to me in dreams... three times now... asking to be baptized... each dream is different, but what he is asking is clear."

"*Guslé* wants to be baptized? And at a *Mormon* Church?"

"Yes... actually the proper name is The Church of Jesus-Christ of Latter-day Saints."

"Well, *that's* a mouthful... you've got to admit."

"Yes..."

"Why not something shorter, easier to remember?"

"Every word counts—every word carries a specific necessary meaning."

"Okay but *"saints"*—sounds presumptuous... I don't mean to argue..."

"Not at all... but actually, if you look into the New Testament, the apostles did not refer to followers of Christ as *"Christians,"* but as *"Saints"*—the *saints* have done this or that, at this or that church, Ephesus and what not... Our church tries to be really The Church of *Jesus Christ*—we try to make it as exactly as possible as it was instituted by Jesus... and *"Latter-day"* refers to our modern days—the last days before Christ's second coming."

"Humm... Anyway, it's an odd request to hear out of the blue...."

"I understand... but I *had* to tell you."

"Why?"

"I need your permission—you're his sister—it's a rule of the church—sacred ordinances for the dead must be performed by a closest living relative, or with the permission of one."

"What's this baptism about?"

"It's a modified version of the ancient Catholic rites of Prayers for The Dead ... a ritual by proxy."

"What do you mean, 'by proxy'?"

"Someone stands for him in the water... in his case, a man... But nothing is imposed, the ritual is an opportunity to choose, the dead can refuse the offer... and if they do, the ritual is void."

"It's been an eternity since I have given any thought to religious stuff Little Sis…"

"Don't worry, it's not a problem… just so you know, baptism for the dead is spoken about in the New Testament. There is biblical evidence that this ordinance was practiced in ancient times— for example, Saint Paul mentions it in Corinthians—he is addressing a group of apostates from Corinth who did not believe in the resurrection, although they still practiced baptism for the dead… he is worried because apostasy from the church had started…"

"What *'apostasy'*?"

"The abandonment of their religious beliefs and practices… Saint Paul asks the Corinthians why they would perform this ordinance if they did not believe in the resurrection."

"Where do *Mormons* fit here?"

"The Church of Jesus Christ of Latter-day Saints has revived the old ordinance of the baptism for the dead spoken of in the Bible."

"But my brother was baptized as a *baby*."

"The Mormon Church's view is that a great apostasy developed dramatically soon after the apostles died, but it started even before they died… the progressive abandonment of doctrinal beliefs and practices by Christians led to the loss of spiritual power, or *keys of the priesthood*… Then the potentially continuous line of succession from one apostle to the other was interrupted… You and I grew up in a kind of rogue church, yet we find *amazing* people throughout Christian history!"

"'Rogue'? You're not mincing words! So, my brother's baptism was worthless?"

"In a sense…"

"You people must vex a lot of folks with this…"

"We do… but history supports this view…"

"Well Sis, besides not being religious, it's good for you that I grew up Catholic… and not Protestant…"

"Why is that?"

"The Catholic Church has indeed already lost much credibility with their dirty laundry being all out in the world, and turning a blind eye for decades on the sexual abuse by priests all over… and when they found out, they just moved the priests to another parish."

"Well, Louise, that's not all they did wrong—what about the mass killing during the crusades, or the Spanish Inquisition? God could not have been well pleased by this use of priestly power?"

"I already agreed with you about Catholics... But Sis, what about the Reformation? Luther... Calvin... the whole revolt against the worldliness of the Catholic Church... wanting to go back to personal holiness? Wouldn't God have been pleased with that? And bless *that* church?"

"The *Protestant* Church? ... Okay, I mentioned the Spanish Inquisition. The Inquisition's tribunal was created as a consequence to the Protestant uprising, they even called it the *Holy* Office... Thousands were burned at the stake, and tens of thousands were condemned to suffer horrible tortures... The persecution of Christians in the first centuries after Christ's death was nothing compared to what the Inquisition did."

"Okay Sis, but the Inquisition was not done by *Protestants*..."

"I know Louise... still, you sound like a defender of the Protestant Church when you speak of their quest for personal holiness, you seem to forget that in that same 16th Century, a refusal to conform to the established worship was regarded by Protestants as much as by Catholics as treason against society."

"Treason?"

"Yes—*treason*. Michael Servetus, a Spanish theologian, physician, cartographer, and a Renaissance humanist of the *greatest* order was burnt at the stake for heresy, and at the personal instigation of *Calvin*, all because he had published views considered heretical."

"Hey... I am not defending them... Don't get excited..."

"I am not... just telling the facts... At the same time, in England, Anglican Protestants behaved the same way—they persecuted horrendously not only Catholics, but *all* Protestants who refused to conform to their established Church... Then what can we say about *holiness* or *priesthood power* in a church that propagates its faith by torture and death?"

"I agree—God and torture don't go together."

"And Louise, what kind of a church worthy of the name, Protestant or Catholic, would martyr men for their belief or their race?

... Inquisition, dictatorships, colonialism, is it not all the same spirit? Pope Jean-Paul II shaking hands with Baby Doc Duvalier at the airport? *Really* ... and look at Calvin... proclaiming the doctrine of absolute predestination and justification by faith alone—he basically nullified the rights to free agency God gave us, he gives a zero for the importance of individual efforts... we need not even try to become better people."

"Sis, I seem to have touched a nerve here?"

"No... I am fighting for your brother. Your questions are fundamental. In order for anyone to believe that Joseph Smith restored the keys to the priesthood, one must see how these were lost to begin with. I get that."

"But still, even if one agrees that the keys were indeed lost, that does not mean Joseph Smith restored them?"

"Hold it there... I am still addressing your original outburst about Guslé's baptism being worthless, and whether priests and ministers are powerless... the validity of Joseph Smith is another related issue, but the issue of the loss of priesthood power comes first, right?"

"Right. Granted."

"Alright... and you more or less said that the loss of the keys to the priesthood is easier to concede in regards to the Catholic Church, but not so much for the Protestant one. Did I get that right?"

"Truthfully... I don't really care..."

"It's okay... I do for both of us... so, about the Protestant Church and its priestly powers, do you remember Henry VIII, king of England?"

"What about him?"

"Pope Leo X was so happy when Henry VIII published a book in opposition to Luther's claim, that he awarded him with the title of Defender of the Faith... But when that same Henry thought the pope was taking too long to grant him a divorce from Catherine so he could marry Ann Boleyn, he sent the pope to hell, and married her anyway."

"That-a-boy!"

"Right... So, the pope excommunicated the king.... and then, to obey the king, the English Parliament passed the Act of Supremacy in 1534... and this happened only seventeen years after Luther came out with his rebel-rousing publications, the *Ninety-five Thesis*... The English parliament then declared absolute termination of all allegiance to papal authority. And this is the way the Church of England started... in *revolt*... without regard for or *any claim* of divine authority, without even a pretense of priestly succession... unlike the Catholic Church mind you... and my own meeting with a pope did not impress me favorably—kings or popes, they are all politicians."

"What was going on between Baby Doc and Jean-Paul II back then?"

"Baby Doc was worried about world opinion over his regime. He wanted to win the pope's favor so he'd look good, so they struck a deal. Baby doc agreed to give back the power to appoint all church officials in Haiti that Pope Paul VI had given Papa Doc... the closer we look, the more we see how religion has been reduced to politics and money matters..."

"You're hitting hard, Sis!"

"Maybe... But, going back to Henry VIII, notice that from the 16th Century down to our present time, Protestant sects that profess to have been founded on the tenets of Christianity have multiplied. There are hundreds of them! Some churches took the name of their place of origin, like the Church of England. Other churches are named after their promoters, so you have Lutherans, Calvinists, Wesleyans. And others are known from their doctrine, like the Methodists, the Baptists... But from the 16th Century down to the 19th, there was not a single church called the Church of Christ, even though it should seem the most obvious name... And the only church that asserted their authority by apostolic succession was the Catholic Church... But if the Church of England, the mother church of all Protestant churches did not have divine authority from the start, or did not even bother to claim it, how can her children gain from her the right to conduct in the things of God?"

"You've got a point..."

"And who will dare claim that man can start and develop a whole priesthood that God did not agree to first? Therefore, if the church's power and authority are of human origin, then the ordinances they perform, like baptism, are nothing but empty forms."

"Amen, Sis!"

"But you know Louise, at least the Roman Catholic Church is consistent in claiming a line of succession in the priesthood that goes back to the age of the apostles, and that it comes through an unbroken descent from Jesus's apostles, and even if the claim is untenable in the light of a rational analysis of history, mind you… However, when it comes to the Church of England, chief among the Protestant sects, they are by their own admission, *man-made* institutions, they have made no semblance of claim to the powers and authority of the holy priesthood. I'll even go further in this argument…

"I am listening."

"Think back as late as 1896 when the validity of the priestly orders in the Church of England was officially and openly discussed, both in England and in Rome. After endless argumentations, Pope Leo XIII finally issued a decree where he denies any degree of authority of the Anglican orders. He declared all Anglican ordinations to be absolutely null and void."

"What else could the pope do?"

"Of course! He'd be shooting himself in the foot… Be that as it may, the issue here is not that the pope denied authority to them, but that the Church of England would *not* have sought official recognition of its priestly status if it felt it had any real claim to the power and authority of the priesthood to begin with."

"Bull's eye, Cousin! … Okay, I'll admit there is a lot here for me to digest. But I have to get going… there's a problem at the pond… a blue heron is eating my fish. I am trying not to shoot the dang bird… But let me ask you before I have to go… did you say that the apostasy started with the death of the apostles?"

"No. It was *before* all the apostles died!"

"What happened?"

"How can I squeeze centuries and so much bloodshed into a brief summary? But okay…. I'll try… You and I agree that we're not dealing here with legends, right?"

"What do you mean?"

"We accept that the premise at the core of this Christian adventure is the *fact* that Jesus Christ established His church upon the earth by personal ministration, right?"

"Right."

"All Christian sects and churches are in agreement on this, yes?"

"I have already said *yes*."

"Okay... the questions therefore at stake are whether Jesus's church remained the way it was established by the Savior himself... and if it has maintained the same organized existence upon the earth, lasting from the time of the apostles up to the present?"

"I agree."

"Okay... and if it has remained the same, and it has maintained that existence, it means that there should be documented proof that priestly authority, or the keys to the priesthood, have been transferred down from the apostles who initially received them from Jesus Christ... Or, is there evidence to the contrary—namely that priestly authority was actually lost, or interrupted, after the death of Christ's apostles... yes?"

"Yes... *yes...*"

"Well, Louise, let me start with *context*—context is crucial. The Christian saga began at a time when Jews were subjects of the Roman Empire, yet they were free to observe their religious and cultural customs... But, Jews stood apart, they were confident that they possessed superior lineage, literature, priestly organization, and law. They saw their neighbors, mostly Romans, as idolatrous pagans who worshipped vacant effigies... Yet, even though they were perceived as one people by the rest of the world, Jews were divided into many contending sects and parties—you had, for example, the Pharisees and the Essenes... But still, pagans were not bothered by Jewish arrogance—for them, Israelites were just bizarre fanatics... So, each group judged the other one inferior... In the meantime, the apostles Peter and John the Revelator, all foresaw the apostasy... the prophet Isaiah already had as well... and apostasy soon showed in the rise of unauthorized teachers who preached false doctrines."

"There we go!"

"Now, stages of apostasy are twofold... There is apostasy *from* the church, and apostasy *of* the church—in the first you have people abandoning the truth, and in the other the church itself is moving away from the *divine* laws instituted by Christ, and becoming more of a *human* institution."

"Which of the two apostasies came first?"

"Hard to say... you can imagine that unity and peace could not last long in a church made up of Jews and Gentiles who had contempt for each other... The persecution of the Primitive Church was both Judaic *and* Pagan—it was competition for power and control... The unauthorized teachers who preached false doctrines were not outside rivals, they were adherents to the church, but wanted the influence and authority the apostles had... You can see why they would want the apostles dead."

"Yes... get off that chair so I can have it!"

"Exactly! Jewish priests and rulers persecuted and condemned to death as many Christians as they could... But the opposition coming from Jews was more Judaic than Jewish. The conflict was between systems, not between nations... *Judaic* hostility was fueled by a secret fear of the progress of Christianity and that Judaism might lose credit... You see, the belief in a single living God had distinguished Christians and Jews from the rest of the world. Therefore, Jews saw Christianity as a rival religion. They were perhaps also afraid that if Christianity came to be accepted as the truth, they would be seen as killers of the Messiah."

"Yeah... we've heard that..."

"Of course... however, *pagan* hostility came from a people essentially idolatrous. The Roman Empire was the main persecutor. It's strange if you consider how tolerant Romans had been before. But the intolerant zeal of Christians themselves, and the simplicity of their ritual, might have been very irritating pagans."

"Like that blue heron of mine! I am very irritated by it."

"Don't make me laugh, Louise, I am trying to focus... Anyway, on the subject of killing, you can identify eras of persecutions by the ruling emperor—we had Nero, Domitian, Trajan, Hadrian, Marcus Aurelius... Christians continued to suffer throughout the second and third centuries. Severus and Decius were brutal... They used the metal rack, scourging, fire, plunging and drowning, decapitation, starvation, upside-down crucifixion... The last persecution was under

Diocletian. It was so severe that when it ended, people thought that the Christian Church was completely eradicated."

"Jesus!"

"That's right... so seeing that *context* Louise, you can understand better the causes for the apostasy *from* the church, and why people left the church."

"For sure."

"But then, as to why people left the church, we have external causes *and* internal causes... the primary *external* causes of the apostasy were the persecutions. People simply feared for their lives, so they went back to the safety of their former religions... And yet, hundreds of Christians still manifested their faith publicly, and accepted their martyrdom... And then, another external cause, of course, was plain human greed—provincial governors and magistrates began profiting from selling certificates, testimonials, and exemptions to wealthy Christians who could afford to buy immunity from the persecutions... you can then well imagine that Christian started fighting among themselves—some of them saw the purchase of immunities as cowardice and betrayal."

"Guslé died because of betrayal!"

"Ah Louise... but your brother is beyond all that now... our conversation is precisely about that—he wants to be cleansed of it all, in a church where it *counts*."

"Alright... continue your story..."

"Where was I? Ah... yes...so now, the *internal* causes of apostasy *from* the church were Greed's dancing partners—Vanity, Licentiousness, Avarice, Deception, and Usury... Cyprian was bishop of Carthage in the middle of the third Century when already he was complaining how the discipline given to Christians had been corrupted, how bishops who ought to be guides had given themselves up to secular pursuits... Cyprian was eventually martyred—he argued that Jesus had foretold us the coming apostasy, he refused to sacrifice to pagan deities, and stayed with Christ. When he was sentenced to die by the sword, his answer was the same as Oliver Plunkett's, my ancestor, fourteen centuries later, 'Thanks be to God!'"... Perhaps Oliver got it from Cyprian?

"I did not know you had a saint in your family?"

"On my mother side... Anyway, a multitude followed Cyprian to an open place in the city to witness his execution. They watched him remove his garments without assistance, kneel down, pray, and then blindfold himself."

"Sis! Men's courage at times is beyond belief..."

"Yes... but it is *belief* that gives courage... belief in something larger than oneself... I feel proud that the history of Christians can boast such men... But Cyprian's concerns were merited—there remained little evidence already of any close alliance between Christ and the Church towards the end of the third century... Faith in Christ appeared to be used for ordinary traffic, or as a profession... Human vice caused a general rot of godliness."

"But Sis, *then* came *Constantine!*"

"Right! *Constantine*, A.D. 306—end of persecutions, official protection for Christians, and Christianity becomes the religion of state... And what Christian at that time would have cared whether Constantine's conversion was for politics or out of true faith?"

"Yep! And didn't Constantine get baptized only shortly before his death... after thirty one years of his reign?"

"Sis? I thought you did not care about religion? How do you know this so precisely?"

"Memory is a strange thing. Why does something stick or not beats me...memory is an ally or an aggressor, depending on what comes up... but about Constantine, I know the story. Perhaps it was all those Christian movies we watched when we were children, Christians thrown in the arenas, fighting against lions... remember?"

"Yes I do... But when Constantine became the head of the church, pagan temples were transformed into churches. Idols were demolished. Bishops suddenly were more esteemed than generals. Competition for church promotion became intense. Twelve thousand men, women, and children were baptized in Rome within a single year... But even if the Christian Church was transformed after Constantine, it had already shown a lot of evidence of apostasy, especially if you examine Christ's original principles. Historians wrote a lot about that... Eusebius, Greek historian, and then Milner too... but greater apostasy still evolved with Jewish converts to Christianity who were still attached to the Judaism of their childhood. They tried to modify it. Many sects and parties evolved, cults, schools… Each one had different theories about the constitution of the soul, the definition of sin, the nature of Deity… and then a horde of philosophical perversions grew in complexity—the *Gnostics* showed up—they brought some of the worst adulterations the Christian doctrine suffered. No absurdity seemed too much. They even denied that Jesus had a body whilst He lived as a man… Then they introduced the idea of antagonism between body and spirit—the body came to be viewed as an incubus and a curse… Men started practicing all sorts of self-tortures—the several orders of celibate recluses, hermits, and monks came out of this view of life… And as if all that was not enough, the *Platonists* and the *New Platonists* showed up with a new conception of the Godhead… And then it was *Arianism* with discussions about the Holy Trinity… It got so much out of hand that Emperor Constantine was forced to summon a council—it became the Council of Nicea, in 325… They composed the Nicene Crede we learnt when we were kids…"

"I don't know about you Sis, but I only remember the beginning of that Credo!"

"Not me. I can recite most of it, but in French…"

"Good for you!"

"Nothing to boast about… However the council of Nicea didn't solve much. The travesty continued—*ritual perversions* were added to philosophical ones. Unnecessary added rites and elaborate ceremonies made a mess of the simplicity of the original gospel and worship… Then sermons by rhetoricians replaced testimony bearing… and then Christians got back to idolatry and started devotion to images and effigies. That began in the fourth century, and became general in the fifth… And now we arrive at *Baptism*—our original bone of contention."

"It was not contention. I just want to understand…"

"Of course… Baptism was done originally by complete immersion to symbolize death before resurrection, but only after a conscious profession of faith and repentance. Yet, baptism of newborns became the norm, and only with a mere sprinkling of water."

"I don't remember my own, but I remember my children's…"

"Well, for my Mormon baptism, just know that I was *completely* immersed! … But other ordinances that characterized the original church were also modified or plain abandoned—the imposition of hands to bestow the newly baptized with the Holy Ghost, for example."

"Was this done at your Mormon baptism?"

"Of course! … And the Sacrament of the Lord's Supper too was transformed—long prayers were added, there were ostentatious display of gold and silver vessels, a lot of pomp… Remember how I told you that the original gospel was simple and might have annoyed pagans? … But then, another form of idolatry became accepted with the doctrine of Transubstantiation—the host is seen as the actual flesh and blood of Christ. I read somewhere that Roman Catholics claim great antiquity for the belief in Transubstantiation, but the historian Milner explained that it was taught in the ninth century, became dogma in the eleventh, and made an article of creed in the twelfth (d)."

"I'll admit to you, Sis, that I never bought the idea of bread and wine being Christ's flesh and blood… a bit creepy too."

"But didn't you do all you could to avoid letting the holy host touch your teeth?"

"Oh yes!"

"Isn't that funny if you consider that you did not believe in it? It shows how deep religious concepts anchor in our subconscious, and why it is hard to convert… But I am not quite done with apostasy…"

"I really need to go, Sis…"

"I have *one* last point about church *organization*!"

"Alright, go ahead…"

"Thanks… now, church organization was greatly modified too. In the Primitive Church, there were apostles, pastors, high priests, seventies, elders, bishops, priests, teachers, and deacons… and we have no historical evidence that the presiding council of the church, namely the council of the twelve apostles, no indication whatsoever that it continued beyond the ministry of those who had been ordained during Christ's life, or soon after His ascension—there is no record of any ordination of individuals to the apostleship, nothing beyond the people whose callings and ministry are already chronicled in the New Testament... and as a historical record the New Testament ends with the first century. Peter and Paul organized the church at Rome, but Peter never ordained or transferred the priesthood keys to another apostle he wanted to succeed him... And in view of all that, the question of the papacy is shown as a troublesome affair, to say the least..."

"Ah, Sis, you and the pope!"

"Laugh at me all you want, my dearest Louise, but the fact is that the contention made by the Catholic Church that the present pope is the last lineal successor to the Rome bishopric, *and* to the apostleship, is a falsehood—the first time that the rightful supremacy of the Roman pope was questioned was under *Constantine*, it was not during the Protestant Reformation, or even by Henry VIII... The question with the rightful supremacy issue started when the bishop of Constantinople declared his equality to the bishop of Rome. Then the quarrel between bishops of the East and of bishops of the West increased during the next centuries, until the bishop of Constantinople finally had enough, and in 1054, he broke all allegiance to the bishop of Rome... That's why we have the distinction between Greek Catholics and Roman Catholics lasting to this day."

"I see..."

"Yes... but the question about the pope's rightful supremacy does not end there initially, the Roman pope was elected through the vote of the people... then it was by the clergy... and finally, the College of Cardinals took it over in the 11th century. The title of Pope was adopted. It means papa, or father. This way, an unprecedented form of paternalism was implanted in our Christian subconscious... Even as a girl, I felt compelled to bow to a mere *photo* of the pope..."

"Not me!"

"Good for you, Louise... But regardless, Roman pontiffs showed more interest in power than in faith—they had already begun trafficking in the fourth century, selling indulgences, pardons and God's forgiveness, and then the pope assumed authority over purgatory itself—he handed temporal pardon, and *eternal* pardon, and he canceled penalties of the afterlife—he was basically selling license to sin... No wonder Luther's blood cell count exploded! ... Then the pope's power gradually increased in the 12th Century, and more so in the 13th.... And soon enough these popes were no longer satisfied with supremacy in church affairs, they wanted *temporal* as well as *spiritual* sovereignty, they wanted to be arbiters of the fate of kingdoms and empires, they wanted to be rulers over kings and princes, and direct the internal affairs of nations... and this is how I met a pope... who seemed quite okay with giving only a kiss in passing to the island soil of an abused population, and be feasted by their pleasure-mongering autocrats."

"Watch out Sis! Your blood-cell count..."

"But doesn't that make you angry, Louise? ... And do you remember the urge Joseph Smith felt when he was confused by the differing opinions in the many Protestant Churches? ... Do you understand now why he prayed in a secluded grove, asking God, 'What church shall I join?' And why God might have answered, 'None of them'?"

"Okay Sis... you win... I give you permission to baptize Guslé... If it doesn't help, it won't hurt either."

13 Debout Les Morts!

Rise Up, Ye the Dead!

1. Baptism for the Dead

The experience of doing baptism for the dead was different than going through my own baptism. I was able to focus on what I felt, rather than on "doing it right."

Each time I descend in the baptismal waters in the name of the dead, I affirm anew the worth of this journey. Entering the water, feet standing on the first step going down the baptismal fonts, the water's warm caress seems eerily unsubstantial whilst it also steadies me.

My calves are embraced on the second step. Clothes feel suctioned, adhering to my skin in singular intimacy. Imagine that you are a child inclined to suck your thumb. The inexpressibly warm, all-around enfolding clutch, clasp, and cuddle are the same: your whole being is somehow gathered in that one thumb, all of you contained in the moist, cushy encasement of your mouth for a timeless moment; stare all the while at the wild world around, and you nevertheless still experience yourself enclosed in a protective separateness; shut your eyes, and sense the enduring ease in being shielded. Yet, let an exacting adult suddenly pull the thumb out like a plug, and you again experience your body as no more than a quivering portion of exposed flesh that endlessly yearns for a return to the fluid into which it once was immersed in the womb. Such was the yearning evoked on the second step.

On the third step down, my knees feel held in between odd kisses that ascend my body while I descend in the water. It is as if a thousand invisible lips were waiting to apply themselves to my body to express their infinite gratitude that I have come to do this in their name. The body is most vulnerable at the knees; there, we may be inviolable if we bend yet shattered if inflexible and proud. Articulations seem to be the soul's insight into, and physical expression of, crossroads of the mind. A great intelligence has, through the knees, afforded us the timely might to succumb, bow, and genuflect. Within its architecture, man's skeleton stumbles on an array of emotional and spiritual intersections and standpoints.

Following the knees, my thighs are soon seized like tree trunks, silken water creeping up my skin by increments depending on how fast I proceed. Then it is the groin and stomach. Memory is stirred insidiously at that point, recalling pain buried deep within. And yet, this is when I relax most in the descent. Weight begins to wane, time dissolves. Fluidity becomes part of my sense of self.

When the water is at the waist, that is the moment when I meet face to face with a man waiting there, endowed with the priesthood, a strong arm onto which I may lean and abandon myself. First my head falls back, crown of my being, then all of me feels pulled and plunges backwards into the baptismal waters, to be cleansed, reshaped, contrived anew.

The scriptures refer time and again to the arm of God. I find that in the closed-eye experience in which I am then willingly briefly immersed, the arm of God is a benevolent one, the believable extension of a creator who dreamt the inexpressible velvet feel found inside the hand of a newborn. It becomes possible, at those times, to think that infinity may be a liquid state where breath and vision are mental sensations of being, rather than a function of organs, causing me to wonder if the unborn smile in the womb.

Coming out of the baptismal water is like being born out of that womb, it takes courage, resignation, and obedience. The baptismal clothes are wet, cold, and dense; they unevenly adhere and cling to my shivering body, like an ill-fitting skin, a shield in which my body trembles, cloistered.

When I find myself alone in the shower shortly afterwards, I begin to peel off this curiously resistant shell, standing naked behind a white curtain drawn shut, and I remember the long ride home waiting for me, a desolate amble in a wintry parking lot, cars like war bunkers halted in rows, little tanks meant to tackle the freeway, the speed, greed, and fury of thousands of beings embattled like me. However, within my heart, I feel that all I am experiencing is a journey to which I consented; the primary obedience is to myself, the word of honor given and sworn before birth to the heavenly presbytery—I believe I came to earth with an inherent, resolute design.

2. The Love of Children

On a day filled with intent, I went to the temple for my father. I stepped into a large, unearthly house. I walked through the luminous reception hall to where two white-haired men dressed in white suit, shirt and tie, welcomed me with uncommon courtesy. They stood behind a white marble-top reception desk; both their eyes were blue; tales of ghostly entities meant to usher the dead came to mind.

It is an old idea, the one claiming that we will all be given back our youthful bodies after death. I have joined others in that belief. A belief for example, that my father's mother will again be the shapely, fine-featured, lively young woman Jules Phipps married long ago. World War I was a wholly different enterprise that started soon after their marriage. A man of honor had no choice but to participate in that carnage. Jules spoke little; his goodbyes must have been sparse in emotions. He returned to Haiti with a medal for bravery, and the address of a war companion with whom he exchanged letters until one of them died a lifetime later.

My father's own battles were a whole other matter. Father and son were different men. Ships bringing soldiers from oversees took so long to reach France that the Caribbean troops arrived at the time of the debacle. Of his circumstances during WWII, my father remembered his horse best. Back in his country, it is unclear whether or not young women resumed lining up to catch a sight of him on his way to the tennis court at the Turgeau Club.

Baptism for the dead is done by proxy through a living person standing in the water in place of the dead. For my father, as for Guslé, the proxy had to be a man. I had been the proxy for both my grandmothers, but could only sit and witness from the sides of the baptismal fonts when a man endowed with the priesthood stood in the water with the proxy for my father, and invoked, "Brother Morales... in the name of Jesus Christ... for Louis Marie Alexis Delmar Phipps, who is dead..." Tears were clouding my eyes when I suddenly discerned the painting of a mountain hanging on the wall across from me.

Seeing the painting of a mountain transported me some fifteen years back to the afternoon of the second anniversary of my father's death. I had walked the streets of Cambridge like one both unseen and blind, when I suddenly found myself on JFK Street, opposite a bookstore of esoteric literature in front of which a floating banner flapped high up in the moist air of a rainy Spring afternoon. "Medium's Day," the banner advertised; its bright colors clamored joyfully under the grey sky.

I had always enjoyed that bookstore: Helena Petrovna Blavatsky's theosophist writings could be found along those of anthroposophist Rudolph Steiner; how-to books on astrology and other unusual sciences; all manner of bronze Buddha, Krishna and Parvati; giant crystal balls mounted on eagle-claw tripods, surrounded by batik cloth hangings, painted scrolls of Tibetan mandalas, lithographs of lotus-enshrined deities in the company of multiple avatars, consorts, and lesser divinities, all of them enveloped in emanations floating from bottled essential oils and boxed incense; the mixed scents would linger on clothes for days afterwards. I went in with a firm step.

Medium's Day turned out to be an uncommon event. In a large, bare room stretching above the entire length of the actual bookstore below, an assortment of mediums sat. Stationed behind a variety of small tables, they quietly observed the few customers entering; some were curious passersby like me, entering hesitantly, eyes shifting right and left, trying to asses the situation at a glance, and then feeling moved to select a medium, as if absentmindedly; others were reluctant to stare for fear of being judged rude, unwilling to feel a circumstantial obligation in the eventuality that their eyes met those of a medium to whom they were not drawn. An empty chair waited for a client in front of each table. The choice rested between various readers of playing cards, tarot cards, hand-readers, or star-readers like my late friend Ali, the astrologer. My eyes fell on a young man whose body took very little room behind a narrow table; he seemed shy, uncomfortable almost to the point of wanting to excuse himself and leave; small hands with translucent skin on fingers of fine porcelain held a deck of Tarot of Marseilles cards. I recognized the cards with a slight ache; Ali had taught me how to read them at a time of life when the upside-down body of The Hanged Man card came up often enough during readings as to seem my alter ego. The young medium's large, watery blue eyes were of the sort that made one think them likely to slip out of his face at any moment; their impermanence moved me. "May I sit down?" I asked him. He startled, but smiled encouragingly.

Tarot cards were invented in northern Italy in the 15th Century. They were introduced to southern France when the French conquered Milan and the Piedmont in 1499. The name of the Marseille Tarot deck of cards was coined as early as 1889 by the French occultist Papus; it was used to refer to a variety of closely related designs then being made in the southern French city of Marseilles, a center of playing cards manufacture.

I was not aware of it at first, but found out soon after, having had it explained to me once the reading was over, that the young medium in front of whom I had sat, thinking him a Tarot reader, was actually a member of the Spiritualist Church. They are people who believe in the survival of personality and physical appearance after death, a fact that they feel proven through mediumship; I now know that this belief is also shared in the Mormon Church. A reading by a Spiritualist medium follows a general pattern: the Spiritualist medium sees and hears the dead who at the start of a séance identify themselves in subtle but unmistakable ways; whether they present themselves at times in their aged or in their youthful form, it is imperative that the departed give ample personal information to allow their being recognized beyond any doubt by the living relative present. What happened to me next was part of that classic pattern.

"The man I see is asking me to thank you for Schubert's Ave Maria sung at his funeral," the young medium said, looking up and gazing past me, both startling and confusing me.

I quickly understood however that something had shifted. I wondered what had happened. Was he having a vision?

"His eyes are green." He said again.

"Ah... my father..." I murmured.

The ensuing conversation was brief, but lasting in memory. The medium began listing a series of particulars he later explained to me had been either shown or whispered to him. "The presence is displaying mangos and avocados he picked off trees from his garden. He is putting them in a drawer full of his socks."

"This is indeed my father ... Why he is here? ... Ask him..."

The medium took a pause, eyes closed. Then he said softly, "the presence tells me 'I am here because you need me.'"

A short-lasting exchange then continued between the ghost of my father and me, with the medium acting as intermediary. Overall, most of the dialogue had to do with identifying the presence.

I soon, too soon, sensed a growing heaviness in the air after only too few words had been said; I felt that my father was about to fade and go. At that point, the young man's body twitched slightly; a kind of opacity came over his eyes; he was almost inaudible when he murmured, "the presence indicates that he has to go... but he will remain close."

I quickly implored, "Ask him to say one last thing!"

The medium hesitated, turned his ear to the side, and said in a whisper, "Remember the mountain... the presence tells you to 'remember the mountain'."

The last time I saw him alive, my father and I stood on the mountainside south of Pétionville, in Thomassin. He was building a house of which he was proud, and meant to be his last. Loose chickens from neighboring farmlands had invaded his rock garden already blooming, daring to peck at our feet, looking for worms. My father died of a stroke and the subsequent car crash when the house was nearly finished, and he already had imagined his life there in several ways. However, that last day we had together in Thomassin, his face glowed in spite of the pervading sadness in the moment. I was flying back to the US early next morning, and it was not known how long it would be until I might return. Nevertheless, he was showing me with one sweeping gesture of the arm how clearly one could see the Port-au-Prince bay from that high mountain on which the house stood, and how much of the all-around landscape was circumscribed in our view as well. Surely, my heart was breaking that day.

I have pondered over this last moment we shared, both at the time of his funeral in Port-au-Prince, and again after receiving his message through the medium on JFK Street. There were many possibilities of interpretation: Was my father telling me to always observe things from a distance? To remember the view we had? To perceive how clear and sharp the world is when one examines the situation from an elevated stance? Was he suggesting I should enjoy how the eye and mind can encompass much more if one stands high up? But I also realized then, that whether or not all these questions were part of his message, he was surely asking me was to remember Haiti itself, the land of my, and of his birth, the land of our common ancestors, the earth of my beginnings and lineage, the springboard of my destiny, the country of my roots, and the roots of this story.

These memories of my father, and associated thoughts, were stirred all over again when I saw the mountain painting during the baptism for the dead I was performing for him at the temple. It was as if he was beckoning to me anew to remember the mountain, revealing to me then what he had always meant—remember your father. But now there was an added tenor; "remember the mountain," meant, "remember all of us, your family, all of us who are dead."

Not on Mount Moriah, site of the Temple Mount in Jerusalem, but on a Haitian mount eternally gathering dust, did I come to understand how a child is bound to the father, and that we are all images of Isaac, all of us coming to be Abraham's assenting lamb. My father said, "Remember the mountain." But it was God then who asked, "Remember *Me*."

My godfather died in great bloodshed. When I see icons of John the Baptist, I remember my family; not only he, the saint, whose head was brought to King Herod, but also Oliver Plunkett, whose head was demanded by King Charles II, and Guslé Villedrouin's, flown to an impatient Haitian dictator.

It was not just betrayal of those who trained them, or the lack of food and munitions that turned my godfather and his twelve companions into prey, nor was it Duvalier's men and might. The young men who fought alongside my cousin had offered their lives from the start. They were compliant lambs, obeying an insistent ideal about family and brotherhood: Charles Forbin was one of the twelve; so were the Armand brothers, Max and Jacques; Geto Brière; Jacques Wadestrandt (once Edward Kennedy's friend at Harvard); Jean Gerdès; Mirko Chandler and Yvan D. Laraque; last to die in battle in October were Roland Rigaud, Charles Jourdan, and Guslé Villedrouin, their leader; but last to die that year 1964, on November 12, were Louis Drouin and Marcel Numa, executed in front of the Port-au-Prince cemetery.

All of them were men who grew up under the sinister reality of a murderous government. All were men able to make the ultimate sacrifice of their lives at an age hardly older than that of Mormon men who at eighteen decide to be missionaries; men like Elders Langford and Fenn, becoming members of the Melchizedek Priesthood, an honored role in Abrahamic religions, modeled on Melchizedek, the mighty king and priest who appears in the Book of Genesis, the first man in the Hebrew Bible to be given the title of high priest.

3. The Bird Who Did Not Flee

It was Memorial Day, and overcast. A lonesome stroll under a grey sky towards which I repeatedly lifted my gaze, filled me with thoughts about the Mormon belief that families are connected forever, finding each other after death, remaining together for all generations of time, and throughout all eternity. It may be that for some, this would be hell; however, another axiom attached to this belief is that we are taught and guided further, expected to continue growing spiritually after death. When we meet again in the afterlife, we therefore meet on novel terms, and may reconstruct our emotional connection.

The drizzle was expected to last all day. I had gone for a stroll to a nearby lake that is crossed in its middle by a bridge whose timber links opposite shores with a soft arch. The bridge's seasoned planks and wooden resonance under my steps evoked aspects of monastic life and esthetics. I saw no one, but a bird.

The heron seemed to have been waiting for me on that early morning hour. The tall bird observed me motionlessly with a round impassive eye as I drew closer. Wet and doubtful on thin parallel legs, elongated neck swelling into a greater feathered body mass at one end and a minimal head at the other, comprising eyes and beak, the creature's whole body traced a stunning sinuous white line against the somber backdrop of the water behind. He stood on a small mound of marshy ground shared by sparse, winding weeds and sticks. The concentric circles drawn by each raindrop falling on the lake's motionless surface echoed my sense of self, one expanding, growing more delicate until it would vanish, seeing God in everything.

The bird appeared to be foregoing the use of wings. We watched each other in unspoken recognition and acceptance one of the other. I stayed there, pensive for a long while with gray bird and fine rain as sole, discreet, uplifting company. I wondered is this bird was other than what he seemed?

The male given name Zechariah is derived from the Hebrew, and means, "The Lord Has Remembered." People in all ages have given their children names that carry the force of an idea. Some names were received through divine inspiration, or such was the claim. The phonetic beauty of the name "Zechariah" reveals how little sound is needed to evoke a vast notion, such as the Lord remembering us— can it then be said that if we are in God's mind as memory, He is therefore aware of us, and can also be assumed to be watching us; and can it thus be deduced further that if His eyes are watchful, His mind accompanies us and, unavoidably guides us. The name Zechariah alone, encapsulated all this.

Twenty four years before his death, a commanding angel come in a dream to my godfather's pregnant mother wrote in red letters on a wall the name "Guslé," leaving it to history, and not to language, to decipher its portent.

In the Book of Zechariah whom the Lord has remembered, it is said that on the twenty-fourth day of the eleventh month, November, the very month when the last of the Jeune Haiti rebels died, Zechariah had a vision in the night: he saw a man riding a red horse among myrtle trees. Myrtle grew on the hills about Jerusalem; they produce snow-white flowers bordered with purple, which some say emit a perfume more exquisite than that of the rose. Behind the man in the myrtle, there were many more horses, some red, some speckled, and others white.

"What are these horses, my Lord?" Zechariah asked the Lord's angel near him.

It is however the man riding a red horse among the myrtle trees who answered Zechariah, "These are they whom the Lord has sent to walk to and fro through the earth."

I wondered how I was to recognize those whom the Lord has sent to walk to and fro while I observed the gray bird unmoved by the drizzle. Were some of these messengers born among my family? Were some others my friends? It was startling this way in which the bird looked at me in the eyes, staying still; his ways could not be confused with the fleeing ways of birds. How will I know the messenger from the rest? Will messengers be known by their fruits?

The bird seemed to have felt that my thoughts were veering; his feathers lifted slightly, and he appeared to shiver. The faces of Guslé, Victoria, Ali, Father Lespinasse, Father Campion, Michael Miller, Elders Langford and Fenn, Clayton Christensen... and even those of my godfather's twelve rebel companions presented themselves to me.

Were they messengers? ... What does it mean that they came from different churches? ... I suddenly felt the cold. Within that chill came other faces and questions. People who had a violent, or simply a deterrent effect on me and the choices I made, may they too be considered messengers, or instruments, if in the end they unwittingly pushed me towards the fulfillment of my destiny, and towards the accomplishment of any good that may have been prophesied in regards to my life?

The idea of possible fulfillment brought me calm. The bird opened his beak as if to swallow, or expel, what he only felt. Ask your own questions, Clayton Christensen said. And this came to mind: among his many visions, Zechariah also saw Joshua, who one might describe as charged by Moses with selecting and commanding a militia group for their first battle after leaving Egypt. I looked up to the skies. "Was Guslé inspired by angels to lead his own militia group?"

Joshua was addressed as a high priest in Zechariah's vision, while he stood in front of the angel of the Lord. Satan was also there, creating tension. Joshua was clothed with filthy garments before the angel of the Lord. Seeing this, the angel ordered that Joshua be given clean garments, and that an immaculate turban also be placed on his head. "Behold!" the angel then said to Joshua, "I have cleansed you of your iniquity. I will therefore change your garments, and replace them with festive ones. And if you walk thereafter in my ways and obey my orders, you shall be a judge in my house and in my courts. You will walk among those you see here standing by, they are men to be wondered at. I will use them as signs."

I suddenly marveled about how wonderfully personal my reading of scripture had become. "Men to be wondered at!" the angel said. How comforting it is for me to imagine Guslé wearing festive garments forever, walking among men whom the angel revealed to be, messengers, and sent as signs.

I let myself be transported, my body keeping company with the bird, but my mind flying with new freedom. I thought how we all may be cleansed in water, adopt festive garments, walk near God and angels, stand among the myrtle trees, reveling in fragrance more exquisite than that of the rose. . It is a choice we can make.

14 Belonging

1. The Way We Mourn

I remember my father's back most vividly: his warm, smooth, honey-colored skin stretching over a muscular, triangular structure expanding upward from the waist, fanning widest at the shoulders, until it rounded into smooth contours extending powerfully to strong arms capable of carrying much. At the nape of the neck, a wine-colored birthmark showed afresh after each haircut.

If I could have spoken to him before he died, and thanked him for all his ministrations, I might have borne his passing better; as it was, it oppressed me. I certainly tried to make as light as possible of my loss, but clearly without success. I became a coywolf—a hybrid creature surviving on the outskirts of civilization. It is clear that I have nonetheless acquired an unprecedented independence, and the freedom to be the person I choose to become.

It occurred to me that the only thing remaining was to transform myself before the world could intervene, mocking or disturbing the new balance I'd found; rework myself just enough so as to wean myself further each day, even if it seemed unthinkable. It was not as if I was so pleased with myself as to be unwilling to change in the first place, even though I should be doing so, not because I no longer found it all satisfying, but merely to propitiate God.

But changing course has been arduous. Mormon theology sensibly answered my questions about human existence and our destination in the universe, yet it has been a challenge to find my place in the family-centered Mormon culture, when converting meant the progressive death of an old sense of self I had previously assembled, and trying to reorganize again. It may be that the need for reassembling oneself rises up periodically in one's life, and that I will be challenged in that way again in the future.

But for now, it is as if I have come to live in a vast new house with solid walls, but whose furnishings are unfamiliar; these give the house its great character while they are not required for it to stand. Within the house, I communicate in an alternative doctrinal language I chose to learn, its grammar being a powerful one, but the vocabulary still feeling most peculiar.

Mourning takes time. It is a slow weaving of mental processes acting towards a reconstruction of the self. The internal undertaking makes the same demands on the mind, whatever the loss incurred, whether of parents, country, moral compass, or one's former beliefs and religion. People mourn around a particular story that explains their loss. That story becomes the fabric of the new being who eventually emerges, and protects one's ability to survive loss and continue living. My own story of loss has been woven around the way I am able to recompose my childhood in Haiti and in France, translate the meaningful experiences that shaped my spirit, acknowledge gifts unwittingly received from true people of God whom I have met.

I had the opportunity to meet Elder Langford's family at the end of his mission. In spite of their divorce, his parents had decided to come as a family, all the younger children brought along for the reunion with the oldest child and sibling. "I am apprehensive about their coming," Elder Langford said. "How am I going to relate to them as the son they knew? During the two years of my mission, I have had to redefine the true character of the childhood I remember. Are the new pieces going to fit?" He chose a popular doughnut shop as the place for us to rendezvous. The time we spent there was brief, and he laughed a lot. Every mouthful of his donut made him grunt and marvel. His parents were very kind and well mannered.

"I am glad to have met you," the father said during our goodbyes. "You are a very courageous woman."

"How's that?"

"Converting is a bold act. Meeting you makes me miss my own mission days."

"Where did you go?"

"Paris."

2. New Family and Heritage

It was only after I converted to the Church of Jesus-Christ of Latter-day Saints that I started learning about the history and culture of the Mormon people, and found myself wondering what I had gotten myself into. My initial inquiry had been purely theological. It can be argued that I observe Mormon cultural heritage from a skewed perspective.

I see Mormon money as "new money." Their children are not heirs to ivy-covered castles, coat of arms, or portrait galleries. Mormon merit and access to privilege is not inherited, it is personal, and comes as a result of individual choices. All that Mormon children inherit is the gospel; the best of them see it as the only lasting wealth.

The Book of Mormon is on my nightstand. It now forever rests there in the company of a leather-bound copy of the King James Bible that Roderick gave me to celebrate my baptism. The Bible is a necessary companion to the Book of Mormon, spoken of as *another* testimony of Jesus Christ; it is not a new gospel, and not a replacement. I only began reading it after my baptism, its sacredness still left for me to discover personally.

I was charmed to enter a story that begins in 600 BC with the prophet Lehi at a time when this prophet obeys the Lord's order to leave Jerusalem, and go into exile with his family before the city is destroyed. I was also stunned to discover that it contains writings of ancient prophets who lived on the American continent from approximately 2200 BC to AD 421. My Catholic education had been scant; there was much that was left for me to understand about Christianity, its prophets, and its books.

I realized with great emotion that it is not just Haitians who bear a hard legacy—heirs of slavery, racism, and colonialism—but that Mormons also have a troubling history of bloodshed. They have been a persecuted people, men, women, children, either killed or chased out of their homes into exile in the middle of winter without protection from rain or snow, or sufficient clothing and food.

It was fitting that these people should be my new family; they were completely familiar; not that I had experienced such physical hardships in exile as they did, but I knew all about emotional tearing. I am part of the U.S. community of Haitian exiles, many of whom also ran from terrible deprivation and threats of violence. I had lived all these years entirely unaware of Mormons' existence and martyrdom, yet a modern-day, Christian martyrdom. They are indeed latter-day saints.

While I remain conscious of the negative press spreading in the world about the Mormon Church, its history, its theology, its leaders, or its missionaries, I have personally neither suffered nor witnessed any of the intrusiveness and aggressiveness in the behaviors of Mormons that one hears about, nor I have found sound historical proof to the negative propaganda about their history as a group that are spreading on the Internet, or by word of mouth. I find that Mormons are an immensely gentle and patient people. They live what they preach.

The negative press may arise from the world's misunderstanding of the deep character of the Mormon Church's members, their commitment to purity, their continued preparation for being worthy of the Lord's presence, in this life, and in the afterlife. The church is run purely on a volunteer basis; church leaders are there to offer guidelines usually drawn directly from Christ's teachings; their insistence on "proper" conduct in this world has to do with pleasing the Lord through obedience to His stated requests, rather than to pleasing or obeying the church. If the behaviors suggested in Christian scriptures to achieve deep inner purity and deep joy in this life are not to one's liking, one is free to leave the church and choose something else. If being honorable in God's eyes is of no interest to someone, then the Mormon Church is not the right place for that person, and nor are Christ's teachings.

In 1823, the angel Moroni warned the 17 year-old Joseph Smith that his name should be had for good and evil among all nations, kindreds, and tongues. I found it mind-boggling that the young Joseph had very little formal education, and was incapable of dictating a coherent or well-worded letter, at the time when he translated the Book of Mormon from its original text written on metal plates, through a process of revelation.

Joseph Smith was killed at 39 year-old. After his death, the cup *runneth* over again in the history of Christianity. Men again conspired, betrayed, lied, killed and butchered people of this new Christian faith, as they had in the first centuries after the death of Christ, a time when patriarchs reworked existing holy texts—they amended, cropped, modified, or plain discarded some, until we are nowadays presented with a Bible that is 57 translations away from its original texts.

American Mormons still reflect the culture of exiles that marked their beginnings. They can be found in the comfort of functional contemporary housing with young trees growing in the garden, and no moss. Taking exception with recent converts from old world cultures, or people of unusual means and tradition, American Mormons I have met seem partial to sensible living rooms furnished with enough modern sofas to accommodate regular gatherings of their spiritual brothers and sisters. On muted-color walls, they hang family portraits and genealogical trees, alongside reproductions of a painted likeness of Jesus. Mormons are on the move; forever ready to go where God sends them. They travel light, taking computers, cookware or heirlooms, more concerned with building up eternal homes in heaven than decorating temporary ones on earth. Nomads of the desert need their camels, rugs and tents; gypsies need their horses, caravans and violins; Mormons will take the clothes on their backs, powdered milk and canned food for the children, the Book of Mormon, and go.

3. God's Beloved Children

When I was a child in Port-au-Prince living with my family in an old Victorian house painted green, I made a mental assessment about my possessions at night before sleep. It was crucial that I knew in advance what I should grab if a fire erupted. If such an eventuality had come to pass, I would have been seen rushing out of my pink bedroom, clutching Suzy, my dark-haired Christmas-gift doll as tall as me and, as far as I was concerned, my child; I would then be running down wooden stairs, negotiating my way through a living-room furnished with antiques, fast speeding past its towering Venetian gold mirror, crossing through high French doors, scurrying along the gallery secured with white latticework and rail, until I stood outside in my nightgown, with Suzy safe in my arms.

Considering this, it seemed then oddly fitting that my first calling to service in the Mormon Church was with the children's Primary Presidency, Mormon children's Sunday school. I held the position of counselor. "Teaching our children is an important position," Bishop Johnson said to me at the time. "A lot of trust is placed on you. My counselors and I have prayed about your calling. We all received the same answer."

Seeing dozens of innocent eyes staring at me indifferently that first day on the job, I felt I was standing at the edge of the Grand Canyon. I quickly came to admire how Mormon children can absorb and learn to juggle abstract thinking early. In his book, *Christ and the New Covenant*, Jeffrey R. Holland writes about Jacob who, in his youth, was introduced to the grand concepts of the creation of Adam and Eve, the role of moral agency, the inevitability of opposition in all things, the design and purpose of the Fall, the consequence of transgression, the immutability of law, the demands of justice, the gift of mercy and grace, the need for mortality and children, the purpose of probation, and, through it all, the joy of redemption. Now living in AD 2000 of the Christian era, Mormon youths are being introduced to these same concepts.

The children I taught had such names as Seth, Jared, Grace, Ruby, Jane, or Jordan. Ruby was Jane's identical twin; she wore a deep-red velvet dress with a large sage-green satin bow at the waist. I have not met a child called Nephi, Alma, Lehi, Mosiah, Abinadi, Enos, Helaman, Ether, or Mormon, named after the prophets in the Book of Mormon. But I have not met a child called Isaiah either, even though Jeffrey R. Holland writes that the current edition of Latter-day

Saints scriptures indicates that some 433 verses of Isaiah, roughly a third of the entire book, are quoted in the Book of Mormon, and that one student of Isaiah documents that no less than 391 of those verses refer to attributes, appearance, majesty, and mission of Jesus-Christ.

Spencer Harrison, a professor at Boston College, a Jesuit school, was one of two counselors to Bishop Johnson at the time when I was baptized, and started my first calling in the church. He had three little boys when his daughter was born. He named her after one of his ancestors who had been a Mormon pioneer. One-month-old Marie-Alice was brought to church for a blessing one Sunday. Brother Harrison performed the blessing for his daughter at the start of the Sacrament Service. He stood in a circle with several men of the church; his eyes were bright from tears, but his voice firm when he addressed the infant daughter cradled in his arms. "I bless you with courage and leadership. I bless you with the desire and strength to serve others. I bless you with faith in God. I bless you with the ability to get on your knees to pray for help and revelation. Five generations ago, there was a Marie-Alice who was a woman of courage, faith and loyalty. She abandoned the comfort of her home to follow the pioneers of the church in their exile following repeated persecution. But you now live in a different time than she did. Your challenges and the demands made on you will be different. I bless you with the capacity to face everything with courage, independence of spirit, and love."

4. New Music

My expectations of silence during Sacrament Service, modeled after my Catholic experience of church, were greatly challenged. The level of noise coming from small children that is tolerated by Mormon parents required adaptation. I had never encountered a church that instituted a difference between worship at the temple or in church. My initial thought about the temple was to see it as a cathedral—just a larger place of worship. Well… it is not. Mormon Churches are for the gathering of the faithful for Sacrament Service and the remembrance of our covenant with Christ; the Mormon Temple is the house of God, it keeps a sacred quiet.

I sat in the front row in church. I would start the hour by closing my eyes to evaluate the sound backdrop. After a couple of Sundays, I began abandoning the use of earplugs, and allowing the children's rustling, cries, cooing, and continuous babble to penetrate me; it would, eventually, becoming the hum of a trapped orchestra rehearsing in a giant hive.

In time, I came to appreciate the hum, and developed a growing pleasure in this novel form of sound evolution spiraling and reaching a kind of accidental harmony, a music of the spheres at its infancy. I came to feel the wonder of being led, Sunday after Sunday, to the very midst of the continuing effervescence, ebullience, and irrepressibly charmed force of life itself, God's creation. The children's were the bountiful sounds of the universe, euphonies of atoms, challenging me to redefine and realize a personal music that is nevertheless part of a whole, relax into the source of all life, the generous origins of my being.

It has been a great many moons since I was born at a pre-dawn hour on a distant Caribbean island. Those times of childhood when I went to bed early are far past, laying on a cotton mattress, contemplating stars through cedar shutters, hoping that my father would come to rub my back before kissing me goodnight. Dolls sat in rows like ladies-in-waiting. When he came, my father found me ready, stretched on my belly, arms folded close to my ribs, hands tucked flat under the spongy pillow. I was a thin little girl; my shoulder blades protruded like organs pushing out. My father was awkward with affection. Ah... if only he could see me now! A woman in my maturity, carried indelicately by life until I could do nothing else one night but fall to my knees, admitting defeat, asking that friends of my soul be returned.

5. The Original Egg

Man is born with a hand free to do the bidding of his expanded brain. With its elaborate nervous system, the human brain coordinates man's eye and hand. Said to be the highest achievement of primate evolution, research to date shows the human hand to be no more than a variation of a primitive vertebrate plan. The morphological pattern of man's hand also reveals its affinity to the "hands" of other tetrapods.

In birds, the hand became a wing.

There is a great scarcity of fossilized primate hands; these bones are small, fragile, easily destroyed by the action of the forces of nature. Hands are as indeterminate as the many art forms. Yet, hands point, lead, command, strike, crush, and beg; they also fashion, hold, caress, or lie quietly sleeping; hands mold clay into a bowl that will contain the essence of something rare; hands make music; hands pray.

"…Juliette, Simone, Marilène… by the power of the Melchizedek Priesthood which I hold… I give you a blessing..." were words I heard as if in a dream while Bishop Johnson's hands rested lightly on my head. It seemed to me then that my entire being was contained in my head, and the whole nothing but an egg. We were at my house. The bishop stood behind me, while I sat with folded arms and crossed feet in a church pew seat I bought at a church antiques auction; a cross, cut from brass, nailed on the backside of the chair, showed that it was donated in memory of a woman who died the day my father was born; I noticed the November 10 inscription after I brought the seat home; no one else had bargained for it. A larger than life head of a Nepalese Buddha hung above the bishop, facing us, eyes half-closed like a cat curled for its nap, and smiling the calm, pained smile of the gods. The hands of the bishop cradled me. My being seemed dissolved but for my head, alive only where I felt a touch as if from something that had neither temperature nor texture, but had an essential emotion—it knew me.

The world originates from an egg. Throughout the world, the egg is a propitious, dominant symbol used in mythology to evoke the mystery of original creation. Alchemy's great cosmic egg symbolizes the birth of life, the place wherein the entire cosmos formed, and grew to maturity. An egg's static outer form belies the active movement and radical transformation occurring inside its shell. What is growing must be treated cautiously.

Dreams about eggs mirror the fragility felt by the dreamer in the world; they can be a reminder that isolation and enclosure may be keys to the attainment of spiritual goals. In mythology, magical eggs of pure gold are guarded by dragons; from eggs, gods and heroes are born. Helen of Troy came from an egg that had fallen from the moon. What about me? Can a mythology of my birth be written?

6. Going Back to the Old That Once Was New

Thoughts about eggs, creation, the fragility of primates' hands, came when I requested a priesthood blessing from Bishop Johnson. I would soon be flying to Arizona, and see the Miller family again. It had been many years. I was anxious about a visit to these old friends that would feel like a return to a time that carried still a certain taste of blood. Being in their embrace would surely bring me back to the season when we first met; wrenching stretch of days implicated with the sale of my family land and home; emptying all that was held within walls my father built, dismantling rooms; desecrating the life they had witnessed, sheltered, and contained. At this juncture of my life, it felt like I was gathering on a single wall all features and memories of people I loved, and places I cherished, in order to paint them over; I was aiming for the peace of a white surface that evoked nothing, stirred nothing, abandoning the comfort and daily reassurance of being part of an established, honored lineage of souls.

In going back to Arizona, having been there once before soon after the sale of the land, I would be brought to face, and feel anew, those days of letting go when I shed a vast part of my identity and lifelong attachments. Loss, Guilt, and Betrayal were the three Graces who accompanied me during my departure from Haiti, having signed the deeds of my family land to Michael and Sarah Miller.

They, not I, were now in possession of the earth where my ancestors walked; where my brother, mother, father and I had grown together awhile, close, and then apart. The Millers were now the keepers of the steps. They were to hold all geometries of irksome relationships drawn there; to continue the tradition, in our place, of evenings under the stars with the barking of dogs, and the longing calls of donkeys from the hills; to be haunted in my stead by traces of all the glorious mornings when my mother came out of the bathroom as if ready for the curtain to open on the stage, fully dressed, but inside, naked still.

The Miller family had also bought my father's grave, that small slab of pale-gray cement under the Caribbean apricot tree that grew by the river, and over which the wooden cross above it casts a faint shadow at a particular time of day; the cross on which were carved his names and surname, dates of birth and death, fashioned out of a branch from a mahogany tree he planted by the gate of our house when I was a seemingly carefree child walking over the land with yellow flip-flops.

Emotions are resistant like insects; they indent our flesh with sharp scissor claws, leave marks in the body that last longer than images in the mind. For lack of chances to create other memories with them, the Millers were still only linked to loss.

7. Renewal of Blood

Baptism had brought me to a differing state of being; like silence, it has a quality, a weight, a mood, a touch. In that new awareness came the sense, or temporary illusion, of having left familiar people behind, beings restricted to a long-ago realm, prevailing in the mythology of my existence. I felt an immense, lingering tenderness for them, yet irreversibly parted.

I now dwell in another liturgy. I hold a place in an enlarged family. I have seeped into a people who embrace me more profoundly than my mother ever has. But the particular fondness felt from individuals with whom one grew up is untranslatable, uncommonly sweet, even whilst it may lack the scope and sustaining power of emotion between people who share a spiritual framework.

Michael and Sarah Miller became the new parents lording over the land. They seemed to have appropriated something I felt would always be intimately, irreplaceably, mine. The fact is that they took nothing away; they added to my being instead. Through the Mormon Church, I have expanded and deepened my experience of belonging. I did not *sell* anything to the Millers; they did not *buy* anything from me; it is more like I *entrusted* them with a vulnerable land and charge of soul, and they took on the responsibilities and tasks comprised in that charge.

I was adopted, not replaced. My spirit could now rest, thirsting for growth.

15 Homecoming

1. A Bird's Wish

Sweet Pea thinks he is a king. How could he not? —Looking as he does, all feathered up in a spiffy cockatiel coat of gray, head topped with a zestful yellow plume that curves upward with panache and pomp. Add the fact that he lives in a mansion, the door of his cage is wide open, his screech gets to be heard all over the rooms, and when it is at its most piercing, Sarah Miller comes to offer her finger for him to climb over, clasp, and perch his tiny self.

Of the Holy Land, Arizona possesses the arid mountains, palm trees, cypresses and bougainvillea. Dawn paints a rose glow on the curvy mountain-horizon before laying it tenderly on the cheeks of the earth. The sun is quick to rise. The sky is vast. I feel at home.

During this December visit to the Millers, tall Chinese vases were lined up in the entrance hall like a watchful guard set against a wall, having given up to an abundance of crèches the spaces they normally occupy on shelves, furniture, and the fireplace's mantel. A prominent carved olive tree crèche from Bethlehem was spread on the grand piano; its gentle-faced, gift-bearing Magi proceeded towards an infant laid in straw, baby Jesus's welcoming them to his vulnerable breast with open arms, at the spot where he would one day be pierced.

"Had I grown up in this house with Michael and Sarah as parents, home and family endowed with a kind of perfection, I might never have married," I said to Roderick on our first night in Arizona. "Why leave home when all the earth's goodness is already here?"

Roderick chuckled, arching his brows. "I see that you're not the sort of Eve who would have made the bold choice, and given up Paradise. It's a good thing that the birth of humanity did not depend on you, my love. And what about me then, your modern-day Adam?"

I had to smile. "Ah yes… indeed… Yet, I think I understand God's decisions about me. I was to be given a home I would only want to leave if I were to ever get out of my cage of quiet contemplation… go into the world in order to define my character, build my own home. Oscar Wilde said, 'Be yourself; everyone else is taken.' Ha!"

"What a marvelous tease, that one!" Roderick said laughing. "An incomparable Englishman."

I discovered during our stay that Sarah has a studious temperament I had not suspected. Obvious elements of her appearance and demeanor must have distracted me: a kind, pretty woman; a soft brunette, hair cut shoulder length, a warm brown gaze startlingly intent on piercing through what one hides.

Having raised five children with complete devotion, she was then applying herself to earning a university diploma through correspondence courses with Brigham Young University. The greater part of her days were spent alone, with Sweet Pea as company, his plumed-highness perched high in a sizable cage that rested on a commode across from her desk. During the time that I spent with her, Sarah revealed herself as a woman with a sense of self and identity inextricably woven to her husband's, her family's and the Mormon faith.

The way she welcomed Roderick and me into her home was a perfect model of the Christian idea that one should see Jesus in all travelers. She opened up for us the large bedroom that had been her youngest daughter's, Ruby, now a mother. The soap bar in the shower stall was sweet pea-scented. We were fragrant every morning when we stepped out of the house into the outside world.

The other surprise was Michael; to discover him as a husband at home, and a leader in the church. I recognized well enough the outer man I knew. First were these limpid blue eyes I remembered, carved beneath a broad forehead framed in white curls; eyes so crystalline and open, they make the interlocutor feel like an intruder into his unveiled psyche. The man's vitality and spirit are unique, filled with curiosity about everything, caught in perpetual movement, acting in a being whose natural eloquence is rare, and whose sole desire seems to fully grasp the many intricacies and pressures of another person's reality; one has hardly finished answering a question that demanded earnest reflection, that Michael asks another; in this way, he affords one the continuous illusion of being interesting, cherished, a person he is happy to know, and rediscover endlessly. It is somewhat intoxicating this temporary illusion of being the center of this unusual man's focus. And when he stands up to put an end to the meeting—it is always him who gets up first, as if responding to a sudden, irrepressible urge—one remains a little sheepish after he left, slightly shamefaced, realizing that one has not had the opportunity to ask him anything about himself, but also wondering of it was intended?

Considering the circumstances in which Michael and I first met, as well as the role he played in regards to taking over my paternal legacy, it is not surprising that I may have seen him as larger than life.

During my first visit to the Millers in Phoenix, right after the sale of the land, I still enjoyed a privileged position and role in their lives. They had wanted something I had. I was the person of the moment, one whose complex knowledge about their new surroundings was needed. As buyers of my family land, they and I had become profoundly connected, and we were still involved in an ongoing process of transformation each of the other. I most likely saw the Miller couple with the veil of one in love, the eyes of Sleeping Beauty awakening, saved from the evil spell by a chivalrous and altruistic spirit. In situations such as these, one sees the essential of what there is to see, remaining blind to the simple human dimensions of the person, what the being would become when blemished by the dulling effect of daily life and chores.

When I saw the Millers again during my second visit to Phoenix in December, I no longer was "the person of the moment." Our lives had evolved separately. They had served as God's agents towards me, but had gone on to affecting other lives.

It must be said that Michael and Sarah had been disappointed with their experience in Haiti. I even worried whether this might have created discomfort and distance between us in their hearts. They had been deceived, robbed blind by greedy, dishonest people who took advantage of their trust and generosity. The Millers were people who are the product of a society of plenty; they could not even have begun to imagine what easy prey they would be for people harassed from birth by economic destitution and desperation, beings whose imagination is solely focused on finding ways to survive each day, and seizing opportunities sprung in the moment. In that situation, it could have been expected that a world's classic scenario unfolded: money the Millers were sending to keep the hospital going was not reaching those to whom it was destined. Michael and Sarah finally understood the goings on, and progressively detached themselves from the ship. The 2010 earthquake finished the sinking job.

As a business investment, the Millers' purchase of the Haiti property proved profitable. American insurance companies reimbursed the value of all properties collapsed during the earthquake, the very buildings for which, in the past, no Haitian company had been willing to insure me. The eventual sale of only half the land (whose total value had increased with time), and by then cleared of any buildings—all of them collapsed in the earthquake—actually returned more money to the Millers than they had initially spent in buying the whole lot—land, buildings, and complete furnishings—all the mahogany doors, windows, wall paneling, chests of drawers, cupboards, beds, bedside tables, dining tables, living room tables, chairs, rocking chairs, and desks that I watched, crouching near, my father's woodworker, Arnold, build throughout my childhood, and which the Millers insisted having.

Furthermore, they would have been able to use as tax deductions their charity donation of the lower half of the land where my father's remains rested. Michael is a shrewd businessman whose cause is the building of God's kingdom. He does not complicate his life with useless emotions. He was the first to tell me how, "We are in this world, but not of this world." And this world is vast. Michael and Sarah just "rowed to other shores," finding other people needing their help.

While I was flying to Phoenix, worried about reviving old emotions, I remembered with lingering bitterness the promise Michael made that my father's grave would always be honored. I however now understand better that we are not time's rulers; there are promises that make sense, or are true, only in the moment, in that time and space when we express our good will, the magnitude and profound meaning of which in the hearts of others we have a limited appreciation.

Maturity perhaps involves our making the apprenticeship of disillusion and betrayal, in a manner resembling Christ's; accept that we lose meaning in the hearts of others, while our own set of values continually shift. I may therefore not begrudge promises made long ago, and not kept. I must remember only the good will shown to me, and the infinite's indecipherable generosity from which I benefited undeservedly.

I learn more and more that what God manifests to me, I must also demand it of myself, forgiveness not the least of it. This may be what I retain most vividly from my visit with Clayton Christensen: what is confessed is truly forgotten; what God himself has let go, I should not allow myself to remember.

2. Leaving Home to Cry in the Desert

Sally was over seventy when we met at a Radcliffe College poetry workshop. A spinster who lived a cloistered life in a Cambridge mansion with her one hundred and five-year-old mother, Sally's one life goal was to craft a perfect poem. As a matter of habit more than faith, she submitted a selection of her works to the Grolier Poetry Prize every year.

Sally's father, an internationally known psychoanalyst, Harvard professor, and father of three, had long been dead when I befriended her. Of her two brothers, one committed suicide in his late teens, the other deserted the family. Sally however never felt compelled to leave her childhood home. She made an attempt at independence only once, renting a studio apartment in Boston, occupying it for one year until she decided that leaving home wasn't worth the effort. She went back, never left again, and spent the next sixty odd years transforming the stately family home into a bunker. With newspaper fortifications built all over inside the house, she elaborated on aspects of loneliness, and created a novel bastion of lyricism, albeit one visited periodically by social workers she despised. Their insolent intrusion, and broadly debasing opinion of her home, only gave Sally further justification for shunning the world, and pile more newspapers up.

By the time I met Sally, her mother lived on the second floor of the house, ensconced and immutable in a dilapidated armchair. There was no space to move about anyway; her bedroom had been progressively suffocated with newspaper stacks, reflecting the state of all the other rooms in the house. The original spacious floor plan of their home, basement included, had been transfigured into a maze of narrow, serpentine hallways whose high hedges, standing from floor to ceiling, were built from stacks of the Boston Globe's yellowing paper marred with ink.

Were it not for the indiscretion of social workers, this would not be known outside; no one was ever invited to the house. It is also not clear who called Social Services in the first place. It can be inferred that it was a neighbor. In any event, Social Services would periodically visit the two women, and force Sally to trim more space out of the heaps.

The first time they came, they could not open the front door because the mounds of paper butted right against it, filling the whole entrance hallway. They had to slip through a narrow space left through the back door that opened into the kitchen, the one out of which Sally slinked twice a week to join the poets at the workshop.

She was fond of Boston Cream doughnuts. Each time the poet's group had a reunion, she brought a fresh one, nibbled all around it during our break like a bird would peck, saving the center for last, then gobbled it in one mouthful, smiling faintly afterwards, before carefully folding the paper bag to store it in her sweatshirt's pocket. Her enchantment was extreme when a poet of the group invited the rest of us in their own plush Cambridge living rooms, serving cucumber sandwiches, oatmeal cookies, and tea. Sally sat slim in her forever gray, stained sweatpants, limp and long graying hair hanging on either side of black-rimmed glasses anchored to the tip of her bulbous nose.

A few stray, embattled facial hairs claimed her chin and upper lip over a small number of blackheads.

In Harvard Square, Sally blended in with the homeless. She never bought herself anything new to wear unless she had to; what the factors were which determined when that point was reached were never discussed or discovered. But it was then that she ventured out of the plush Harvard Square neighborhoods where she lived, heading for the Salvation Army store in Central Square.

Yet Sally's breath was always fresh. She created rare, delicate poems that seemed to have been breathed directly out of the chest of an immaculate angel. It is unlikely that the world will ever know these precious poems of rare sensibility and intelligence.

Remembering Sally who lived in a suffocated mansion, its window-blinds always down, I think of God who made us all to His image, and loves his children equally: the physically-malformed, the psychologically-handicapped, the spiritually-dysmorphic, all those who bravely litter their way through life with an abundance of words, attempting to articulate the indeterminate absence within.

My old fragile friend came on my mind while I hiked up the rocky path of the Phoenix Mountains, looking for the divine, as in a way, Sally also was. In sacred books, God manifests Himself on a mountaintop. In the purity, clarity and strength of the air, God is already in the mountain. There, the vastness of the landscape echoes the human desire for internal amplitude.

The desert bares all pretenses, and imitates our nakedness. Cactuses enrobe themselves in needles to appear invulnerable. They raise to the skies the eerie, stiff, deformed, ineffective hands of unwrapped mummies who eternally trust that God will listen to prayers and poems equally.

3. Elder Rhein's Temple

Elder Rhein and his wife were hosted by the Millers at the same time that Roderick and I were. As a member of the Quorum of the Seventy in the Church of Jesus Christ of Latter-day Saints, like Clayton Christensen once had been before I met him, Elder Rhein was sent by the Quorum of the Twelve Apostles to attend the Phoenix area's stake conference.

As Stake Mission President, Micheal opened the conference; he grasped both sides of the pulpit with open arms, and spoke for a half hour without the use of notes. I sat next to Sarah. Roderick had stayed at the house.

A gentle, unassuming doctor of internal medicine no taller than me, Elder Rhein's spiritual stature shows in the glow of his eyes. At the conference, he spoke about the apostles of the Mormon Church whom he once met. "I took the hand of one, and gazed into his eyes. He seemed to be looking through, and into me. I took the hand of another, and the same thing happened. I felt love streaming into me, and filling me like never before."

"Elder Rhein, how does one receive revelation from God?" I asked at the church. It had been pure chance that he was sitting at a table next to me after the conference. We were eating sandwiches and cakes offered at a small reception for the organizers of the conference.

"You must do your homework," he said. He put his food down, and turned to face me. "There are two keys. The *first* key is that you must obey the commandments… You'll often read in the scriptures how 'no man receives a fullness' unless he keeps God's commandments. And the person who keeps God's commandments receives truth and light, until glorified in truth, and knows all things. You will also read that man is called the tabernacle of God, His temple even. It is therefore logical to see how whoever defiles one's body, or spirit, also defiles God."

I gave out a deep sigh.

"Why do you sigh?"

"This is a very full and sobering answer you have just given me."

"The question and the answer are equally important. But don't be intimidated, it is all rather obvious, wouldn't you say?"

"Yes, and inspiring too."

"Ah good…" Elder Rhein spoke with great simplicity, sitting with hands folded in his lap, while his food waited in his plate. His hair now gray, his waistline unclear, the upper rooms of the house his own to occupy freely, he admitted that he still goes to the basement to pray.

"The *second* key is that you must find a place of proper reverence… Take me, for instance: in my old age, I find myself again living in the house in which I grew up. As an adolescent, I had adopted the basement of the house as my room. No one else wanted it. It was windowless and damp. But it was totally my own. In that space, I had my first communications with God."

Picturing Elder Rhein in his childhood house almost with envy, I also imagine Sally inside hers. I thought how they are similar souls caught within different frameworks—indeed, Elder Rhein kneels down and prays to God from his windowless basement room, while Sally crafts poems about birds, and flights of spirit. She chooses her words as carefully as if in prayer, and offers them from an invisible altar, in a bedroom that was its own form of windowless basement. She built newspaper ramparts to silence her house, and protect the poetic muse living inside; hers was an unconscious, poignant attempt to establish her house and being as holy ground, bolstered by a barricade of printed words. She profoundly understood the power of words in our lives. One might think that her error of aloneness was to have addressed the profane, rather than the sacred, and she thus never received answers.

"I have another question, Elder Rhein. "How do you know that the communication you receive is indeed from God?"

"If it invites you to do good, you know it's from God."

I later learnt that Elder Rhein and his wife are bird watchers. They seek encounters with these endothermic vertebrates as often as they can, and thus regretted not meeting Sweet Pea; especially after I described how singular a prototype of an "avian dinosaur" I found that bird to be, demonstrating such marked personality, at once coy, tenacious and tender. They were also sorry to have missed the chance to admire the Christmas lights at the Mesa Temple, when the gardens are turned into a fairyland.

The dedication of the Mesa Temple in Arizona, on October 23, 1927, was an event of great portent. This was one of three temples constructed in the early part of the twentieth century. One easily imagines that demands had been put forward to serve what were then thriving Latter-day Saints settlements outside Utah. Announced in 1919, only a few years after Arizona had achieved statehood, the relief this news would have brought the faithful must have conjured tears of joy and blood. A large circus with its enormous traffic of men and animals could not have inspired such jubilation.

Temple attendance is an important part of the Mormon faith. Mormon Churches welcome all, but the temple is maintained for God's use. The Prophet Nephi's words were sharp, yet filled with logic, when he explained that people must be judged by their actions and their lives, which, if unclean, reveal the uncleanliness of the people themselves. The unclean therefore cannot be allowed to enter the kingdom of God, less it would mean that the kingdom of God too is unclean (4), and so, the temple is not open to all.

The costly, dangerous, long and arduous trip to existing temples located in the state of Utah were probably and appropriately considered an undue hardship for the faithful of the era. Numerous colonies had been set up in Arizona by the church during the last half of the nineteenth century. It seemed therefore necessary to construct temples in these communities.

Upon its completion, the Mesa Temple was the third largest temple in use by the church, and the most sizeable outside of Utah. Cathedrals of Europe had already exhibited what ambitious and bold-spirited men are capable of, and what excruciating sacrifices people are willing to make when it comes to house and love their God. It was perhaps to remind us of the roots of the Mormon faith that a departure was made from the style of temples constructed prior, and so the Mesa Temple was built in a style suggestive of the temple in Jerusalem. And why not? An intuition is what these builders must have had, else why do away with the spires that have become a feature of temples built everywhere since?

An eleven-foot white marble statue of Jesus Christ looking down onto the world with gently opened arms stands at the visitor center of the Mesa Temple, evidencing a point of view that finds reasons to craft large symbols. The painted blue sky and soft clouds in the Christ's alcove revived in me a sense of enchantment that in my world has fallen into desuetude. It was also inevitable that it might evoke in me the vast skies of childhood, and the charmed Immaculate Virgin's grotto in Turgeau.

The Mesa Temple's statue is a replica in white marble of the nineteen century Christus Consolator statue carved by Bertel Thorvaldsen in Denmark. It was adopted by leaders of the Church of Jesus Christ of Latter-day Saints, and placed in many temples to emphasize the centrality of Jesus Christ in the church's teachings; show to the world that Mormons are Christians. And still, when I tell people that I am a member of the Church of Jesus-Christ of Latter-day Saints, they invariably ask, "So, what is it you believe in?" turning their faces in different suspicious curves.

4. The Making of a Christian

Being a Christian was a simpler affair when I was a child, unless I am deluded in my thinking. Still, upon close evaluation of distant reminiscences, it seems that the few requirements exacted had to do with wearing a lace mantilla on Sundays, a gentle pastel dress, white shoes, and be passive during Mass for a boring hour of incomprehensibly frequent sitting-downs, and getting-ups, interspersed with impenetrable discourse.

When Catholic Mass said in Latin was eventually dropped, and I understood the priest's invocations and admonitions, it was admittedly a disappointment. I missed the many avenues of meaning in a language I could not understand, and it soon became evident that my imagination had both enlivened and plagued me. But in terms of church requirements at the time, however simplistic matters of faith seemed to be then, it cannot be denied that I also had to contend with the ever-increasing malaise, disheartening complexity, and distorting theater of Saturday afternoon confession, yet an unavoidable prerequisite to attending Sunday Mass in the recommended clean state of mind.

In those days, I was made to confess to a heavily perspiring priest. This must have been on account of the Caribbean heat and the long black robes priests wore. God's representative spoke in a toneless voice, muffled behind a wooden screen in front of which, when done with me, he drew a red curtain sharply shut. Within the short span of time I spent on my knees while the priest sat sideways in his dark, narrow booth, his shoulders leaning towards the obscured window on the other side of which I was straining to hear him, I appreciated how adroit he seemed at insinuations of depravity in the behavior of the eight year old I was. He mentioned vices the existence of which I had remained unaware until then, referencing them with words I had not yet learnt. During that time, I could faintly overhear my cousins and my brother whispering in the back pews while I confessed to sins I barely could construe, and they were comparing their own lists of ill-deeds prepared earlier at home with the help of a dictionary. These lists demanded skill and artistry—a marked sensitivity to word choice, allied with the keen desire to avoid punishment that involved too many rosaries to recite, countless Ave Marias, Pater Nosters, or *Actes de Contrition*, all the while preserving God's trust and delight in us. When finally the others saw me edging my way to the side of the confession booth, wearing a frown over sweaty brows and clutching my blue rosary, they knew that another's turn had come. Either my brother or a cousin came forward, the loser of a brief, hushed argument in a competition to be last.

There were many wild ideas and customs around being a Christian then. These converged during feast days and religious holidays. On Ash Wednesday, for example, I felt distinct from the common people that make an ordinary crowd, when my forehead displayed an ashen cross all day, initially drawn by a priest during the early morning Mass. But in truth, the real happening of import for me during all of Ash Wednesday was "*bat tonè*—beating thunder"—the 4:00 pm excessive neighborhood raucous we would create to our heart's content. Even my father felt he could not interfere, no matter how much it irritated his ears, and strained his nerves. Perhaps he felt a kind of nostalgic reverence for the very cacophony he too enjoyed in his own childhood. We used sticks to pound on buckets, tree trunks, cooking pots, anything that resounded famously. This was evidently not about music, but about chasing the devil away; it was about fear and release, blaming hell for the yearlong weight of parents on us, of religion and morality, of a culture of restriction that relished the punishment of sin.

When Christmas came, greed and awe combined in a very special way in our bosom. It was the enchanting and puzzling stretch of days when God himself turned into a helpless child, just like us; but a time of intense emotions when the lust for toys would never be contented, and the hunger for an indefinable love shown with material gifts never satisfied. Still, the rapture I felt from a life-size crèche glimpsed between mantilla-covered heads during Midnight Mass was indescribable, causing the meaning of the entire, mysterious Christmas story to solidify in me, a meaning the depth of which I felt deeply, but could not articulate.

There were nevertheless many requirements attached to the possible fulfillment of my Christmas hopes; human rules on how to be good and deserving; surprisingly silly rules when one considers their connection to a god-centered, immutable event; rules that always involved the negation or deprivation of something tempting, and from whose pressure I could only lift by busying myself with dreams about the ocean stretched at the Virgin's feet, the indecipherable stars at night, or the burning flight in the dark of insignificant fireflies.

It is therefore inevitable that my idea of being a Christian would dramatically evolve in adulthood. It is evident that my passion would become greater for having eventually understood principles of faith that before were mere rote or theater. Excitement was sure to come from developing my own ethical purpose. Home is both a reality and a concept I would continually be drawing on.

5. The First Gate

It is here that our story began. It is also here that nothing will ever be as it once was. Prayers have frittered away long ago, scattered from the mahogany alleyway where I now stand, observing the horrid building that suddenly confronts me, unnaturally emerged from lower down, and eying me up from that very area of the garden that had been the most beautiful, the sky above it prim and blue.

I used to crouch on that same spot when I was a little girl, at the beginning of our time here, when we had just moved to this new land, and I loved to espy my father while he gave orders to men maneuvering tractors. He seemed to me one of the great pharaonic builders portrayed in my illustrated Egyptian story book; he organized the digging, transporting, and shifting around of large amounts of earth, in order to stretch the many verdant terraces where we later played, running naked in the sun, and where there had previously only been an arid slope tilting towards a consuming void.

I have known all too well, how all that my father built during his lifetime had crumbled in 2010. Miraculously, the newer construction where my mother and brother lived together remained intact. Three people however, tenants at the time, were buried alive under the collapse of one apartment building that overlooked the swimming pool; one of the three was a woman, and it is not known how long it took for her to suffocate alone in the dampness of this internal silence. She lived by herself in the basement apartment I used as an office before the sale of the property; the very walls between which I once schemed with Boss Michel, and bargained with a *kazèk* to keep the slums silent from dusk to dawn. The woman trapped under rubble used the remainder of the charge on her cell phone to say farewell to her daughter. One of the United Nations rescuing crews operating all over Port-au-Prince had come to help, but the overall mass of debris was too much for human strength alone to affect, while all the required mechanical equipment were not yet available in the country at the time.

Since the earthquake, I had never yet come to view damages occurred on the grounds where my childhood played itself out. I only made quick trips to inquire about my family's wellbeing; doing occasional repairs, providing additional comfort; but during these brief visits, I quickly went in and out of my mother's house, looking straight ahead like a horse with blinkers.

I had not had the heart to take a look before today, six years after the fact, and walk again on the narrow path of childhood where *kaka zombie* mushrooms once grew. I have not seen these since childhood, enough so that I wondered if they ever existed, until I found photos of them, their exact likeness, on the Internet; it is possible that they only thrive in wilder ecosystems than the neighborhood has become, with pavement replacing dirt.

So I found myself going down the stone-paved alleyway once again; glancing at the electric post on which my father's car crashed, the shock killing him; going past the neighbor's low property wall edged by tall, skinny, sage-green *paresseux* bushes, where we, cousins of differing ages, sat waiting for Tonton Pierre. We were in awe of this old man wearing rags, foul-smelling and toothless, whose straw bag was as filled with impious surprises as his memory was of stories whose heroes populate the shadow-world: fanged flying devils fawning at the crossroads, mermaids that murmur where oceans meet, and werewolves that feast on fire and blood.

At long last, I now gently pull open the tall, white gate the way one might lift a tender scab, noticing how chipped and rotted it has become. My brother liked to stand at dusk by this upper-level front gate ever since he was a child, and watch the flux of humanity moving by. It is by that gate that we took the first photos of each other with a new camera gotten at Christmas. As a grown man, he could still be counted on to stand there, hoping for an encounter, friendly to anyone passing by. He was a natural storyteller, keen to entertain beggars come to him with the hope that he might intercede with the gods in their favor, or better yet, simply give them alms. It often gave me pause to realize how the poor saw my brother as an elect sent to suffer for others, regardless of apparent family riches and support, regardless of how eccentric, fragile, and traumatized a being he seemed to those who knew him from the start, and saw him grow up.

And so, he was indeed at the gate the day his father's car came speeding down the alley before it crashed onto a pole. He was among those first to rush up to the wreck, pull his father out of the car, still breathing. It was also at the gate that in later years, a beggar, angry at all the promises his own life had never kept, assaulted my brother with a stick, insulting and beating him furiously, breaking the few fingers with which he was mildly attempting to protect his face.

And so it is in the year 2016 that I finally enter what used to be our home; that land which Michael and Sarah bought, and which they wasted no time disposing of after 2010, selling the uppermost part of the land where all the constructions stood and then crumbled, and giving to charity the lower half, that part of the garden that had been our tropical nature reserve, and where my father's grave nested.

Everything I see before me appears blasted by some incomprehensible spell. Rot reign in pits left yawning. Cocks and dogs cry furiously by day as well as night, daylight is no longer a crossing; a breakdown of barriers between good and evil has occurred. Rats, scorpions, ants and cockroaches crawl over spaces where we used to live, whisper, and delight. What is left of foundation or basement walls is covered with bramble, vermin, stagnant rainwater, broken glass, empty plastic juice bottles, and odd packaging materials thrown by visitors content to dirty this place they envied us. I discover what advanced stage of decomposition this land and its ruins suffer from, and how summarily it had been cleaned up of rubble by the new buyer, who apparently lost all interest in it soon after. All that is left are vast gaping holes. The pool that looked so grand to me, now seems the smallest of these holes; suffocating ferns surge there in a last defiant effort of life, out of the cracks in the walls fouled with fragments of a blue-color paint that once made the water tempting; the steps we descended in bright bikinis are strewn with piled excrements over which noisy swarms of flies cluster to feed. The entire front wall of the apartment by the pool in which I lived, and under whose door Ali would slip quotes from the Koran on bits of white paper, now displays several wide cracks from top to bottom, as if the giant machete of an angry marooned slave had repeatedly slashed its face; long, curvy trails of black mold are mushrooming, progressing like clouds that can only predict further misery; all the windowpanes are broken, now mere hanging scraps of glass covered with dust; spider webs agglutinate over them, withholding carcasses of old winged insects eaten alive by the arachnids. But the trees look taller than I remember them.

"Ki moun ou ye—who are you?" I suddenly hear a man's voice questioning. He is standing at the doorframe of the poolside apartment, but the door itself is missing.

"I have come to see my mother... she lives here... lower down, next to Healing Hands Hospital... I came in through the upper gate. It was open."

The man makes no reply, and looks at me with mistrust. He throws spit on the ground as quickly as an iguana might flash its tongue. He then slowly ascends the few steps leading to the pool's terrace. He keeps observing me while he lingers by the cement balustrade of which my father had been so proud, having copied its design from a magazine about French castle gardens; but it is now cracked, chipped and shaking-loose, like everything else here.

"Se pitit ansyen patron an—it is the daughter of the old boss," I hear him say to a woman I imagine to be his wife, after I overhear her answer him, "An wi... li pa move moun. M konn tande yo pale de li—Ah yes... she is not a bad person. I heard people talk about her."

I try to walk by discreetly—it is their place now—and to ignore my upset at seeing the dilapidation, disrepair, filth, detritus, the layer of dry leaves rotted by successive rains that are now covering terraces once so carefully planted, and raked daily. While I am passing by the tall, ancient breadfruit tree, my old friend, with its scarred trunk under which I would set my easel down, and where I did paint large canvasses of the Tarot's major cards, I catch a glimpse of the watchman's wife. She is crouched in front of a single cooking pot, fanning the coal burning under a small rudimentary stove, the gray dreariness of her skirts gathered between her uncovered thighs. The breeze suddenly lifts, and surrenders a red bean scent. The woman's face looks chiseled, framed in gray by hair sticking out from under a washed-out flowered scarf; her thighs are muscular and stringy like an old leg of lamb. Not a single bird has flown or cries overhead. I sense not even the shadow of a crow, a black species of birds once so abundant and noisy in the trees, living under alert. This silence almost has texture and temperature, spreading furtively between the barking and other calls from creatures in the hill slums across from us. The terrace on which the watchman's wife is cooking her meager meal had been paved all during one Sunday, and the next; several birthdays were celebrated there, with a great number of guests smelling of French perfumes; my brother and I were hiding on a balcony overlooking the pool, observing with delighted eyes all the large platters of delicious foods being passed under our noses. It is hard for me not to feel that some sort of curse and damnation happened here. But why would that be?

In spite of the destruction from the earthquake, there had been great hopes of reconstruction and transformation in the country. Yes, the city had been leveled, but so seemed to have been the social classes' separateness and neglect of each other. For a brief period when everyone had suffered from the same evil, Haitians showed signs of being one people united by the same drama, and to be discovering each other's common humanity.

Yet, besides having not improved, the order of things has worsened. Instead of reconstruction, there is abandonment. It is the Jahr's house syndrome all over again—the people have deserted the ruins, and the city has sprawled towards empty areas in an unprecedented, crowded way. The old Port-au-Prince is a vacant lot of ruins left to beggars, and to the stalls of street vendors competing for the few customers available among an already destitute population. And I should not be surprised at the state of my childhood garden, as it reflects the larger phenomenon observable outside: ruins are not repaired, but cast aside and given up to the poor already caught in a continuous hustle over the next day's meal; those unable to afford medical care or education, let alone effect any kind of repair or upkeep on properties they do not own, and from which they will be expelled without hesitation once the need for land reestablishes itself. In the meantime, empty spaces where gardens once flourished became quickly overbuilt without planning, or any concern about esthetics; neighborhoods now connect to each other at random, through streets seemingly squeezed by the throat, and that can barely let one car go by in a one-way traffic without a gasp.

I walk down a few more steps, away from the terrace with the breadfruit tree, and find myself in front of the bungalow where Ali lived. Its chest has also been slashed open, and the carved mahogany front door has given up its guarding job. The mourning doves' cage is gnawed by rust. After Ali died, and perhaps moved by the same deserting instincts that I reproach Haitians now, I had opened wide the doors, relieved to see, as the doves escaped without hesitation, that they still knew how to fly.

6. The Lower Gate

At Healing Hands' gate, another watchman sits, a rifle up between his legs, aimed at the sky. The gate is accessed from Marcadieu Street, and opens into the garden just beneath Ali's bungalow. Cars must honk at the closed gate for the watchman to get up, and inquire about the driver's purpose before he will open. The new Healing Hands Hospital is built on the lower half of the land, the section that Michael Miller gifted to the Red Cross.

Without Michael's inflow of money, this hospital has not been able to survive as a charitable institution any better than the hospital formerly housed in my father's apartment-buildings above, all of them now collapsed, and that Michael had already stopped funding before the earthquake. Presently, amputees who cannot afford care are not treated at Healings Hands Hospital.

"His name is Philippe," My mother told me about the watchman a few days prior to this day's visit. "He has been working here for a couple of years. Usually, watchmen come and go. But Philippe is lasting longer. I am glad. I like him." This was said the time I first came to see my mother by entering through the Marcadieu Street gate, keeping my eyes closed to the upper level of the property, still gathering strength until I could face seeing it all, as I just have. But even when I have entered through Marcadieu Street, I tried not to notice what construction has emerged past my mother's house, which stands right at the gate.

"Philippe looks a bit phlegmatic for a watchman," I told my mother that first time I met him at the gate.

"Yes, but he is very nice," she insisted. "He protects me. He warns me if there is trouble, or if there is going to be trouble. He may be sitting inside here, and you can't see anything through that sheet-metal gate, but his eyes and ears are tuned onto the streets… You've got to understand… this is crucial—that gate's entrance is right above my house. So anything, or anyone, who enters the gate, passes by my front door, before getting to the hospital, or anywhere else down here... If there is danger coming from the street, I am the first in line."

Today, Philippe recognizes me right away, and draws a large smile. "Bonjou Madanm... Ou vinn wè manman w? ... L ap kontan!—You came to visit your mother? ... That'll make her happy!" Philippe is not tall, and his overall frame is small. His forehead is unusually broad, and his bright eyes seem dwarfed in contrast. He is not in a uniform, but he wears his starched white shirt and dark pants as if they were.

"Bonjou Philippe... m vinn wè manman m tout bon... kouman ou ye?—I did come to see my mother... how are you?" I am not in a talkative mood, and I keep this exchange perfunctory, albeit friendly. I soon turn towards the alleyway of mahogany. Today, I can't ignore my surroundings.

The trees so powerfully associated with my father have been cut down on the entire length of the right side of the alleyway. The architect presumably intended to take advantage of the greatest possible width of the land for the hospital, and would not lose land for trees. This bright orange, painted-cement creature staring at me out of dark-eyed, mean, angular windows, was brought to existence after the death of a great many trees; the arrogant beast takes its ease, stretching on the whole lower part of the land, this selfsame garden through which Michael and I had walked, sharing with each other our great, ancient dreams.

All those years of life... I realize with outrage. All the struggles and devotions... and we end up with THIS? ... An oversized bullfrog would have been better! The monster's mouth is off-center, pulled to the left as if by a rictus, yet it has been able to devour everything in order to exist, spreading from one perimeter wall to the next, like a cancer defining amorphousness. All bets are off, nothing is left: neither the verdant plateau and terraces, nor ample fruit-bearing trees parading golden ornaments yearlong; no more fireworks explosions of ferns on the ground; no boldly-painted cheeks of croton leaves imitating my imagined face-decorations of Arawak Indians at war; no hibiscus either, yellow, red, or salmon pink, their pistils reaching out for the touch of elves; no pink laurel, no blue hydrangea, no tall tamarind tree whose underarms we tickled to shake him with laughter, and cause his tart brown fruits to fall on the ground; and I can't even glance any longer at the river's serpentine line which the sun's finger would trace in gold—our fairy godmother along whose banks we ran free, drunken by sunlight, taunting birds with chicken feathers stuck in our hair. No more of any of that! The orange building's belly blocks the horizon from all directions; no more sky, no more birds, no more foliage, no more ocean breeze, or fragrant winds, they cannot reach us; we are damned up behind too much concrete; nothing remains but a continuous rumble of generators and air-conditioners busy warring with silence in order to keep cool air in, and mosquitoes out.

Have I only imagined the existence of this favorite place of mine at the edge of the *zorèy bourik* plants? Is this where I would lie in the grass, a mock-creator commanding clouds streaming through the vast heavens of my entire childhood? Was it really here, in a night of adolescence, that the three of us, my brother, my cousin William, and me, brought Ti Paris and his ramshackle group of street musicians, to offer a dance party to our friends? All night long, we overheard the river in its tireless rush to reach the ocean, while inebriated, rag-wearing Ti Paris's raspy voice rose above drum and guitar to sing his politically incorrect compositions about anger at the rich. "Mwen wè tout sa ki ganyen. Bam pam ladann—I see all there is. Give me my share!" Or a song about Pè Ilè, a Priest who stood at the pulpit, crying out, "Dominus vobiscum, all women have honey!"

Could it indeed also be the same spot where my brother buried alone, without a single witness, the first of his two sons, both of whom he named Ramses, after the Egyptian Pharaoh of the 19th dynasty, and both of whom died in infancy in spite of the hope held in the power of a name? Might they have fared better had they been called Zechariah? But is this really, the very area of the ravishing small clearing that glowed from sunlight at the first break of dawn… now covered over by the hard slab of a paved cement surface—a parking area created for one delivery truck and two administrative SUV's? Even when the motors are turned off, surely the dead infant buried underneath holds in the remaining dream of breath he briefly had, and that suffuses still his poor, disintegrated chest, while he suffocates under the weight of sorrows perpetually pouring from a Caribbean family.

Lower down, and to the right from where I am surveying the land and the orange monster, my mother lives cloistered in three large rooms through which she limps without complaint, holding on to a gray metal cane whilst she walks amidst dogs deaf to her protestations when they trip her. Each wants to be the first in line when she puts their food down. She cooks corn meal for them, with choice pieces of meat bought fresh at dawn by her house servant.

At this time of day, she often sits on the terrace outside her bedroom, looking down at her small-apportioned garden section of her former land, and where her son's remains lie buried near those of his second child's tiny coffin. In her bedroom, a mahogany box identical to that holding my brother's ashes waits on a dresser. She gives that box a long, pensive look at least once each day.

I am so overwhelmed by the pragmatic ugliness of the site, that I may not go see her today after all. She must not know how helplessly dumbfounded her child felt, hesitating between conflicting impulses, only a few feet away from her. Were it not for the fact that her windows turn their backs to the old mahogany alleyway, and open onto the riverside with mango trees bordering it, I would not be able to avoid this visit. She had been the queen of this land; so beautiful she was resplendent. It was vertiginous how I loved her!

But the family land is now no more than an extinguished arena, an invisible graveyard. My father lies beyond the bright orange demon. I will not go check, not today, whether his cross is still up, or whether the gardener I pay to clean and water the grave area has kept his part of the bargain; what for? My father will not be waiting there for me; what ghost would have wanted to stick around this place, hover above such hideousness, in the hope of one more of these rare, brief visits from his beloved daughter, the one who escaped far away, and so long ago?

I tell myself that hell is made up of a collection of incoherent gestures, a shapeless accumulation of survival mechanisms experienced blindfolded. There are many ways of being immured alive. It is not here only, or in 2010 alone, that creatures die, horrified as they suffocate. That which was my Eden, this on which I built myself up as a person, a dreadful thing has been done to it.

Disgrace has been added to injury that only demons could have wished for, creating a scandal of emotions inside of me. That too is what hell is made of: being forced to live what one has not conceived, or *chosen*, and that which one hardly has time to process, and survive, before another thing is piled on top of this existing accumulation of hurts, ill-understood, and therefore eternally fresh.

7. Home's Gates

And what choice is there left for me in a world where the wonders of science do nothing to disprove the existence of another dimension of being? What choice do I have when confronted with an inacceptable reality? What choice but to abandon familiar weapons, habits, and malaise; what is left to lose in choosing unprecedented modes of prayer, and go where space is truly cleared of this evil I see? Indeed, when one's tangible world has collapsed, the only building blocks remaining are those of the spirit.

A Mormon baptism is a point of departure, not a destination. The ill loved, ill interred, and broken-hearted beings line up for a chance to assimilate existence in a reinterpreted way.

To repent is to open up.

The digestive cancer that came to kill my brother will have been his repenting. He aspired to another realm, and looked for another gateway. How could he not yearn for more, and be cleansed of *this*?—Scum and foulness proliferating around him; the dishonor was too great! He chose to reject, make clean, no longer absorb and embrace all this waste.

He refused all cancer treatments, saying, "Only God can heal me..." My brother thereby made the desperate, bold choice of loving completely one last time—to love with his *entire* being this childhood garden, and the symbolic image of self it represented for him.

He must have thought he had the answer!—I will end my sufferings with one last, great one... it will be my way of the cross... And so my brother let his organs feel, reflect, exhibit, and demonstrate within, in the very fabric, and depth of his being, all that the land suffered, and could not escape. He painted with his own flesh a picture of the horror he had witnessed, and lived intimately each day.

Christians are brothers and sisters who pray to a common Heavenly Father. But Gaëtan was my first brother. He came with my father to the Bourand Maternity Clinic to identify me in my crib, verify that I had indeed come to rejoin him on earth, as in heaven I must have promised I would, and where he did play his own part with courage to the end. He suffered so my heart would burst, and increase. He came to earth first; he went back first too. Again he waits, and watches at the gate.

"But what shall I do now?" I ask the heavens out loud, poised at the gate below.

"Pray," the Lord answers, "and be in quest of my face."(5)

Standing as I am over the land, underneath the mahogany planted in my childhood, it can be said that I have returned to the origins of time. "Alas…" said I to God, feeling little more than a mouse. "The world is growing bigger every day. I am nothing if not a broken creature. Walls of my being have crumbled like dry bones, confirming ancient fears of my adolescence in France."

I remain at the gate quietly a long while, listening, waiting for signs. I want answers to burn into me like fire descended from the night sky. Instead, a quiet voice comes inside that tells me, "when it seems that your life has lost all sky, and there is no rain, I will heal your land."

My reply comes loudly like a cry, "But the work is hardly begun! And alas, we all live together in such a great heap! I feel like I am again outside the Mesa temple, wanting in. I want to be like Solomon in Jerusalem, vouch that I too shall build a house to your name, O Lord, my God! … But will it matter that Solomon had fir wood to build his house, and pure gold to overlay the walls… when all I have is mahogany?"

And here suddenly, I find myself recalling incidents of my life when I harmed my spirit, seeing how I have run in darkness for a long time, but filled with presentiments of great things. I felt that something extraordinary was needed, if only to justify my wild expectations.

And so it had to be told, how and why one day, I came to a stop, hearing an intoxicating music of ideas, mystified as to how it had been produced; how I bowed my head, giving in to the call of angels, so that I too might wear fine linen of purple, crimson, and blue. My being is the delicate carving I lay at God's feet. Science has little use for it. But surely, God does.

Solomon's timber for the Jerusalem Temple came from cedar out of Lebanon brought to him in floats by sea to Jaffa. But mahogany is *my* timber. The Caribbean ocean need not cling to it, and push it along to new shores; mahogany travels *in* me. My father planted these great trees to border the path and lead us home, revel in their noontime shade, rest a while under, lean on them, write about, or be buried with. I am the mahogany in God's garden.

Christian musings about the garden of Paradise inevitably leads to a Biblical story of expulsion. Yet Eden was not a garden, it comprised a garden, called Paradise. God planted it himself, on the East side of Eden, whose waters were the source that gave life to the world around.

Haiti was my Eden, and the valley where I grew up was my Paradise; through it, water also ran. I feel their loss like one expulsed. "Was there indeed no other way?..."

"There was not. Paradise is where the challenge takes place, and where the shock of revelation must occur... But, do not worry, I stand at the helm..."

"Where? When?"

The answer comes; it resonates inside. "You are the journey, the boatman, and the boat. It may be night where the boat is tied, but the boat is my own... I know it intimately... I know you intimately. I know the corner in which rot hides, I know where the source of the nail iron is to be found, I know the curves in the body that can espouse my own, when I choose to rest there."

I did not trouble to answer. It is enough that the beast will not be parted from its master, for I am the stranger come from a far country about whom Solomon prayed. His supplications were heard, and mine as well. The Book is in everybody's hands at this time; why even speak of it? It is plain what God meant when he spoke to Solomon, the temple-builder, and said, "I shall do according to all that the stranger calls to me for, so that all the people of the earth may know my love, and that the house in which I dwell is called by my name."

References

(1) Red Heat: Conspiracy, Murder, and the Cold War in the Caribbean; Pages 325 to 326. Henry Holt and Company, NY, ***p. 27

(2) Red Heat: Conspiracy, Murder, and the Cold War in the Caribbean ***p 56

(3) —Mathew 7: 15-20

(4) 1 Nephi 15:33-34: "if their works have been filthiness they must needs be filthy; and if they be filthy it must needs be that they cannot dwell in the kingdom of God; if so, the kingdom of God must be filthy also. But behold, I say unto you, the kingdom of God is not filthy, and there cannot any unclean thing enter into the kingdom of God."

(5) 2 Chronicles 7:14 (My translation from a French Bible — "...*cherche ma face*")—James E Talmage: The Great Apostasy; page 121

Acknowledgements

Profound gratitude goes to my husband Roderick Kettlewell for his unending, patient support and belief in the value of my work. A surprising bestowal from God to me each day, his name spells life, joy and song.

To my late father, Delmar Phipps, and to my mother Viviane Pauchet, for enabling my passage on this earth and instilling in me a deep need for beauty as well as the desire to express it in any way I can—in thoughts, in gestures, in art, and literature.

To my late brother, Gaëtan Phipps, who taught me about love's inviolable realms; the glow in his eyes when he spoke about me is an enduring gift.

To Bishop Seth Johnson who encouraged me to keep a journal. This was the start of a process that unwittingly led me to write this book.

To Richard Kaplan, a most uncommon man. His refined, complex and playful sensibility allied to a profound love of great literature were a stimulus and support for this book from the start, and throughout its followings stages.

To the late Jonathan D. Langford who generously offered to read the earliest draft of Unseen Worlds, and without whose professional editing observations and comments this book would not have become what it is now. His sudden passing continues to be a great loss to his family and to his friends, as well as to the future of Mormon Letters.

To my cousins from Haiti and in France whose love has buoyed me through the years; their keen interest in reading Unseen Worlds while still an unfinished manuscript and their enthusiasm about it afterward were crucial in giving me heart to continue the work.

To family members, friends, and all people mentioned in this book (even whilst some names were changed to maintain privacy). Their lives have brought invaluable richness to mine.

Last but not least to my publisher, Calumet Editions, where the hard work and enthusiastic response to this book of Gary Lindberg, Rick Polad and Ian Graham Leask was luminous and opened the door wide.

About the Author

MARILÈNE PHIPPS held fellowships at the Guggenheim Foundation, and at Harvard's Bunting Institute, W.E.B. Du Bois Institute, and the Center for the Study of World Religions. Her collection, *The Company of Heaven: Stories from Haiti*, won the Iowa Short Fiction Award. Her poetry won the 1993 Grolier poetry prize, and her collection, *Crossroads and Unholy Water* won the Crab Orchard Poetry Prize. Her work is published in England by Carcanet Press, and is found in American anthologies and collections such as *The Best American Short Stories*; *Haiti Noir: The Classics*; *The Beacon Best*; *Ploughshares*; *River Styx*; *Callaloo*; and *Harvard Divinity Bulletin*. She was the editor of the *Jack Kerouac Collected Poems* for The Library of America. Phipps is the recipient of the NAACP's Award of Excellence for outstanding commitment in advancing the culture and causes for communities of color. Her website is www.marilenephipps.com.

www.ingramcontent.com/pod-product-compliance
Lightning Source LLC
Chambersburg PA
CBHW031946080426
42735CB00007B/281